Fun & Games

with

Alistair Cooke

Fun & Games

with

Alistair Cooke

On Sport and Other Amusements

Arcade Publishing • New York

First Arcade/Skyhorse edition 2015.

Arcade Publishing books may be purchased in bulk at special discounts for sales promotion, corporate gifts, fund-raising, or educational purposes. Special editions can also be created to specifications. For details, contact the Special Sales Department, Arcade Publishing, 307 West 36th Street, 11th Floor, New York, NY 10018 or arcade@skyhorsepublishing.com.

Arcade Publishing® is a registered trademark of Skyhorse Publishing, Inc.®, a Delaware corporation.

Visit our website at www.arcadepub.com.

10 9 8 7 6 5 4 3 2 1

Library of Congress Cataloging-in-Publication Data is available on file.

Cover design by Bet Ayer
Front cover photograph by Dr. Carl E. Borders
Designed by Bet Ayer

Print ISBN: 978-1-62872-442-4

Printed in the United States of America

Foreword

In my early twenties I worked for the *Manchester Guardian*, as it then was. Nowadays the office in Cross St, Manchester, is, like the rest of the world, a supermarket. Then it was a Dickensian place with dull linoleum on the floors and sombre timber desks. Portraits of C. P. Scott, Haslam Mills, a Montague or two and others who formed the Praetorian Guard of *Manchester Guardian* style gathered dust on the wall. When I first joined the newspaper I was given the job of late duty reporter, which meant keeping in touch with the emergency services throughout the night and reporting on such momentous events as a runaway heifer causing chaos in the streets of Rochdale, or a pan of beef-dripping catching fire in an Oldham chip shop. In between ringing the ambulance service, the police and the fire brigade, I whiled away the time by looking through the cuttings library, searching out articles by my two great heroes, Neville Cardus and Alistair Cooke. One night Cardus swept into the reporters' room. He was wearing a black opera cloak with a red silk lining (or am I imagining things)? He had been to the Free Trade Hall to hear the Hallé Orchestra conducted by his great friend Sir John Barbirolli. I sat quietly in the far shadow of the room while the great man wrote his review. I hardly dared to breathe. That night Oldham and outlying districts could have been consumed by chip-pan fires and the readers of next morning's *Manchester Guardian* would have been none the wiser. That was as near as I ever got to Neville Cardus and as much as I dared hope for.

Alistair Cooke was another matter altogether. It seemed to me that he did not so much report from America as beam down messages from another planet. He had in abundance what we lacked in our Cross St office: mystery and glamour.

[v]

Not only did he hobnob with presidents, but he knew Chaplin, adored Garbo, worshipped Duke Ellington and, most impressive of all, was able to argue the case for Sugar Ray Robinson being, pound for pound, just about the best fighter who ever made the ring. My admiration for this polymath reached new heights when browsing through a second-hand record stall in Manchester and finding a recording called, I think, 'An Evening with Alistair Cooke at the Piano'. I struggle to recall the title only because the record was nicked from my collection some time later. My consolation is that the thief must have been a fan of Mr Cooke's and therefore the record found a good home. On it Mr Cooke is heard yarning, playing piano, singing and whistling. At one point while he was whistling and playing a blues on the piano, the recording was interrupted by Buck Clayton, the splendid jazz trumpet player, who put his head round the door of the studio to see who was making the noise and said: 'Boy, that's a mean piano and a dirty whistle.' Cooke regarded this as a tremendous compliment. I saw it as yet further proof of my hero's versatility and felt a warming pride that I worked for the same newspaper as one of the few men in the entire world acquainted with the work of both Isaiah and Irving Berlin and able to write about the two of them with the same enthusiasm.

The problem with meeting your heroes is that sometimes they let you down. Alistair Cooke didn't. I interviewed him first for BBC television in 1972 and twice more in the next ten years. It was during that time that I had the idea of gathering together a collection of his writing on sport. He had the better idea of including a selection of his work across a wider range of the performing arts.

Thus, in the book, there are accounts of Alistair Cooke watching Ali fight Frazier at Madison Square Garden and Cooke talking jazz to Duke Ellington. Garbo rubs shoulders with Nicklaus, Groucho Marx with Johnny Wardle. We are introduced to both Charlie Chaplin and Arnold Palmer, Randolph Turpin and Fred

MacMurray. We are present at George Gershwin's funeral: 'I remember it as one of those midsummer mornings in New York when the skies can take no more of the rising heat and dump on the city a cataclysm of warm rain', as well as being ringside when the end came for Sugar Ray: 'When it was over Sugar Ray flexed his calves for the last time and did a little hobbling dance over to embrace the victor, who was pink and sweaty and very happy, identifiable on the score card as Denny Moyer, of Portland, Oregon, but on closer inspection was that bearded figure with the scythe Sugar Ray had dreaded to meet.'

What we have in the book is further proof, if it be needed, that Alistair Cooke is both a magnificent journalist and a unique stylist. To paraphrase Kenneth Tynan, if there is a tightrope bridging the gap between being a good journalist and a great one, Alistair Cooke would make the trip in white tie and tails with a cocktail in one hand and a quill in the other. I have not had many good ideas in my life but this book is one of them.

MICHAEL PARKINSON

To the reader

About ten years ago, Michael Parkinson asked me if he might put together a collection of pieces I'd written on various sports down the years. He added the, to me, surprising information that he had his own publishing company, which would be happy to oblige. But I had my own publishers: in England, Max Reinhardt and his Bodley Head; in the United States, I had never been published by anybody but Alfred A. Knopf. In those far-off days, your publisher was also your friend and protector. I had no cause to jump the reservation, and no more was said.

Just before Christmas of 1993, I had a letter from Colin Webb repeating the proposal. I should have turned it down as effortlessly the second time as the first if he had not sent along an accompanying catalogue of Pavilion Books. I was astonished. Here was a company that put out beautiful books at a time when publishers on both sides of the Atlantic appeared to be ravished by what H. L. Mencken called 'the libido for the ugly'. This spring I was in London one week and New York the rest. In both cities I had mooched through the bookshops. Practically all the new books displayed the current mania for embossed titles on garish jackets. The typical product of the publisher's art today has a slightly bloated (embossed) title in silver lettering on a strawberry jam background. The Pavilion catalogue, on the contrary, paid zealous attention to the aesthetics of design and a loving concern with typeface worthy of the late, and greatly lamented, Alfred Knopf himself. A discovery that prompted me to think there might be something in the Parkinson–Webb campaign after all. Here is the result.

The question of an American publisher had barely occurred to me when Richard and Jeannette Seaver came into my life as if by divine intervention. The first thing I heard of them was that they shared my distress over the absorption of the old-time publishers, wholly devoted to books, into conglomerates that see no reason to look on a book as a marketable product different from a soft drink or a vacuum cleaner. Once I learned that the Seavers had retreated respectfully from the prospect of such an absorption the better to retain their own identity as independent judges of worthwhile writing, the signing of a contract was a formality. To my delight, they chose to leave the book exactly as Colin Webb and Bet Ayer designed it.

Seeing all the sporting pieces together, I am struck by their steady light-heartedness. Of course, they were written far apart in time but always in grateful relief from the daily grind of a foreign correspondent, who lives in the jungle of politics and who, during this whole period, worked in the menacing chill of the Cold War. For more than fifty years, I can truly say that scarcely a day has gone by when I didn't think about government, its plethora of ailments and its depressing range of failed panaceas. In politics, nothing is ever settled for keeps, nobody wins. In games, the problems are solved: somebody wins. Hence the 'isle of joy' offered by a sport in an ocean of anxieties. Down the years, I have found no haven more therapeutic than an absorption first with fishing and, in later years, with playing golf and watching tennis. I have come to feel a deep, unspoken pity for people who have no attachment to a single sport, almost as sorry for them as I am for teetotallers.

I hasten to express my gratitude to my beloved old friend, Max Reinhardt, for so gallantly permitting me this one-time defection. To Bet Ayer my debt is obvious in the appearance of the book itself. Finally, I must pay tribute to my devoted secretary, Linda Wichtel, who has nurtured and watched over these pieces as solicitously as if they were her own.

A.C.

Contents

CONTENTS

In Memory of
Pat Ward-Thomas
and
Carroll J. Lynch

The maniac: Central Park, New York City, February 1975

PART ONE

Days in the Sun
(mostly)

1

Fun & Games at Blackpool

[1972]

I don't know when I first became aware that my mother's morning battle with her bronchia was abnormal: that people do not usually bark away like a pack of wolves on getting up in the morning. It was a frightening sound to strangers but, being a small boy and therefore accepting almost everything about our family life as normal, I took it for granted, just as I took for granted the endless dark mornings, the blanket of smog, the slippery veil of mud on the streets, which only later did I discover were not typical of life on this globe but only of life in Manchester.

'It was her cough that carried her off,' my mother's friends would chant, with that peculiar cheerful grimness of Lancashire people. Happily, it took quite some time. She bore it for eighty-six years. But it was her cough that first took us from Salford to Blackpool. Towards the end of 1916, after a particularly harrowing bout, the doctor told us that the Manchester climate was not meant for her (the implication that it was meant for *anybody* is another interesting facet of Lancashire phlegm; and phlegm, I think, is the right word). He solemnly announced that she should move to either of two places: to Blackpool or Egypt! Since my father, a lay preacher and an artist in metal work (who fashioned the flagship that serves as a weathervane atop the Town Hall), had gone into an aeroplane factory by way of doing his wartime bit, Egypt was not on; or, as the politicians would say, it was not 'a viable option'.

So we moved to Blackpool, in March 1917. And in spite of the War, and the fierce rationing (also normal), and the dark nights, and the sight of every other housewife wearing widow's weeds, it was for me an entry into paradise. For Blackpool was a luxury granted only once a year to the ordinary mortals of Lancashire. It was now to be my daily circus. Sand castles, and the sea, and the Pleasure Beach, and laying down lines on the sands at night for catching plaice, and ducking the high tides on the lower Promenade. A little later on, and in the crowded summertime, there was a special Sunday-evening pleasure, all the more intense for being at once sinful and delayed. In those years, the Wesleyan Methodists held an overflow evening service in the Grand Theatre. By then, I was old enough to be an usher and hymn-book dispenser, a duty that relieved me from the compulsion to stay sitting through an interminable sermon. It was possible to hang around in the foyer and not even hear the man droning on with his promise of life eternal—for mill workers earning a pound a week. Such sociological ironies never crossed my mind in those callow youthful years, but I'm pretty sure that the younger bloods in the congregation were as impatient as I was for the blessed sound of the benediction, which was like a starting gun that sent two or three of us out along the Promenade and towards the sandhills (there were big rolling dunes then, both at the Squires Gate end and the North Shore) where you could get an eyeful of the promenading, and sometimes reclining, birds.

A Freudian item occurs to me here that may explain my later affection for all games both indoor and out. It was noticed by some concerned parson that as a small boy I played only with girls. (After adolescence it was, of course, big girls.) So at some point, care was taken that I should meet and play, for a change, with little boys. I took to marbles, then to flipping cigarette cards against the pavement, and then, when we moved to Blackpool, to fishing and cricket on the sands. And then to bagatelle. My father bought me a table for Christmas, a splendid thing of mahogany and green baize that I would gladly buy back today at its no doubt ruinously inflated price.

[4]

After that, though notorious from an early age for my addiction to books, I never felt any conflict between work and play. And so, in the course of time, and with my father's encouragement, I went on to play soccer, rugby, and cricket for the school; ping-pong, badminton, squash, tennis, you name it. But, for a happy period, between I should say the ages of eleven and fifteen, my particular mania was gymnastics. Next to the public library was the town gymnasium, and, since I lived up the road, I came at a tender age under the sharp eye and expert instruction of one H. Gregory, father of Alfred Gregory, the Alpinist. By the time I moved to the Secondary School, as it then was, I was pretty good on the horizontal and parallel bars and had gone through the whole genteel gamut of country and folk dancing. During my years in the second and third forms, I must have been an odious figure to the giants of the Sixth. We had at the time a regular master who, until the sensible importation of H. Gregory himself, 'took' us at gym. He knew a few Swedish exercises and what he could recall of the army's routines. He was chronically fatigued and was always making excuses to skip his sessions with the Sixth. So he would get permission of the headmaster, a small bouncing figure of Roman imperiousness named J. Turral, to fork me out of class (any class) in order to take the Sixth at gym. It must have been galling for those seventeen- and eighteen-year-olds, already sprouting the down of the first moustache, to have to obey the hip-hup instructions of a twelve-year-old, who now recalls with relish the mean pleasure of showing some hairy giant how to vault the pommel horse, perform hand-stands and cart wheels, not to mention the hopeless attempts to give them the elements of doing up-starts and 'hocks off' on the horizontal bar. I realized very much later why, for a time, I came in for a delinquent's share of 'lines' from the prefects, smarting under the helpless giggles of their contemporaries every time they demonstrated their ineptitude at climbing a rope or crashing from a hand-stand.

Football, anyone? It took quite a while to get around to it, didn't it? But then it took me quite a while too. I had picked up from Hal Gregory a firm prejudice about the distinction between athletics and gymnastics. Athletics were for gorillas; gymnastics appealed to a subtler breed that appreciated grace and timing. After I had spent long Saturday afternoons at the gym, my father would come home from Bloomfield Road, and pretty soon I was converted by his ravings about the speed of little Mee, the walloping defensive tactics of Tulloch, and the hair's-breadth retrieves of Mingay. I began to skip Saturday afternoons at the gym, except when we were in training with 'the girls' for the folk dancing division of the Lytham Festival. (Of all those enchantresses I recall only one, because she was a knock-out and was the first girl to knock me flat. As old H. L. Mencken put it: 'A man always remembers his first girl; after that he tends to bunch 'em.' Her name was Mamie Woods, and down the vale of fifty years I salute her. If she is still around, all she has to do is whistle.)

So I became, with my father, a regular Bloomfield Roader. Of that 1920 team, I remember only Mee at outside-left, then Heathcote (who bore a surprising resemblance to Henry Edwards, the reigning British silent-screen star), Barrass with his curls, and Benton. The name of Donnachie has been suggested to me, but if he was there in my time he must have been on the injured list throughout the season. Robin Daniels also informs me that Blackpool had a goalkeeper, around this time, by the name of Richardson. I am sorry to say he has left no impression on me. Mingay was *the one*, alternately the hero and the butt of the Bloomfield Road crowd. He was a glum little man with ping-pong-ball eyes, and lids as heavy as Sherlock Holmes got up as a Limehouse lascar. His regular expression was one of gloomy contempt for the game and the crowd. No footballer I remember, except possibly Harry Bedford, lurched so unpredictably, from one week to the next, between brilliance and bathos. One Saturday he fumbled

[6]

everything; the next he slithered, darted, plunged, leapt, in a series of jagged but wonderful recoveries.

Bedford, of the permanently furrowed brow and the prison haircut, came to us, I guess, in 1921. He was, after Cecil Parkin, my sporting hero. And I watched him till the dizzy day he played for England. After that, the 'regulars' became hypercritical of him, as Lancashire people will of anybody who has acquired an extra-local reputation and might begin to put on airs, which Bedford never did. I don't know if it's true of Lancashire crowds in general but the Bloomfield Road mob never lost its head over any idol. Either he was a 'reet champion' or he was 'disgoostin''.

I'm afraid my memories of Blackpool football fade after that, along with my enthusiasm. I played for the Secondary School and cannot truthfully say I was crazy about standing between the goal-posts on witheringly dank afternoons. Then the inimitable J. Turral, who was a terrible snob but an absolutely Dickensian original, decided that soccer was gross, fit only for cave-dwellers. So the school changed over to rugby, and I didn't enjoy that much either, breaking my back and weaning arthritis in the mud on other shivery Saturdays, as I heeled the ball out to Ken Jones or Norman Hinton.

When I went to Cambridge, I swore never to play football again, and I never did. There was, astoundingly, no gymnasium at Cambridge, so for a brief spell I turned to long-jumping. I had the honour of jumping for Jesus (the college, not the Superstar) but, since sport was no longer compulsory, I gave it up, what with the humid-steaming Fen country and the jolt to the system of thudding your heels in the sand-pit twice a week.

Years later, by the time I'd become the New Yorker guide-in-residence to visiting Englishmen, I would incite them to watch American football because it was, and is, such a fascinating combination of chess and armoured warfare. But I always warned them that they might take understandable offence at the nauseating

American habit of using substitutes every time a man bruised an ankle; and the even more odious custom of bounding to embrace each other after every touchdown. Well, two years ago, I saw my first English soccer match in decades and, sure enough, the players had followed the usual English procedure of first ridiculing an American fashion and then adopting and exaggerating it. To watch any soccer player in the moment after he has socked the ball into the net would give a man from Mars the impression that he was seeing a film clip of VE Day or the arrival of Lindbergh at Le Bourget.

Since my family died, I have not been back to Blackpool. But on the last trips, I had a regular sensation, as the train wheeled around the coastline, and the Tower came into view, that I had never known in all the years I lived in Blackpool or travelled there. In the interval between the Bloomfield Road days and my last few visits to my ageing mother, I had taken up golf in the most maniacal way. Being still incapable of keeping books and sport apart, I read everything I could find on the game. And now, some years later, I regard myself as having earned a creditable Master's degree in the history of golf. On the last visits, when the train gave the lurch that takes it alongside the green undulations of Royal Lytham St Annes, I got up and dropped the window and peered out. This was the very place where Robert Tyre Jones, the immortal one (and all the more immortal now that he is dead), fired his devastating iron shot from a bunker or sandy swale on the seventeenth to win the British Open of 1926 and obliterate Al Watrous. On that very day, I was four miles away, playing cricket amid the yeasty odours of the abattoir that adjoined the Secondary School field. How dull, blind, and insensitive can a boy be?!

There is, they tell me, a plaque in the bunker today to commemorate the feat. I have never seen it. I have never played Lytham St Annes. One day, I hope to. And, if the weather is right, maybe I shall drop in again at Bloomfield Road and see if Mingay is still at it.

[8]

2

A Lesson for Yale
[May 21, 1951]

The rivalry of Yale and Harvard is going into its third century and has been bloodied down the years by many a student riot and pitched battle on each other's campus, to say nothing of the more routine muscle-matching of football games.

By the end of the last century the typical Yale man had evolved into a human type as recognizable as a Cossack or the Pitcairn skull, and there was a tense period in the late twenties and early thirties when Harvard could no longer bear close proximity with these well-developed anthropoids and primly refused to play them at anything. The football and chess fixtures were summarily cancelled. But by now even a Harvard man has heard of 'one world', though of course he recognizes no obligation to belong to it. So today, in a wild lunge of global goodwill, Harvard recalled the sons of Elihu Yale to their common heritage by suggesting a revival of the ancient joust known as cricket.

Not for forty-four years have Yale and Harvard together attempted anything so whimsical. But a far-sighted alumnus lately gave $100 to revive the match and encouraged Harvard men to learn how the other half lives. Accordingly, with this bequest, pads and bats were fetched from Bermuda and Canada, and a roll of coconut matting was bought wholesale in Philadelphia. These props were assembled today on Smith Field, which is a dandelion enclosure lying west of the Harvard football stadium.

Here at 1.30 in the afternoon came ten of the visiting Yale men, various sets of white and grey gentlemen's pantings, a score-book and a couple of blazers for the sake of morale. Fifteen minutes later, and two hundred yards away, the Harvard team arrived in two old Chevrolets and a Cadillac. They carried the matting out to a weedy airstrip devoid of dandelions; stretched it out and pegged it down; made Indian signs at the glowering Yale men and, discovering that they understood English, formally challenged them to a match; spun a dime, won, and chose to go in first.

The eleventh Yale man was still missing and the Harvard captain, a mellifluous-spoken gentleman from Jamaica, offered to lend them a Harvard man. The Yale captain suspected a trap and said they would wait. Ten minutes later the eleventh man came puffing in, swinging from elm to elm. Everything was set. It was a cloudless day. It had been 92 the day before, but Providence obliged with a 35-degree drop overnight and we nestled down into a perfect English May day—sunny and green, with a brisk wind. The eleven spectators stomped and blew on their hands at the field's edge. And the game began.

Mr Conboy and Mr Cheek put on the purchased pads. Conboy took centre and faced the high lobbing off-breaks of Mr Foster, who delivered six of these nifties and was about to deliver a seventh but saw that Mr Cheek had turned his back and was off on a stroll around the wicket. This mystery turned into a midfield conference at which it was found out that Yale expected to play an eight-ball over and Harvard a six. An Englishman on the Harvard side kindly acquainted the Yale men with the later history of cricket, and they settled for a six-ball over.

This shrewd act of gamesmanship effectively rattled the Harvard team for a while, and Conboy was soon out for three and Cheek for a duck. But Frank Davies, from Trinidad, knew a sophisticated ploy that shortly demoralized the Yale men. He came in slowly, hefted his pads, squinted at the coconut matting, patted it, rubbed his right shoulder, exercised his arm and, while the Yale men were still waiting for him to get set, started to cut and drive the Yale bowling all over the field.

[10]

Yale retorted by occasionally bowling an over of seven balls and once an over of five. It had no effect. They were now thoroughly cowed by Davies's professional air—once he cleverly feigned a muscle spasm and had the Yale side clustered round him terrified at the prospect of a doctor's bill. They were so trembly by now that they thought it only decent to drop any fly ball that came their way. Davies hooked a ball high to leg, but the Yale man obligingly stumbled, pawed the air, and gave a masterly—and entirely successful—performance of a man missing an easy catch.

Davies tried another hook with the same result, but the agreement was now so firmly understood that no Yale man would hold anything. Davies accordingly cut with flashing elbows, secure in the new-found knowledge that considered as a slip fielder, a Yale man is a superlative bridge player. Davies went on to cut fine and cut square and drive the ball several times crack against the cement wall on which two mystified little boys were sitting. This, it was decided, was a boundary, and the scorer was told to put down four runs.

Davies did some more shrugs and lunges with his shoulder-blades, and, though there was a fairly constant trickle of batting partners at the other end, Davies had scored never less than two-thirds of the total. Suddenly he let go with a clean drive to mid-on for 2 and the astonished scorer discovered that the total was now 68 and Davies had reached his half-century.

There had been so far a regrettable absence of English spirit but Bruce Cheek, a civil servant, formerly of Peterhouse, Cambridge, was signed up to repair this omission by shouting 'Well played, sir!'—an utterly alien sound to the two Boston small fry on the cement wall. This cued the growing crowd to rise and applaud the incomparable Davies. All fourteen of them joined in the ovation.

Ten minutes later the Revd Bill Baker, a Baptist from Manchester, went in to receive his baptism of fire from Foster, who had suddenly found his off-break again. The result was that Mr Baker

[11]

was walking back right after walking out. Then Davies hit a short ball into a Yale man's hands. He failed to drop it in time. And the whole side was out. Harvard, 102—Davies, 70.

The two small fry dropped off the cement wall and came into the field to investigate the ritual. One of them stayed in the outfield and the tougher one came on and asked a question of the retreating umpire. It was a simple question. It was: 'What game you playin', mister?' He was told, and turned round and bawled: 'Cricket!' at his pal. The pal shrugged his little shoulders and went off and picked up two Boston terriers from somewhere, for no reason that anyone discovered then or since. They did manage to invade the field during the Yale innings and had to be shooed off.

Meanwhile we had taken tea, from a thermos about the size of a city gas tank. From nowhere a parson arrived, wearing an old straw boater. It was a heart-warming sight, and I found myself mumbling through a tear the never-to-be-forgotten lines '. . . some corner of a foreign field that is forever Lipton's'.

With a knightliness that cannot be too highly praised, Yale maintained the dogged pretence that they were playing cricket. It entitled their going out to the matting and back again in a slow though spasmodic procession. The continuity of this parade was assured by one Jehangir Mugaseth, a dark supple young man from Bombay, who had one of those long, beautiful, unwinding runs that would have petrified even the nonchalant Mr Davies. At the other end was a thin, blond man with another long run, an American who distrusted breaks but managed a corkscrew baseball serve in mid-air.

Between them the Yale team fell apart, and your reporter had no sooner looked down to mark 'McIntosh caught' than he looked up to see Allen's middle stump sailing like a floating coffin past the wicketkeeper's right ear. Yale were suddenly all out—for 34. They followed on, more briskly this time—they were catching on to the essential tempo of the game—and were out the second time in record time for 24 runs. It was all over at 6.40.

No excuses were offered from the Yale team. They had fine English names—Grant, West, Allen, Foster, Parker, and Norton—and true to the Old Country traditions they lost magnificently. Nobody mentioned the mean Colonial skill recruited by the Harvard side. Nobody, that is, except a Yale man who dictated to me the exact tribal composition of the Harvard team: one Indian, one Jamaican, one Australian, one Egyptian, one Argentinian, one from Trinidad, one from Barbados, a Swiss New Yorker, two Englishmen, and a stranger from Connecticut.

But after all it's not the winning that matters, is it? Or is it? It's—to coin a word—the amenities that count: the smell of the dandelions, the puff of the pipe, the click of the bat (when Harvard are batting), the rain on the neck, the chill down the spine, the slow, exquisite coming on of sunset and dinner and rheumatism.

3

An Epic of Courage
[September 14, 1951]

Sugar Ray Robinson on Wednesday regained his world middle-weight championship from Randolph Turpin, by a technical knock-out after two minutes fifty-two seconds of the tenth round.

No myth dies harder, and none is more regularly debunked by the facts, than the one about international sports contributing to international friendship. White-headed Frenchmen will bear up bravely under the conviction that all the gallantry of France was outraged by pitting the gentle Carpentier against the bruiser Dempsey. The fact that Carpentier was hopelessly outclassed has never been allowed to interfere with the growth of a legend that is now as much a part of French history as the piety of Joan of Arc, another astonishing discovery of hindsight.

Last night Sugar Ray Robinson, tiring to the point of panic before the concrete insensibility of Turpin's massive flesh, wrung everything he had from a brave heart, fought from his finger-tips, and at last had Turpin helpless against the ropes, his arms by his thighs, his stubborn body reeling back and forth like a badly beaten bull when the flags go in. I have never seen a human being receive so much punishment with such dumb bravery. For almost a whole minute Robinson crashed and shot and pounded on him until his head sagged from one side to the other with the flopping rhythm of a broken pendulum.

An old man sitting next to me lit a cigar with precision, keeping his eyes steadily above the flame on the crumbling Turpin. 'Thirty seconds more,' he said quietly, 'and we'll have another Flores on our hands.' Flores was the young boxer killed ten days ago in a similar act of bravery before just such an onslaught. It did seem then that Turpin should be rescued to fight another day. If there had been another minute, I do believe that he would have gone down and out for a long time to come. But pride never lacks pretext, and there were only eight seconds of that round to go when the referee bounded in and scissored his arms to stop the fight. Turpin fell on him in a face-down dive, and it seemed to one no more than twenty feet away that it was a gesture of oxlike gratitude.

Pound for pound, the experts say, Robinson is the best boxer we have seen in many a long year. In victory he is incomparable, in trouble resourceful, in near-defeat—as we saw last night— indomitable. He is Robert E. Lee with the fighting reserves of a Montgomery or a Patton. The point about scoring him, though, is that nothing he does goes unseen or unrecorded.

With Turpin, you have to look beyond the awkward stance, the heavy, burrowing style, and watch for what he's doing when he gets in there. Then you see, if you are close enough, that his short-arm jabs to the belly are faster than the eye and heavier than lead. A flashier fighter than Robinson might appear to be dancing easily around this approach until the sudden moment when the man keeled over, in absolute exhaustion, from the invisible pounding at his middle. Turpin appears to do everything wrong. His left leg is always out, whether his weight is forward, dead centre, or moving over. An undercut consequently sends him down on one knee— this happened twice in the early rounds—but a thoughtful judge might score a point and cancel it when he saw Turpin with his big glass eyes calmly using that knee to rest on.

In the first four rounds the comments of old and young fighters and veteran sports writers sharpened this dilemma, of how to identify as confident pauses what in another man would be help-less postures. 'You can't box this guy,' somebody said, seeing Robinson's long left punching the air to the starboard side of

Turpin's right ear. 'He's all flesh,' somebody else said. 'All body, you mean,' another man capped, 'I never did see a man fight more with his body.' You note these good remarks and look up to see Turpin, his gloves somewhere around his thighs, moving in wide open for the sort of murder Joe Louis used to execute on any man two feet away with one arm down.

But this is Turpin's normal approach to artillery fire in the clinches. Time and again he came on last night, with that modest homely face, and those wide glassy eyes, as untouched by the possibility of human interference as Marley's Ghost clanking up from the cellar, or Boris Karloff wheeling into the petrified drawing-room. 'He's not a man,' an admiring youngster cried. 'He's The Thing.' And the mind winced at the memory of Hollywood's latest terror, the monster that has an arm blown off, then grows another.

This always-moving, never-blinking mechanical man sent anxiety flashing into Robinson's eyes. We saw Robinson's muscles tighten for action, the shower of spittle that grunted out of his mouth after each careful body blow and set the moths darting in terror through the white rectangle of light. And they sucked their teeth and said, 'He's all in. Two more rounds and he's through.' It was then, with an old cut opened, that Robinson summoned up the last cry of courage to brighten the tension of style. He wrung tattoos from his knotted stomach. He missed many times. But he landed many times more.

Even then, Turpin tottered, like a man in a nightmare lifting iron legs up an endless flight of stairs, over towards Robinson's corner. There was an ugly misgiving that Turpin was lurching after his conqueror. But he was merely going to embrace him. 'It was,' wrote the New York *Herald Tribune*'s Red Smith this morning, 'a genuine gesture of sportsmanship from a first-class fighting man. There haven't been many better fighters than Turpin seen around here in a long time. There never has been a pluckier loser.' That, I think, is the accurate truth of it.

[16]

But recollection in tranquillity, though it may be the making of art, is just as often the death of truth. Turpin may well see the newsreels of those last two minutes and wonder who was that all-in giant who fell into grateful oblivion on the referee's chest. It was Randolph Turpin, a very game young man, nobody else. And all the dressing-room philosophy will not change it.

Turpin's recovery from the event was as dramatic as the right to the chin that sent him down for a count of five and left him panting on one knee for a further count of four. Three minutes after the fight Turpin was standing in mid-ring with his arm around the smiling Robinson. He stood up straight and he was breathing at a normal rate. In the dressing room he admitted to having been 'a little foggy, but I was not hurt. I didn't want to go down again because I knew they would end it.' Without haste or ill will he thought again: 'If I were the referee I probably would have stopped it, too.' He most certainly would.

But out of this act and the reconstruction of it by people with fierce transatlantic loyalties will be built another myth: that Turpin was denied his right, and robbed of the victory, by a referee too susceptible to the home crowd and the howling fringe of Harlemites a mile away against the bright sky. Again the vivid fact remains. Referee Goldstein did as fair a job as I have ever seen. And alone among the judges he gave Turpin four rounds to Robinson's four, with one even. One judge gave Robinson five, Turpin three, and one even. The other gave Robinson five and Turpin four.

My own less confident count was three each and three even, with a footnote to the effect that one or two more rounds and Robinson would have been a ragged frame of flesh, all co-ordination gone, twitching possibly, but from the viscera and nerves, not the mind and will. My doubts about the three even rounds could easily be extended to a fourth and fifth. It is the nasty problem of how you score two men who might have learned their fighting on

[17]

different planets. How do you compare rare roast beef and crêpes Suzette?

Robinson is still a great and delightful boxer, with the stress on the noun. His stance is the textbook stance drawn in quicksilver. When he jabs with his long slippery left, his neck goes down for cover and the muscles ripple down along the waist. He dances lightly according to the subtle demands of balance. When he comes close he rat-tat-tats in a protective flurry before resting in the clinch. In open fighting he has a left and a right, a wicked hook, a perfect uppercut with belly deflected, and the guard up over his heart.

Finally Turpin came out of a clinch and Robinson flew in like Mercury. Turpin's glazed eyes rolled over—the dragon's last squirm, with the nostrils high and flaring. He pitched forward and Robinson jerked him down, down on to the glaring mat and rolling over. Then he was up on one knee, and up again. Robinson, stretched and taut in the corner, paused for a fraction and came in again to bang him against the ropes. Three more thunderbolts, to the head, the chest, the sagging neck. And Turpin staggered across a right angle to be bounced against another rope.

Turpin seemed almost sick with the concentration of his own frenzy. But he stayed with it and flung all he knew. His left eye was showering blood, so that the four gloves looked as if they had been dipped in paint. Turpin's gloves were up against the hailstorm rattling around his head. Then they were down and limp and gone for ever. Two, three, four more rocketing blows, and Turpin was slipping against the rope, baying mutely at the nearly full moon and the roaring thousands up against it. And then the man in white came in. And it was all over.

4

Sugar Ray's Downfall
[1962]

As no lover of music this morning will fail to bow his head before the memory of the great and humble Bruno Walter, so no lover of boxing in its squalid decline will fail to yield the passing tribute of a sigh to Sugar Ray Robinson, the one incomparable fighter of our time, whose head this morning was both bowed and bloody.

He was thrashed last night in Madison Square Garden as he has never been beaten before, by Denny Moyer, a game and supple twenty-two-year-old who fought always at a driving angle from the centre of the ring and had Sugar Ray wheeling around in a spry but hopeless outer circle, his back flipping the ropes from time to time like the wrists of a clumsy guitar player.

Before the fight Sugar Ray had said, with no bluster at all, that he was in better condition than at any time since he regained his middleweight championship. He was probably correct, but he was still in no condition for a ten-round battle with a ripe and crafty youngster who had, and exploited, a nineteen-year advantage in muscle tone, respiration, reflex response, and the ability merely to grunt and not expire when a piston hits the navel.

What was charming about Sugar Ray in this, his inevitable farewell to the big time, was that he did not snarl, pout, or claim he was being smothered in the clinches, or indulge in any of the self-pitying bravado that disfigures most champions in eclipse. He was simply puzzled. He kept coming on with that famous left jab, which punctured Moyer's nose in the first round and kept it bleeding to the end.

The youth has springs of blood to spare, and Moyer acted as if the leeches had been put on him to rid him of some plaguey infection. Robinson would dance in again and try his old left-right-left flurry of jabs and little uppercuts. Moyer tossed his blond head with the gesture of a man blowing a hair out of his eyes. And Sugar Ray was truly baffled. Nothing that he knew, no feint or arms thrown wide in that fake invitation to suicide, was any use against this weaving, erect young man.

For only three rounds, and those the first, was Sugar Ray able to weld the memory of his greatness with its current parody and to dazzle, or at least intimidate, young Moyer with it. After that, Moyer heeled at dead centre and radiated every punch in the book around a widening circle. He never grew careless or cocky or was caught moving off balance. In the last four rounds, every punch he delivered ran as fast as a seizure clean from the ball of the forward foot, up through the calf and thigh and shoulder-blade. In the ninth, a dreadful right caught Sugar Ray and for a fraction of a second he rocked and saved himself by falling around Moyer's middle.

When it was over Sugar Ray flexed his calves for the last time and did a little hobbling dance over to embrace the victor, who was pink and sweaty and very happy, identifiable on the score card as Denny Moyer of Portland, Oregon, but on closer inspection was that bearded figure with a scythe Sugar Ray had dreaded to meet.

5

Short History of Baseball
[1952]

In the country south of the Mohawk Valley, in the setting for several of the stories of James Fenimore Cooper, there is a town called—not unnaturally—Cooperstown. It is now a regular port of call on the tourist route because of a museum, sacred to the memory of one Abner Doubleday. He, it says here, was the only true inventor of the national game. The museum has a lot of early relics. It has a home-made baseball supposedly used by the great man himself. It preserves prints of Union soldiers playing baseball in North Carolina during the Civil War. It has bronze plaques bearing the names of retired heroes of the game who have been voted into the so-called 'hall of fame' by 75 per cent of the members of the Baseball Writers Association. Tap an American anywhere between the Canadian and Mexican borders and ask him who invented baseball and he will reverently pronounce the name Abner Doubleday.

Let me begin by quoting the official account as it is quite briskly told in the federal guide to New York State: '. . . baseball grew quite informally from Old Cat, a favorite boys' game in Colonial days, played by a thrower, a catcher and a batter. In 1839, Colonel Abner Doubleday, a student in a local military academy, later a major general in the Civil War, limited the number of players to eleven, outlined the first diamond-shaped field and drew up a memorandum of rules for the game which he named "baseball".' That is the version confirmed by an investigating commission after its researches in 1908. It was not, by the way, a government commission, as most baseball fans like to assume. It consisted of a sporting-goods manufacturer, a bunch of baseball managers and one United States Senator who was mad about the game. Even the *Encyclopedia Britannica* (a Chicago publication) says about this commission: 'It was appointed ostensibly to investigate the origins of the game but really to "prove" its exclusively American origin.'

Well, by 1908, any other inventor of the game who could challenge the Doubleday legend was dead and gone. Cooperstown, New York, was naturally delighted to be singled out for glory. And the commission's findings passed into the record books and the tablets of sacred Americana. However, there is another name rarely mentioned by baseball scholars, and it is not surprising, because he is a dissenter and a sceptic; once you have picked and immortalized a public hero it is an awful nuisance to discover that he is a fraud. The name of the Doubting Thomas is Robert W. Henderson, a quiet fellow who, true to the requirements of his job as a staff member of the New York Public Library, doesn't like to take things for granted. Down the years he had poked around into the baseball story and by 1939 he was ready to launch a shattering offensive against the legend of Doubleday and Cooperstown. He confirmed, for instance, that Abner Doubleday went up to West Point in 1838, the year before he invented and named baseball at Cooperstown while he was presumably on leave from his military education. But at that time, cadets never got any leave in their second year. Mr Henderson also doubted that Cadet Doubleday managed to grow into a colonel in one year as a student. Luckily for the legend, the records of that investigating commission were lost in a fire. All that's left is a small file of papers quoting the main witness. He was a resident of Cooperstown bearing the suspicious name of Abner Graves. He laid it down that his namesake invented the game and that the runner was put out by the fielder hitting him with the ball. Since this doesn't happen in baseball, and

[22]

granting that the man was telling the truth as he had observed it in many a stretcher case, Mr Henderson began to cast around for a game in which it did happen. He found that it had been the normal practice of an English game for a couple of centuries. He then started to go through the English records.

He found out—what even the Oxford dictionary had overlooked—that the word supposedly coined by Doubleday is first mentioned in 1744 in a letter of Lady Hervey in which she writes about the habits and pastimes of the then Prince of Wales: 'The Prince's family divert themselves at baseball, a play all who are, or have been, schoolboys are well acquainted with.' Jane Austen in one of her novels writes about a heroine who 'had nothing by nature heroic about her . . . she preferred cricket, baseball, riding on horseback . . . to books.' Mr Henderson began to pile up a mountain of documentary evidence from English literature, mainly from notebooks and journals and the like, to show that baseball—and so called—was a very popular children's game in England in the early eighteenth century. In the same year as Lady Hervey's letter there appeared a children's book of games, one letter of the alphabet for one game. B stood for baseball, and it has a picture of the player at the plate, a pitcher, a catcher, and two posts for bases. The book was a best seller and was reprinted twice in America. And in 1828, when Abner Doubleday (if he ever existed) was nine years old, the *Boy's Own Book*, published in London, had a whole chapter about the game and illustrated it with a picture of a diamond, with bases at each corner. Many a rearguard Doubleday man will concede that perhaps Abner did not invent the game but certainly invented the diamond. Not old Abner. Colonel Jane Austen, maybe, but not General Abner.

What came out of Mr Henderson's subversive labours was that a game called baseball, which looks very much like a rudimentary version of today's American game, was played everywhere in

England in the eighteenth century; and that it was called 'baseball' in the southern counties, 'rounders' in the west country, and 'feeder' in metropolitan London.

That's all, folks.

6

Revised (Soviet) History of Baseball
[1952]

Fair-minded Americans were taking a second look today at a game that they have long assumed to be their very own, one moreover that was always supposed to mix gallantry, humour, horseplay, good fellowship, and material rewards in equal proportions. The game however has just been identified, after considerable research by a Soviet youth magazine, as 'lapta'. According to *Smena*, the official periodical of the Young Communist League, Russian peasants played lapta in all its classless purity for many centuries before the game was smuggled into the United States and transformed into a mocking demonstration of the class struggle. In its corrupt American version, according to *Smena*, it is known as beizbol.

In its pristine Russian form, a bol is heet by a better who then ron aronn tree becks of send or bessiz. This is nawn ez a hom ronn. The better then rons hawm an earns great glory but naw kesh. In the United States, on the other hand, *Smena* tells its readers, 'It is a beastly battle, a bloody fight with mayhem and murder.' It is played by 'slaves, bought and sold like sheep'. *Smena* does not explain why the best sheep earn as much as 15, 20, or 30,000 pounds a year. These slaves are 'bought and sold and thrown out the door when they become unnecessary . . . after which, with ruined health and often also crippled, they increase the army of American unemployed.' (*Pravda*'s estimate yesterday of American unemployed was thirteen million—one million more than in the depth of the depression. The United States Bureau of Labor

[25]

statistics fall about 12½ million short of this figure.) As an example of the shameless capitalist exploitation of beizbol slaves, *Smena* cites the famous case of the late Babis Rut, known locally as the Babe or the Sultan of Swat. He was 'sold against his wishes to another club for 150,000 dollars'.

The *New York Times* this morning rather academically notes that there has been 'only one fatality in the entire history of major league baseball'. But the *Herald Tribune* more conscientiously sent a sports writer off to check on the Russian accusations and he regrets today to find them well-founded. He attended the game at the polov graundz between the Nieu Uork Djiantz and the Shikago Kubz. The Djiantz were beaten nine to nothing; says Harold Brown, the *Tribune*'s man, 'it was murder all right'.

There were ugly facets to the game the Russians had not mentioned. The slaves were forced to play at night under hot grilling lights. The shoddy official excuse for this torture is that at this season of the year the top teams are trying hard to win the championship of their respective leagues in order to qualify for the test matches and thereby, as Mr Brown frankly admits, 'make extra money. Players like Boby Tomson and Alvin Dok of the Djiantz have been known to play their hardest because they are motivated by a capitalistic desire for ready cash.' It is a fact that the two winning teams, who meet in the test matches, or lapta series, next month, are given big bonuses. They get even bigger bonuses if they win the series and emerge as the champion team.

Mr Brown unflinchingly noted regulation barbarities charitably overlooked by *Smena*: the umpire for instance wears 'a mask over his face and a chest protector'. The spectators freely urge the slaves on to petty larceny with such self-explanatory admonitions as 'steal second base, ya bum'. Mr Brown positively heard one spectator confidentially advise one player to 'Kill the umpire'.

Englishmen may imagine the ultimate cruelty of the game by pondering *Smena*'s surprising conclusion: 'in the number of maiming wounds and bloodletting, this type of sport is not far behind American football—or rugby'!

Rokbje is, of course, the name of the village in the Ukraine which invented in the fourteenth century the game stolen and patented in England by Doktor Tummaz Arnuld.

7

The Sit-Down Fight
[1953]

Rocky Marciano kept his world's heavyweight championship on Friday night 15 May when he knocked out Jersey Joe Walcott after two minutes and twenty-five seconds of the first round.

In what was variously reported this morning as one of the shortest, most farcical, hilarious, or sordid attempts on the world's heavyweight championship, Jersey Joe Walcott sat down on the mat in Chicago last night, cocked his head to hear the referee call a count of ten, and then got up and went home, complaining he had been robbed. It was never quite clear in the following confusion exactly who had been robbed.

The audience contributed at the gate a net $253,462, and Walcott took a guaranteed $250,000, something of a record increment from a sit-down strike. Marciano's reward was a paltry $166,000, or just over half the sum a television network had paid on the firm understanding that they were cornering a boxing match. It was over so soon that millions of families fixing the chairs and beer-coasters for a leisurely session of blood-letting will never know who sponsored the programme, a contingency that the whole advertising industry is mobilized to avoid. Robbery is a word Walcott should never use. It is the least of the indictments the cheated crowd would bring against him.

There is no boo like the boo of a man who has paid fifty dollars for two minutes of aimless shuffling. And when the referee hoisted Marciano's arm and the bell rang, all the tired trans-continental aeroplane passengers, the preening celebrities, and the boys who had traded a week's baseball tickets for a seat against the skyline bared their teeth and let loose like wounded hyenas. They weren't allowed to televise the fight in the towns that ring Lake Michigan, but a thousand and two thousand miles away the boos turned saloons into sounding boards and rattled the windows of spinsters knitting in their ignorance upstairs.

It all began with the usual hoopla. The 'preliminary contests' between boys whose purple trunks nobody would notice. The press hitching their trousers and figuring the size of the crowd. The howling introduction of celebrities. The smoke curling and fainting into the high lights. The sharp little referee holding the mike like a boy chewing an apple and naming the judges, the 'attending physicians', the challenger from Camden (black trunks, white stripes, weighing $197^3/_4$), the champ from Brockton (white trunks, black stripes, at $184^1/_2$). The customary sermon about clinches, the best man, and come out fighting. The bell.

They are both chunky men, but on the television screen, which would flatten a Henry Moore pinhead into a Nazi, they looked like gorillas, though Walcott is a harmless codger, the children's pet. They were both bent over, as if from a severe case of the cramps. This is no position to throw any punch known to the books, and a right hook from Walcott and a left from Marciano must be mentioned as technical warm-up gestures. Marciano pattered after Walcott in the centre of the ring and made a few bunching fee-fo-fum movements and missed again. Then Walcott sat down.

Well, he didn't exactly sit down. He was shoved at by a motion hardly conforming to the definition of a left hook but more reminiscent of a short-armed boy embracing a rocking-horse. Walcott gave every sign of rocking into place again. But something to do with balance, no doubt, surely no disturbance of gravity for which Marciano could claim the credit, sent him on his shoulder-blades. He rocked back to a sitting position and took it easy on his rump while the referee caught his breath. Walcott sat with an arm across his knees and the other on the rope, and all he needed was a pipe to make him any comfortable old gaffer settling in to watch an afternoon's cricket on the village green.

He was already composed when the referee started counting. He shouted off the seconds a couple of feet from Walcott's left ear and his arm swung like a metronome. Joe was thinking sweet thoughts right through eight and nine. Once he heard ten he took his gloves off the floor and jumped up smartly and went over to his corner. If he were new to the game you could imagine him saying to his manager, 'Is this where we pick up the purse?'

Marciano went over to him and Walcott, who was no more dazed than you are standing in line for the pay envelope, flashed his solid white teeth at him in a 'What the heck' smile. Then he padded off to watch his manager and the seconds make big gestures and cry 'Foul!'

This was the sequel to the great fight in Philadelphia last year, when Marciano bled his way to the title through thirteen rounds of terrible slaughter from this same reflective old man who last night sat and pondered till the seconds ticked away. It was an absurdity for everybody. The only thing it cleared up was the question of Walcott's motive in hiding his age. He has been mooning around forty longer than a movie actress. This mystery, it now appears, has nothing to do with coyness. It is just plain innocence. It explains, wrote Red Smith today, 'why there has been so much confusion about his real age. He can't count his years. He can't even count to ten.'

8

Return of the Native
[1954]

Yesterday, so far as I could gather, England was beating Pakistan in a game whose swift conclusion is so foregone that Monday's crowd will have to be shanghaied or coaxed in with free beer. The connoisseurs at my elbow also instructed me that Bedser beat a Test record, that Wardle hit three home runs, that the Old Trafford pitch has astonishing powers of recovery, that the Pakistanis are not as bad as they look, and that the English fielding was as snappy as it ought to be for a team that is going to Australia.

I dutifully quote the experts on these obvious conclusions because none of them was obvious at all to a renegade separated by time, and the corruption of baseball, from the gentle pleasures of cricket. My own impression was one of marvelling admiration for the endurance and gallantry of English crowds, who sit for hours in a dank wind and watch thirteen anonymous men in white, and two barbers with hats on, move in stealthy slow-motion on a public lawn; who ask so little here below that when the pitcher bowls six balls, and nothing at all happens, they rise in grateful applause with all the delirium of a Liberal fête saluting the prize dahlia at a flower show. Walking behind the stands on a circular tour of the field, I would hear these little rounds of clapping, disturbing the general hush at four-minute intervals. I enquired for the cause of them. They were always for maiden overs.

There must be some irresistible property in the drug of cricket, for this ceremonial coma and the grateful murmur that occasionally breaks it is practised all around the world, in the fetid winds of

Pakistan, under the Renaissance skies of Jamaica, alongside the sheep hills of New Zealand. Anyone inclined to make fun of cricket should consider that, though Mr Eden may be having a little trouble persuading the Egyptians, the koala bear is entirely familiar with the sound of a leather ball 'climbing the air from the thick of the bat'. It all goes to support the American conviction that although an Englishman on a trade mission may be easy to handle, the secret agent to watch out for is the cricketer who settles modestly in your own neighbourhood and stays for twenty years because, he says, he 'just happens to like it'. It reminds me of an aged Texas lady asked to recall the types who settled West Texas. 'Mostly,' she replied, 'they were men who had shot their uncle in Tennessee or jumped a mortgage in Maryland. Nice, straightforward people mostly.' Then she elbowed herself up on her death-bed. 'Course,' she said, 'there were black sheep. Ah remember a man came here, said it looked like mighty handsome country, good for goats. Just thought it was a likely place to settle. He was a suspicious character from then on.'

The United States Immigration authorities should be alerted to any incoming Englishman carrying a cricket bat. At first glance, he may seem as inoffensive as Robert Benchley's typical Englishman, whose charm 'is not that he takes his pleasures sadly but that he takes pleasure in such tiny, tiny things'. But give him ten years and a heavy roller and the natives will be drinking tea, voting for a Governor-General and applying for secession.

Thirty years and three thousand miles away from Old Trafford is long enough, and far enough, to qualify any returning native as a man from Mars. And the following account, though strictly accurate in all matters of fact, may possibly strike the cricket fan as naïve or insensitive to the finer shades. I am simply trying to help any visiting American to a deeper appreciation of the game. And then, a man whose eyeballs are burnt by the summer sun—striking him every hour on the hour from May to November at the latitude

[32]

of Corfu—is not likely to figure out very expertly what is going on in the encircling gloom. Cricket has to have 'fine shades' since it is played so often in the dark.

We got to the ground just after noon and saw a long, silent queue. But the cops, and the gatemen, the committee members and the programme sellers were in a dither, arching their eyebrows and hissing some gorgeous secret behind the back of their hands. I assumed that Marilyn Monroe had arrived, suffocating in a bikini. But what they were saying was, 'Twelve thirty!' This miracle was made possible by Harry Williams, the groundsman, who had been up all night sucking away on some new sort of pipette and transforming the wicket from a flood into a treadable bog. And sure enough as the half-hour struck a file of little men in sweaters (and red flannel underwear, I'll bet) trotted on to the field, and were followed by two men carrying long slim spades. One was a Mr Evans, a vigorous hitter, I was told. But he was walking back before I learned to distinguish him from the fielders and the barbers (they turned out to be umpires). A great peace descended for a half-hour or so, irritated only by the alarming shout of 'Shot!' from the men in the pavilion. It was a false alarm. There wasn't a gunman in sight. It is simply what you say when a man makes a line-drive. Ho-hum.

Suddenly, the ball was dropped and they all came striding back to the pavilion again. England, I was told, had 'declared'. They stayed in the pavilion long enough to eat lunch, without a ripple of protest from the spectators. Eating lunch, it seems, is part of the game's strategy. At 2.16¼ (it is essential—in American newspapers it is compulsory—to get these incidents properly timed) they all came out again. But for some unexplained reason, having to do with that 'declaration' of war, it was the English team that came out. Now the Pakistanis were to bat. There are evidently different rules for visiting teams, or maybe there is a limit to the freedom you can grant newly-freed Colonials, but anyway they weren't allowed to stay half as long as the English team. They played with great correctness, trapping straight balls with the left toe perfectly pointed, swinging back to the short-pitched ones, doing everything that would guarantee a couple of comfortable centuries on the hard ground, under the hot sky, of Pakistan. But they were playing on a lake against men bred to seafaring. And the Pakistanis' obedient text-book demonstrations of how they had learned to play cricket were pathetic in view of the obvious fact that Bedser and Wardle were cradled in mud. It is no accident that the television stand is built at the top of two nautical ladders and is a sort of mizzen-mast. It was the best place (and on a wet day perhaps the only place) to watch the Pakistanis all at sea. I went up there once in the hope of sighting a submarine, but achieved no greater distinction than that of stopping the game. The television crow's nest is spotted just above the bowling screens and if you wave an arm there it distracts the batsman as a fly might perched on his eyebrow. So Mr Hanif Mohammad waved at the umpire, and the umpire turned and waved at your correspondent, who hastily beat it back to the main deck.

There were only three other events that disturbed the day-long hush of the crowd. After lunch Wazir Hassan, fortified by English carbohydrates, jumped into a fine drive and while the crowd was springing awake to applaud him McConnon had clapped the ball in his hand. McConnon was on his toes again when Wazir cracked at a half-volley. Apart from these two fine catches, and a couple of routine ones also from McConnon, the fielding looked to a baseball fan as if the English team had been up all night helping Mr Williams to drain the turf.

With wickets dropping like the drizzle from heaven, the game began to take on the appearance of a competition, but just when it was warming into life they all walked to the pavilion again. This time it was tea, even cricketers apparently feeling that if you go much longer than two hours without a meal you will just dissolve

[34]

into the rain and good brown soil from which this happy breed sprang. At 2.34 a strange light broke over the field. And again at 5.26. It was reliably reported to be the sun. At 6.30, when the Pakistanis were going in and out again in an embarrassing procession, they all decided to go back—for tomato juice cocktails, I assumed. But it was the end of play, and now they are allowed one whole day, or six meals, to recover from this exhausting minuet. Will Rogers, I am afraid, had the answer when, on his only visit to a cricket match, he was asked by the then Prince of Wales for any suggested improvements in the game. He pulled at his forelock and said: 'Well, your Highness, if I was in charge I'd line up all the players before the game began and say, "Now listen, fellahs, no food till you're through."'

9

The Road to Churchill Downs
[1960]

I was recently invited to go down to Kentucky as a house guest for a few days and wind up with a front seat at the Derby. In the early days of May this is about as sure a guarantee of heaven as a city dweller, or even a countryman, could ask for on this earth.

Kentucky is technically a border state, lying poised between the North and the South, but it deserves far more than its neighbour, Ohio, the description 'a Northern state with a Southern exposure'. Being not quite in the South it has striven to be very much *of* it. There are no Southerners quite so Southern as the professional Southerners of Kentucky, and by practice as well as by blood they have taken on the legendary pace of Southern life, its customs and cookery, the slow twist of vowels into diphthongs, and that attractive Southern irony which is prepared to believe the best of human beings and expect the worst.

It was a little warmer than usual the day I tumbled down into Kentucky, but the Ulstermen, or as they say here the Scots-Irish, who settled here a century and a half ago soon accustomed themselves to a semi-tropical drowse that would have choked their cousins in Aberdeen. It was at Aberdeen, by the way, that I crossed the Ohio River, and along its banks the Judas trees were in full flame. The town is terraced high on the steep slopes of the hills as they crowd down to the river, as if rushing to make a last stand before they give way to the rolling meadows of the Bluegrass country.

I tossed in the word 'Bluegrass' there in a casual way, but have no fear that it is going to go unexplained. The Bluegrass region for a hundred and seventy years has bred the fastest, proudest, most gleaming of America's race horses. On top of the Fayette County courthouse is a weathervane in the shape of a golden stallion. It is no more possible to go through the Bluegrass country and ignore the horses than it would be to go through Nevada and ignore the slot machines. From Maysville, the first town across the Kentucky line, down to Lexington, the capital of the Bluegrass, is sixty-three miles, and there are some interesting oddities. There are handsome houses overlooking the river that were built in the spacious times when the steamboat minted fortunes as fast as the railroads that superseded them. But this was, and is, trapper country. The first white men who really roamed this hinterland were the French, the fur trappers and traders who made the most of a huge continental landscape where, unlike Europe, the mountain ranges ran from north to south, and the rivers also. There is hardly a river in the main river systems of the American mainland that has not left the relics of the French fur trappers, for they extended Napoleon'· empire up the Mississippi and the Missouri and the Ohio to places far in the north. Even Chicago, it may strike you, is pronounced 'Shick-ago' and not 'Chick-ago' because the first people to come on it were French rivermen. Chicago is an Indian name, but the French had trouble with the 'chi' sound, as they still do (they can't even say 'Good night, chairee'), and they had to say it 'Shick-ago'. The incoming Yankees picked up the pronunciation and it has stayed that way ever since, except, of course, out of the mouths of Englishmen, who live eighteen miles from the French but have had little truck with them.

But in this first valley that I went through, the French had been quietly obliterated by the Scots-Irish, who have a habit of taking over any place they settle in; and if they don't absorb it, they preserve the gift of not being absorbed either. Until I arrived on the edge of the Bluegrass all the names were such as Cochran,

[37]

McConnell, Marshall, and Keith and Duncan. In a charming small town called Washington one of the houses that is a required stop for tourists is a two-storeyed Georgian brick house. It was built at the turn of the eighteenth century by a man who had loaded a large family on a flatboat, sailed down the Ohio, and made a home here. The point of visiting the place today is that in the grounds many of the Marshall family are buried. And there stands still the modest tombstone of a certain Mary Keith, who turned out to be the mother of John Marshall, an early and great Chief Justice of the United States Supreme Court. The epitaphs on Scottish tombstones are not, as I recall, very flowery, not even when they were written in the eighteenth century, which both in old England and in New England consigned its beloved to the care of Providence with grand flourishes of the language. But some of these Kentucky leavetakings are as chilly as the Highlands. That of the mother of Chief Justice Marshall is no exception. It reads, 'Mary Randolph Keith, born 1737, she was good, not brilliant, useful not ornamental, and the mother of fifteen children.' The mind reels at the size of her progeny if she had been ornamental.

Well, by the middle of the afternoon I had come to the end of the winding river-bottom roads and was on a long undulating upland and the true Bluegrass country. You will want to know, as everybody who has never seen it does, if the grass is really blue. It is not. Even the natives admit that it is merely green in summer. But no matter how much the Kentucky guide insists that 'only in May do the blue anthers of its blossoms give the grass a distinctly steel-blue tint', a stranger needs to wear special tinted glasses to make it appear so. The way not to disappoint your friends is to photograph it in colour in the very late afternoon, when the slanting light of the entire Western hemisphere spreads a film of milky blue on anything, even the complexion of your favourite girl. It is only fair to say that you do notice the greenness of the grass, but it would not startle an Englishman or an Irishman and it would not be much of a surprise to a native of Oregon. However, let's not be hoity-toity about this local product. It is as indigenous to this region as the Monterey cypress is to that small coastal stretch of central California. It is not matched as turf, and as pastureland is surpassed, I should guess, only by the two famous sections of eastern Pennsylvania and southwestern Belgium, which a League of Nations survey chose as the finest in the world.

The Bluegrass is a small central plain, less than eight thousand square miles, which lies on a bed of limestone and is richly veined with underground water. And this is the perfect—they say essential—recipe for the two glories of Kentucky: fine horses and bourbon whiskey. It is the limestone which endows the waters that pass through it with phosphorus and calcium. Which, as every stable boy knows (and I just learned), are two ingredients of bone and rippling muscle. This is why the Kentucky thoroughbreds are strong and fast and beautiful to look upon. This is why, as you drop south from the eroded hills of southern Ohio and up on to the downs of the Bluegrass country, the road signs change from advertisements for familiar gasolines and cigarettes to elegant stud farms that say: 'Brood mares, boarding and training'; 'Track entrance, 100 feet'; and 'Blue Grass Seed'.

In deference to people who were brought up in my own self-denying faith, I will quickly explain the essential ingredients of Kentucky's second famous product and then pass on. It may be regrettable but it is also true that the water that courses through the limestone has a distinctive flavour. There are simple, strong people who slake their thirst with the natural product alone and go on, I'm told, to live blameless lives. But there are others, the first of whom was one Jacob Spears, as long ago as 1790, who looked on the Kentucky water as the merest raw material for a confection that has done the state some service. The United States abounds, as you may have heard, in maize, so much so that like the English with their wheat, the Scots with their barley, and the

[39]

Australians with their oats they have adopted it as the usual counter-word for the staple crop: corn. Mr Spears earned the gratitude of uncounted generations by having the wit to take the maize and grind it and mash it and add the magic limestone water, and then distil the compound and age it. And that's how bourbon was born, so called after the name of the county that gave birth to this splendid firewater. Not surprisingly, Mr Spears's first distillery was in Paris. And the heart of the Bluegrass country is between Paris and Versailles.

These towns were so named, as were many others nearby, in grateful remembrance of a stripling boy, a nineteen-year-old Frenchman, the Marquis de Lafayette, who offered himself in the service of the American Revolution to General Washington and beat you know who, and has ever after symbolized the special one-upmanship that the French enjoy in America. This is nothing to dwell on, but you surely can't expect me to toss off the remark that I have just driven from Paris to Versailles without explaining that we are still in Kentucky.

It has a wide undulating green horizon, strikingly devoid of evergreens but spotted here and there with those jetting, fanlike American elms, which, alas, have been blighted by the Dutch bug all the way from Ohio to the New England coast. The Bluegrass is rich country in more senses than one, for it must cost a modest fortune to maintain even the five-barred white wooden fences that ring the paddocks and enclose the fields and swing like switchbacks between you and the horizon. Inside these pastures is practised that strange and compelling ritual of breeding race horses that so obsesses the insider and leaves the outsider feeling that he has been mistaken all his life about what a horse is. In sickness and in health, in affluence and depression, no babies anywhere in Kentucky are so jealously and delicately cared for. After the weaning comes the precisely regulated diet—a mixture of oats and corn, bran and flax seed and vitamin extracts—then the trimming of the

feet, the breaking to the halter, the gentling into the paddock routine, then the exploratory trotting and cantering, and then the
speed trials; all this going on for two years or more before the
magic truth is revealed or exploded: whether or not the blood of
the horse's ancestors and the skill of his training will merge to produce a true race horse, perhaps a great one.

In the late winter and early spring, you could have seen on the
doors of some stalls record charts—for temperature, diet, and
other clinical peculiarities of the tender patient inside—which are
as anxiously consulted as those in a surgical ward; because no discipline is too fussy, no care too excessive to the men who match
their knowledge of blood lines and skill in training methods, in the
gaudy hope that one day the people may flock to see their ward
run on the first Saturday of May in the Derby at Churchill Downs.
And there can be few Kentucky owners and breeders who do not
nurse a faint hope that later on the people may troop to a second
shrine comparable with Kentucky's first.

And what is that? It is Faraway Farm, outside Lexington, and to
some knowing people it is as much of a pilgrimage as Lenin's
Tomb used to be to an obedient Russian. Up against the sky and
standing on a small hillock is a handsome statue of the greatest
race horse of his time, who won nineteen times in twenty-one
starts, collected a quarter of a million dollars in only two seasons,
sired 236 horses, 176 of whom were winners: the fastest, the most
beautiful, the proudest son of Kentucky—Man o' War. You amble
up to the statue with your hands in your pockets and a few other
visitors come up, and the men take their hats off. You are surprised to find that you have done the same.

All this, you will have assumed, is an easy build-up to the climax of
a holiday in Kentucky: the breathtaking spectacle itself, the Derby.
Well, to be quite honest, I can think offhand of a dozen other
spectacles that catch my breath quicker. A hooked bluefish, for

instance, a glass of lager, the dimple in the chin of Ava Gardner. For I was shaken to discover that if, while the race is on, you lose your programme or have a coughing fit you can miss it altogether. If anybody had asked me, I should have guessed that the Kentucky Derby was something like the bicycle race around France, and that we were going to sit through the last day of it. It turned out it takes two minutes, and for this the whole population of Louisville, and several hundred train and plane loads of gamblers from the East and West, and breeders from Ireland and Argentina, and 'kinfolk' from the South, make plans for a year, finagle for tickets, pay regal prices for a bed, and line up for food—for a 120 seconds on the first Saturday in May. Other people's enthusiasms are always a riddle, but I shouldn't take kindly to a sneer at mine. So I will say that the reason for my being in this strange place was a promise I had given, in a wild moment a year before, to my ten-year-old daughter. By the peculiar grace of God, she has not yet become aware of one half the human race—I mean boys. That being so, what else is there on earth to rave about but horses? Her weekends are spent bouncing round the park, the only dress catalogues she handles feverishly are ones for riding gear, her room is plastered with more ribbons and horse prints than a presidential convention with campaign buttons. She flew in on a flawless day over the velvety pastures and the rolling farms and the gleam of horseflesh, and she said at once, 'Why can't we live in Kentucky?' I said, 'I'll tell you why. Because a little later on you'll discover that they breed boys in other places than the Bluegrass.'

The object of this trip, then, was up at dawn and out with Ned, a slim young man in blue jeans and a high-buttoned shirt, with tendons as bowed as the horse he couldn't sell. There was a choice of colts, fillies, ponies, for this was a working farm, and a working farm for other less favoured beasts. Cows sloshed their tails around in the heat of the day, and at night sheep complained to the moon and the air was dense with birds that trilled, barked, whistled, shrieked, and glucked. The sun came up like a yellow rose and fell like a sweating orange. It was 94 degrees the first day, 92 the second, 96 on the great day itself. But the tempo was easy and nobody was going anyplace but Churchill Downs. We lay on the grass and had lunch of Kentucky chicken hash and potato pancakes and the best succotash (corn and lima beans) I'd ever eaten. We had a box overlooking the finishing post, and for the first time since 1880 there was a challenge from the losing jockey, and a very tense pause before the stewards decided that in the stretch Tommy Lee and Sword Dancer were bumping each other in a rhythmical and entirely legal way.

Some people, I don't doubt, will be sensing with suspicion or disfavour the sort of society I seem to be sketching: a horsy, arrogant, vowel-chopping—or vowel-smearing—upper crust. Not your cup of tea perhaps? Not mine either, I assure you. While I feel like a vaudeville clown in the presence of dignitaries of the church and state, I am practically T. S. Eliot in the presence of horsy people. I know less about a horse than—certainly—a horsefly. An Argentinian, in a mad attack of mistaken identity, asked me if I'd brought any promising fillies along. I said I had brought a ten-year-old filly with me. My daughter hopped to my side and growled in a whisper, 'You can't be a filly if you're older than four.' 'How about colts?' I asked. 'Same thing,' she said, and blushed for her city-slicker father. The Argentinian thought he was in the wrong town and wandered off.

But the great surprise, and the delight, of this interlude in the Bluegrass was to mix with a lot of people who were expert and hospitable and easygoing with their knowledge, and impossible to grade socially. You never knew whether the young tow-haired man in the corner was a Yale sophomore or a groom. For three great days, Jefferson's original image of America was restored—that of a pastoral republic where the rich, the poor, and the in-between mingle, eat, drink, joke together, have the same manners, the same idioms, and an overriding gentleness and naturalness. A small, uncorrupted society united in a lovely landscape by a genuine love of the same thing—a horse. (I discovered, much too late in life, that the same sense of an innocent community can be guaranteed by the pursuit of a ball with a liquid centre.)

On the plane coming home, my daughter rattled on in ecstasy till she had to catch her breath. I jumped in with the damping reminder that it was wonderful but it was not at all like life. 'What d'you mean?' she said. 'Well,' I said, as we looked down on the approaching industrial landscape of the Jersey flats, 'we might have had bad seats, or stayed in a crummy motel, or keeled over from the heat, or been bedded down in Louisville, or there might have been no horses to ride. Everything was perfect,' I said, 'but it isn't always so.'

'I don't get it,' she said, and fell asleep.

10

Breton Rules the Waves
[Newport, Rhode Island, June 19, 1964]

At four minutes to ten this morning, a chic 45-foot ketch with a black plywood hull, and a dinky upside-down yellow lifeboat attached, skimmed between Brenton Reef and the reef light tower here, and a slight tremor was recorded on Nelson's Column in Trafalgar Square.

A Frenchman had attempted, and what is worse achieved, the audacity of crossing the Atlantic in 27 days, 1 hour and 56 minutes, or better than five days under Chichester's 1962 (non-OSTAR) record.

He is Eric Tabarly, a thirty-two-year-old lieutenant in the French Navy, a curly brown-haired, brown-bearded, merry-eyed, compact little man of Napoleonic (5ft 4in.) stature, but with the wide-eyed insouciance of Jean-Pierre Belmondo giving the slip to French Customs or blowing up Brasilia. According to a close friend of his, panting for the great reunion as we plunged into a heavy sea towards the reef, Tabarly had two ambitions in life: to cross the Atlantic singlehanded and to 'fight the English'.

'*Comment?* Fight?'

'Yes—to attack, to defeat perhaps?'

'Ah, to beat?'

'Yes—to beat the English, no?'

'Yes.'

He had done it, and when we spotted his graceful *Swallow* ('*pen duick*' is Breton for the bird) coming over the horizon into a 12 mph south-west wind we must say that we also saw at our elbow an ecstatic white-haired French Consul from Boston, and one Captain Chatel, a naval attaché, strutting on the balls of his feet, and a French correspondent pointing with dramatic emphasis to a head-line in *Le Monde*: '*Tabarly serait en tête des solitaires.*'

Tabarly was, without doubt, the leader of the singlehanders. As the French captain put it: 'We cannot understand why we should be winning, and the British cannot understand why they should be losing. It is historic, and it is very droll.'

It was droller than we knew, for Tabarly told us that for the whole month at sea he had no idea whether he was winning or los-ing until seven this morning, when a couple of yachts and a young outboarder went out to greet him and conveyed, by grotesque sign language, that he was indeed *numéro un*. Tabarly had a radio, but he tried once to reach a French station, failed, and switched it off for good. '*Le TSF*,' he said. 'I do not like.'

'Offhand' is the word that the French aboard used to pinpoint the character of the Bretons. 'And is he Breton?' the friend said. 'Typical, a comical character. They don't give a damn.'

We expected him some time last evening, but at seven o'clock he was reported 74 miles from the finishing line and buffeting west-north-west winds up to eight knots. This made it impossible for him to do much more than five knots through the night. Then the wind swivelled round to south-west, and suddenly the coast-guard reported him 'right off Point Judith and going like crazy'.

When we caught up with him, we and a score of yachts, out-boards, put-puts, and fire-boats streaming jets of water in salute, he was ambling in with slack sails towards the harbour and looking up with red eyes to jumping-jack photographers bawling without success, to 'Wave, man, wave!'

At last, he was tied up to the Port o'Call marina, and several thousand Americans in a hundred variations of the colourful native summer costume straddled the rails and stanchions and peered down at the little bobbing black hull flying the tricolour;

[46]

for he was hemmed in by the contestants in tomorrow's record entry for the Newport–Bermuda race, no fewer than 145 yachts of indescribable splendour, a concentration of nautical wealth that must have been very awesome to a Breton lad who wouldn't think of going home any other way than he came. ('Naturally, I will sail back alone, it is my own boat, it would cost money to ship it.')

The characterization of Bretons as 'offhand' took on a stoical grandeur when we got him into port. A score or more newsmen jumped aboard and scuffed the decks and bruised the paint and cracked a spar or two. He paid no heed. He stood there in a blue navy jersey and blue slacks and happily answered all questions in two languages and several dialects.

What was the worst trouble? Like Chichester and every other veteran, the answer was the same: the lack of any prolonged sleep. On the eighth day he broke the governor shaft of his automatic steerer, and from then on he had to steer by hand.

The weather, though, was better than he had hoped. Gales on three days, once the winds went to Force Nine. Still, he had never expected to do it in under thirty days.

His course was just south of the Great Circle, and although he was becalmed a couple of times, he was never frustrated by the winds, and the fog never lasted very long, so he stayed with it. He didn't seem to suffer, ever, from Chichester's chronic bellyache about which leg to take. He did what came naturally. He ate rice, spaghetti, a little tinned meat, and had lots of red wine.

Swallow was designed specially for this race. She has a very deep keel and is very light, perhaps half as heavy as a normal ketch of her size. The hull is 12mm plywood. He has no complaints about it at all. He would like to do it all again.

Was there any special ordeal? He apparently had never heard the word. But, after coaching by the more intense reporters, he got the idea. The worst thing, he said, was the nightmares that come

[47]

from broken sleep. He said it with a chuckle, as if he were describing an unexpected bonus.

As he was led away to the mayor and a reception committee, to receive the seal of the city and the yacht club's tie-clip ('in case he ever wears a tie'), the French friend swelled up like a pouter pigeon. 'This, you understand,' he said, 'is an entirely new sport in France. Five years ago very bad results in the Channel race. Ten years ago, nothing. Now—*mon Dieu*—the sale of boats to young Frenchmen, it will be *sensationnel, sensationnel!*'

11

Player's Puritan Victory
[June 1965]

At Creve Coeur, Missouri, last evening Gary Player, the dapper little perfectionist from South Africa, defeated Kelvin Nagle, of Australia, by three strokes (71 to 74) in the play-off of the United States National Open Championship in which on Sunday both men had finished with a 282 for the regulation seventy-two holes, only 2 over par.

When they came to the ninth tee in the long, silver light of a hot afternoon, Player was five strokes ahead and scrutinizing every lie like a laboratory technician with a blood sample. Some of the six or seven thousand people who had padded along the enormous fairways of the Bellerive Country Club decided it was all over, and they had to be shushed as they stomped off home while Player was crouching for his twitchy address.

But all those who had played and the millions who had watched the four previous days were haunted by the pitfalls, the canyons, the rearing forests, the House-of-Nonsense surprise of this youngest and longest (7,191 yards) course in the history of the Open. They recalled the absurdity of the short sixth, a water hole, where on Friday thirty-odd giants had clouted into the pond, thus causing the memorable crack in the clubhouse, 'Let's go down to the sixth and see how the other half drowns.'

They remembered the misery of their idols with the short sixteenth, which has a green as elevated as a pulpit. They had seen great professionals reduced to weekend hackers by the 606-yard province known as the seventeenth, whose great flanks slope down to water all the way. They would never forget that for the first time in eight years the lordly Arnold Palmer had failed to make the cut and after two days was home in Pennsylvania gawping at his television set, even as you and I.

And Nicklaus? Didn't the *Guardian* man say that the 1965 Open 'might well usher in the Age of Nicklaus'? Well, when the Masters' champion was sixteen shots behind the leaders some time on the third day they decided to postpone the Age of Nicklaus.

And also, if the bored ones needed an extra come-on, there was the reminder that Player had seemed to have the championship in his hand on Sunday when he fumbled into a double bogey. So most of the crowd waited, and it was a long, long wait. For Gary Player won this time by never taking a pitch or a putt or an intrusive blade of grass for granted.

At the end he described it as 'the toughest course I have ever played on in my life'. Its creator, Robert Trent Jones, describes it as 'at worst a tiger, at best a fox'. The forty-odd groaning professionals in the locker room describe Mr Jones as Dr Frankenstein and the Bellerive course as the Monster of American golf. Some of them suggest that it constitutes grounds for a slander suit, on the principle that it tends to bring a citizen 'into ridicule and disrepute with his fellow men'.

All this became acutely well known to little Gary Player in the first day or two, and the chances are that while others blasphemed he praised the Lord for so many ingenious and soul-searching trials. Not for nothing does Player do sixty or seventy push-ups a day (on his finger-tips), study yoga, refuse to sleep on a pillow ('it is more difficult for my heart to pump blood to my brain'), abstain from all 'sweets, pastries, and fried food'.

To the men who cheerfully recover from hangovers and maintain their pars over American fairways as wide as the Serengeti Plain, and with rough as uncomplicated as velvet, Mr Jones's Bellerive course is an affront to their way of life and a tasteless

[50]

sermon. To Gary Player, Johannesburg's Billy Graham, Bellerive must look like the green pastures.

And so into the twilight he pondered his iron shots for minutes on end, climbed hills and knolls and stood on his head to gauge the break of the green, lined up a two-foot putt from the pin and the apron, and back again, and picked up every dew drop or hint of fuzz in between.

Never did hypochondria reap such a rich reward. It made him proud to announce that after the achievement of this life-long ambition ('Even as a boy I would say: "Here's a ten-foot putt for the US Open"') he could now spend more time with his family and less on the tour. It gave him, incidentally, 25,000 dollars, which he handsomely handed back in two charitable packages: one to the United States Golf Association to encourage 'junior golf', the other to a cancer fund ('because my mother died of cancer').

All in all, a very worthy champion, a throwback to the Bobby Jones era; and like the immortal one himself, it is not his carefulness, or the painful putting together of his strokes; nor even his undoubted nuttiness about yoga, health foods, pillows, and the like; but the simple and refreshing fact that in a game which more and more is engulfed by publicity, advertising, and lavish stakes, he is a gent.

1 2

A Mountain Comes to
Muhammad

[February 1967]

In Houston, Texas, last night, Muhammad Ali, of Louisville, Kentucky, became the first Black Muslim priest to be acclaimed as the undisputed heavyweight champion of the world. His comment was in keeping with his holy calling; 'I am a miracle.'

Until the final bell clanged, after fifteen rounds of teasing slaughter, Ernie Terrell, a modest giant from Philadelphia, was the official World Boxing Association champion, on the technicality that he had dutifully fought the opponents sanctioned by the association, whereas Muhammad Ali was disbarred as a reputable fighter when Sonny Liston retired hurt and he promptly signed him up for a lucrative return bout.

But shortly before midnight, when Terrell looked like a broken-down sledgehammer being pawed by a tiger, there was no doubt in anyone's mind, least of all in Terrell's, that his day was done. He has never been knocked down, and it was something of a collateral miracle that his 6ft 6in. frame could still potter around with a left eye as plump as a June strawberry and his right like a bloody slit left by the Vietcong. The mountain had come to Muhammad and been blasted apart in one hour and ten minutes of calculated detonations.

According to his conqueror, it was all his own fault. Muhammad had said earlier in the day that at the weighing-in he would ask Terrell a simple question of three words, and according to the answer he would either dispose of him in a merciful knockout or stretch him out on the rack of a long 'Floyd Patterson humiliation-type defeat'.

The question was: 'What's my name?' The answer, respected by all sports writers and fight fans, is Cassius Marcellus Clay, a very proud name in Kentucky since it is that of the delegate who secured the presidential nomination of Abraham Lincoln, the man who, in a rare act of pre-vision, freed the slaves and enabled the present Cassius Clay to hate the white man and tool round in a Lincoln Continental.

But young Cassius recently brushed off the eminence his parents hoped would brush off on him from his famous namesake. He took his Black Muslim vows, renounced tobacco, liquor, and the wiles of women, and declared himself to be the one and only Muhammad Ali. At the weighing-in, Terrell stared at him as long as Scrooge recognizing Marley's ghost and replied, 'I know him—Cassius Clay!' Clay went into his well-known dance of rage and promised Terrell the sort of slow torture inflicted on Floyd Patterson's crippled back from what appeared at the time to be motives of sheer meanness but which was later explained as an act of obedience to religious scruple.

Muhammad was as good as his sacred word. It took him six rounds to manoeuvre the infidel into the proper position for a ritual sacrifice. Like the roisterers in the old Sunday School lantern lectures, Terrell had the unbeliever's usual early luck. He kept planting Muhammad against the ropes and jabbing at his ribs, not only with the left that everyone credits him with but with right-arm stabs as well. But in the seventh round the rake's progress took its inevitable downhill turn. The man of God was out in the centre now, hopping and feinting and tossing his head back in rhythm with the wild lunges of the 'one-armed bandit'.

The simple sinner could never reach him and pretty soon the slides would show us the falling-down drunk, the mortgage foreclosed, the weeping family, and the triumph of virtue. There was blood on both of them by now but it all came from the spouting eyelids of Terrell.

[53]

In the eighth and ninth rounds Muhammad allowed him a pause for repentance. Jabbing and hooking and belting as he chose, Muhammad started to scream the catechism: 'What's my name? What's my name?' Terrell was too dumb or beaten, to respond. For the six last interminable rounds, his head was hidden behind his gloves and from time to time he would peep through a veil of blood and give little left jabs, like an expiring cat.

Muhammad was greatly troubled by one snag in the plot. 'I had meant to put him away in the eighth,' he said, 'but he wouldn't go down.' By some foul-up of the moral order, Terrell suffered and survived his promised purgatory.

And the next fight? There would be no next fight, said Muhammad's manager or acolyte, until they had gone with other good Muslims into Arabia. Next stop, Mecca (by permission of Muhammad's draft board, which blasphemously denies his divinity and has classified him 1-A: fit for potato peeling or Vietnam).

Come-Uppance for the 'Onliest Champion'

[May 10, 1971]

It is not enough for a lifelong Methodist to wait for justice on Judgment Day. He preserves a deep yearning to see sinners get their come-uppance here on earth.

And last night all the rumbling warnings of his boyhood came meanly, beautifully true: from the Psalms and Moody and Sankey right through to Robert W. ('A fool there was') Service.

The moral of Muhammad Ali's slaughter was so thumpingly obvious that even one of the scarlet-sweatered men in his corner coined a proverb as 'the onliest champion of the world' tottered off to have his bulging jaw X-rayed. 'You must remember,' the man said, 'that a star boxer is a lot of clown and a lot of child.'

For twenty-five years, Cassius Marcellus Clay has been glaring in the mirror and declaring himself to be the prettiest and the greatest. In the past four years, as a holy father, he has somehow managed to manipulate the humility of the Muslim faith to make an exception of its latest convert. His colossal arrogance was in full flower last night as he came prancing into the ring in his scarlet robe. Before it all began, he danced, he sprang lightly on his toes, he cut and stabbed the air with jabs that were marvellous to see.

He granted the roaring crowd a kind of indulgence, acknowledging their presence by looking down his short, adorable nose and lightly nodding his head. He assumed his stool as the heir apparent might await the depositing of the crown by the Archbishop of Canterbury. At the end of the second round, he waved a derisory gesture at the departing Frazier as if to say: 'No way, no way, this punk can touch me.' At the end of the third round, by which time the unbelievers might have thought that Frazier's buzzsaw operations on the Emperor's stomach were threatening his mortality, Ali favoured the minions of the press with a roguish wink.

This, as it turned out, was the high moment, the last *beau geste* in the career of Cassius Clay Muhammad Ali, the unconquered. In the fifth round, Frazier committed an act of *lèse-majesté*. The Emperor had held him off and patted him with his long, catlike paw, saying 'There, there, why so hot, little man?' Then Frazier did a monstrous thing. He put his tongue out, and he grinned. Since Frazier looks like Sammy Davis cast in concrete, it was as if one of the gargoyles of Notre Dame had come down and cackled an obscenity in the middle of divine service. The Emperor winced in a spasm of rage and Frazier dropped his guard and flapped his arms waggishly around his thighs as if to say, 'Well, pretty boy, what are you waiting for?'

In the sixth, Ali recovered his cool for a pretty period, during which he rested his beautiful shoulders on the ropes and playfully pawed at the burrowing little man. Frazier is not so little at that, but his sacrifice of $3^{1}/_{2}$ inches in height and $8^{1}/_{2}$ inches in reach make him seem so. At the end of this round, too, Ali jogged back to his corner and repeated, with considerably less feeling, his old gesture of derision.

By the seventh, even his disciples began to wonder how much of Ali's nonchalance was feigned or true. What the people up close had been seeing for six rounds was a bulldozer battering away at Ali's middle with the impatience of a squirrel burying nuts. We should have been warned by the really remarkable speed that such a bruiser was maintaining through half the fight.

He had started off with something of the absurdity of the old silent newsreels, in which generals reviewed troops, cars whisked round corners, women embraced, in jagged lightning movements. It seemed impossible to me, hunched up close by one of the official doctors, that anyone, certainly any heavyweight, could keep this up for more than a couple of rounds. The doctor nodded at this misgiving but added: 'There's a limit, too, to the pounding a stomach can take.' Another man, a grog-blossomed fight veteran, wearily remarked: 'I used to say that this Frazier fought like Rocky Marciano, but not so good. Now I'm not so sure.'

The crowd sensed something of the sort and improvised a great swelling organ chorus of 'Al-ee! Al-ee! Al-ee!' It reminded me of the defiant cheers that rolled around the ballroom of the Eugene McCarthy headquarters in Los Angeles in 1968 when the down-state returns were coming in and showing him to be a certain loser.

In the eighth round, all the bogeymen predictions of the astrologers and the Book of Job began to come true for Ali. Frazier was bunched over Ali's stomach, his head rammed against the big boy's chest, and rattling away like a piston in heat. Ali clutched his ears with his gloves and tensed his stomach muscles. He was, a weird irony now revealed, too tall to reach down to this murderous midget. Frazier was too small to have to bother about hooks or upper-cuts, any blow from below. 'Talk about endurance,' said old Grog-Blossom, 'this Clay's got a stomach made of whipcord.'

When Ali pattered off on free-floating legs, the crowd roared again. This time it was 'Joe! Joe! Joe!' but it was a tribute, not a scream of defiance. From then on, all the stuffing, the true and the pretentious, the visceral and the egoistical, had gone out of Ali. True, he was facing a bleeding, scarred mug. And, true, his own beauty seemed unmarred, but that was because Frazier did not need to reach so high to ruin him. The epidermis does not so easily show cuts and gashes, but behind its rippling façade there must have been a monstrous clinical picture of ruptures and congests.

All that Ali could do now was to back constantly into the ropes and writhe like Laocoön at the agony that was seizing his middle. Frazier was slowing down now, but he was so much in control that once he lifted Ali irritably from the ropes and planted him solidly

[57]

in the middle of the ring. The eleventh round was a nightmare that no one who saw it will ever forget. Simply viewed as a target, a bull's eye, Ali must be the most unyielding metal since the discovery of iron. He was pounded in the middle and on the shoulders, and his head began to flop like a pendulum. He staggered around like a hopeless drunk—and surely another thirty seconds would have finished him.

But Frazier too was hearing the bell toll. He was moving not much faster than a zombie, though still burrowing away. At rare intervals, Ali was so overcome with the outrage of this performance that he erupted in a flurry of long lefts and short jabs. But these were pure reflexes, the wriggle of the snake's body when the head is severed.

And then in the fifteenth, Frazier caught him with a walloping left hook and Ali was down and kneeling and miraculously up again . . . he could not be downed, not by this exhausted monster. But he surely was whipped, humiliated, massacred. At the end, it would have taken a superhuman effort of recovery on Ali's part to raise a sneer.

On the way down to the Garden I asked my black cab driver how he figured the fight. 'I really don't know,' he said, 'but I'd like to see this Frazier cool him down a little.' That he did. In a brief overseas cable, you could save a lot of money by summing the whole thing up in nine words by Frazier: 'Those body punches. One, two, three. They add up.'

1 4

History of the
Scottish Torture
[1973]

They have been playing golf for 800 years and nobody has satisfactorily said why.

For of all forms of exercise theoretically designed for recreation and relaxation none can be so unerringly guaranteed to produce nervous exhaustion and despair leading to severe mental illness and, in some cases, petulance. The consolation once offered by a helpful caddie to a British Prime Minister that it was 'only a game' was enough to unloose a torrent of obscenity that had never before passed the statesman's lips. After an abominable round, a man is known to have slit his wrists with a razor blade and, having bandaged them, to stumble into the locker room and enquire of his partner: 'What time tomorrow?' Bing Crosby has a friend who has been working on his game for forty years and who, when asked after a long absence if he was playing much golf, moodily replied, 'Just days.'

Why should anyone persist in a game whose aim, in Winston Churchill's memorable definition, 'is to hit a small ball into an even smaller hole with weapons singularly ill-designed for the purpose'? Well, it has been going on for so long that it is impossible to dismiss, like mah-jong or sex, as a passing fad. Bernard Shaw once proclaimed that the propulsion of a ball across open country with a stick was 'a typical capitalist lunacy of upper-class Edwardian England'. As usual, he summarily dismissed all the facts in the interests of a sentence with a lilt, for the lunatics so afflicted have remained a hardy race since Roman times at the latest. Caesar's legions instructed the barbarian Britons in banging a leather ball stuffed with chicken feathers. That ball remained standard until 1845, when an English clergyman who dabbled in Hindu mythology received a statue from India of the god Vishnu wrapped in gutta-percha. The cult of Vishnu—incorporating, as we all know, the notion of 'uncountable incarnations' with the tenth still missing!—is extremely taxing to a mind brought up on the simplicities of the New Testament. And it may well be that the Revd Dr Robert Adams Patterson saw in the gutta-percha wrapping a saving expression of the grace of God. At any rate, he made out of it the first gutta-percha golf ball and so became immortal. (The opposing school of thought, which maintains that the packaged god was not Vishnu but Siva—The Destroyer—is entitled to its opinion. That's as far as we're going to go just now with the effect of Hinduism on the composition of golf balls.)

Anyway, at some unrecorded point during the 2,000-year dominance of 'the feathery' (55 BC–AD 1845) the Dutch banged a ball across a frozen pond at an adjoining post. Since the game itself was called *Het Kolven*, all the Scotsmen since Robert the Bruce cannot howl down the evidence that golf, in its essentials and its terminology, was a Dutch invention. The Dutch pretty soon saw where it was leading (to paranoia and the paralysis of their empire) and more or less abandoned it. By then the Scots had seized on it and, no later than the fifteenth century, it posed a similar threat to the national defence, causing ordinary citizens who should have been off at archery practice to spend all their spare time trying to hit the damn thing straight. James II of Scotland was sufficiently alarmed at the neglect of archery to put out, in 1457, a decree commanding that 'golfe be utterly cryed down and not to be used'. It was too late. James did not recognize what every other Scot knew in his bones: that golf was just what the Scottish character had been searching for, for centuries. Namely, a method of self-torture, disguised as a game, which would entrap irreligious youths into the principles of what was to become known first as Calvinism and then, through *het kolvenism*, as 'golf'. The main tenets of this faith are that life is grim and uncomfortable and that human vanity cannot prevail. The emblem on the necktie reserved for the members of the Royal and Ancient Golf Club of St Andrews—the Vatican of golf—is of St Andrew himself bearing the saltier cross on which, once he was captured at Patras, he was to be stretched before he was crucified. Only the Scots would have thought of celebrating a national game with the figure of a tortured saint. Yet, as anyone knows who has laboured for years to put together a serviceable golf game and seen it collapse in a single afternoon, the symbol is apt. No experienced golfer has ever suggested that St Andrew is a morbid choice as the patron saint of the game. He was a realist moving towards a sticky end, and he triumphantly exemplified the golfer's credo: that Man should expect very little here below and strive to get it. If there is one generalization that may be applied to the inveterate golfer, it is that he is never an idealist. It is impossible to imagine Ibsen, Dante, Shaw, Hitler or D. H. Lawrence sallying out on a Saturday afternoon to subject his ego so publicly to the facts of life. Of all European nations, the Germans are the non-golfing champions. The game is too much for their pride. For every game of golf is an open exhibition of overweening ambition, courage deflated by stupidity, skill soured by a whiff of arrogance. It is possible to fake a reasonable bridge game and to affect a modestly consistent skill at swimming, billiards and, yes, tennis. Even a mediocre chess player can convey, with a little adroit gamesmanship, that he was plotting a combination that didn't quite come off. But every golfer, no matter how impressively he has talked up, or talked down, his game beforehand, proclaims in the simple act of standing to the ball—before he has even started to swing—that he is a 10 handicap or an incurable 25. It does not take a pro to recognize, after a hole or two, that A is a fake and B is a duffer and C—goddammit!—is a golfer.

[61]

(There are baffling exceptions. It is quite clear from watching the swing of Doug Sanders and the stunted finish of Arnold Palmer that neither of them will ever be a golfer.)

These humiliations are the essence of the game. They derive from the fact that the human anatomy is exquisitely designed to do practically anything but play golf. To get an elementary grasp of the game, a human must learn, by endless practice, a continuous and subtle series of highly unnatural movements, involving about sixty-four muscles, that result in a seemingly 'natural' swing, taking all of two seconds to begin and end. Very few of us ever make it, and then not for long. No one makes it for ever. Jack Nicklaus, the best golfer of our day, and perhaps of any day, is at this moment busy working on some puzzling 'defect' in his swing.

Yet the figures on the national addiction to golf are almost as alarming as the hard-drug statistics. When tennis was born, a century ago, the Scots had been at golf for 500 years at least. But there were no known American golfers. (It was tried out in New York, South Carolina and Georgia at the end of the eighteenth century and given up as hopeless.) Twenty years ago, there were calculated to be eight million hooked Americans; today, it is closer to fourteen million.

There must be good reasons. The usual ones given by golfers to non-golfers are three: (1) That the game, unlike tennis, squash, pinochle, chess, *boccie* and practically every other competitive joust, is not played on the same dull rectangle or board or in the identical pit or alley the world over but is played across delightful varieties of open landscape. I should like very much to maintain that all golfers are nature lovers. Unfortunately, while all golfers know the difference between a bunker and a hole in the ground, legions of them cannot tell a cypress from a Cypriot. (2) That there is something tonic and bracing about the fact that you are totally responsible for the fate of the little white ball and that you have only one chance of hitting it correctly (there is no second serve, no third strike, no fourth down, etc.). (3) That golf offers the supreme challenge of playing, not against an opponent, but always and only against yourself.

The second and third reasons simply detail the objections, not the incentives, to playing golf and powerfully confirm what I seem to have been saying all along, that no man in his right mind would ever play golf. That is just the point. Nobody in his right mind does, no mature adult with a grain of what the French call *l'amour-propre*, which has nothing to do with girls and everything to do with self-respect. Right-minded men fish, grow petunias, run the PTA or the White House. (The best thing about Eisenhower's Presidency was his Jeffersonian conviction that there should be as little government and as much golf as possible.)

So right at the start you can be sure, wherever you wander to pick up a game, that there are certain noxious types you will never have to meet. The proud, the self-regarding, the anxious. Anybody concerned for his 'image' gave up golf as soon as he saw that his partners, in a single round, had fathomed his deep pretentiousness. Look at the membership board of any fashionable club and you will see fashionable names, all right. But you will also notice that there is no handicap number against their names. They are non-playing members, for the simple reason that they have no intention of exhibiting, week in and week out, what their friends know anyway, that they are pompous asses. Show me a man in a round of golf and I will give you a character analysis that makes Jeane Dixon look like—well, Jeane Dixon.

The main reason, I believe, for the lure of golf has to do with a unique brand of companionship possible only to a psychological type that unites the little boy aching to be king with the sensible adult who knows he'll never make it. It is the companionship of communal, low-key debunking, a willingness to invest three or four hours in proving to one and all the vanity of human wishes— especially the vanity of your closest friends. 'When a man laughs at

[63]

his troubles,' Mencken wrote, 'he loses a good many friends; they never forgive the loss of their prerogative.' Mencken abominated golfers and did not know them. If he had, he would have discovered the only worldwide secret society that revels in the mutual display of human frailty. By providing every man with the visible proof that his partner is a failing show-off, golf reinforces one of the great joys of friendship; it is all the more delicious for being secret, since the etiquette of golf requires that you keep it to yourself.

Don't suppose, though, that golfers are a particular species of meanie. They are a special kind of moral realist who nips the normal romantic and idealistic yearnings in the bud by proving once or twice a week that life is unconquerable but endurable. For the golfer compresses into a few hours all the emotions he spreads over the rest of his life: hope, envy, betrayal, self-discipline, self-deceit, the Holy Grail in view, the Grail smartly whipped out of sight. You're away, partner.

15

The Missing Aristotle Papers on Golf*
[1967]

The current *Golf Digest* lists thirty-eight books of instruction. Through the northern winter hundreds of thousands of slaves to the marvellous mania will be thrashing on their pillows imagining themselves chanting *Swing Easy, Hit Hard* with Julius Boros and *Never Say Never* with Bobby Nichols, rehearsing the tricks of *Chipping and Putting* with Billy Casper, snatching the *Secret of Holing Putts* from Horton Smith or the *Secrets of the Perfect Golf Swing* from Phil Galvano, and yielding at last to the sure-fire sedative of *My 55 Ways to Lower Your Golf Score* by Jack Nicklaus. Over breakfast, there will be the cartoon 'tips' of Palmer, Snead, and Tommy Armour. And once a month, the golf magazines will rush through the mails the absolutely final word on retarding the right side, swinging the hands, sliding the hips, forgetting the hips, eliminating sway, tension, casting, steering, scooping, slicing, hooking, the loose grip, the tight grip, the flat swing, the upright swing, the lot.

Anyone who has laboured over the literature, and then discovered how reluctant the human body is to see the word made flesh, is bound to conclude sooner or later that the trouble with the books is that they are mostly written by men who play great golf and write duffer prose. It is true, of course, that practically every book that carries the by-line of a champ was ghosted; 'the authors', as Charles Price puts it, 'had as much to do with the actual writing of them as King James did with writing the Holy Bible.'

*Bobby Jones on Golf, by Robert Tyre (Bobby) Jones.

[65]

This is where the failure, and the frustration, sets in. The self-effacing ghost, at his most conscientious, sits and argues with the King for days and months and then tries to set down what he thinks the great man means. The big question is, does the great man know what he *does* so wonderfully? For the raw material they both have to master is not golf but the communication of feelings so fine that they could only be perfectly conveyed by somebody able to handle great complexity of emotion in the barest prose. Donne, thou shouldst be slicing at this hour! At one end of the golf library, you have Ben Hogan analysing a split-second motion as a compressed course in aerodynamics. At the other end, you have Snead, the happy hillbilly, saying, 'Step up to that little ball like you're going to love it, keep saying "you little sweet thing, I'm not going to hurt you".' With the closest attention to these masters, the learner steps to the ball and ends up with only one sure feeling, that of baffled admiration for the fact that Hogan fired balls more precisely than anyone who ever played, and that Snead at fifty-four, in spite of his instructions, still swings the most graceful club in the game.

And now, in anticipation akin to reverence, the learner can take up, surprisingly, the only book entirely devoted to golf instruction to be put out by the immortal one himself. Between 1927 and 1935, Jones wrote two columns a week for a syndicate, which Charles Price has splendidly salvaged and distilled to about one-fifth of the original bulk. He handed the manuscript over to Jones for his approval. Whereupon, to Price's amazement, and our gratitude, the author then 'picked apart every chapter, every paragraph, every sentence, every phrase of his own writing until he was sure that thirty years had not dimmed what he truly meant to say.'

So what we have is a unique manual. One of the handful of very great golfers is also revealed as a literate and intensely thoughtful man who modestly shares the agony of Flaubert: to re-experience a feeling and transmit it with exactness to another person. In other words, unlike the vast majority of golfers, he knows precisely what he is doing. Unlike any other before him, he can *say* what he is doing.

It comes down, I think, to the business of metaphor, especially to the intense form of it embodied in an idiom. Whether a man learns golf from a pro or a book, or supplements one with the other, he is trying to impress on his visual memory, and then on his muscular habits, a series of metaphors designed by the great ones to give him the 'feel' of the swing. Linking only the favourite images of, say, Percy Boomer, Snead, Lema, Hogan, and Galvano, he will arrive at this astonishing picture: of a man standing in a barrel, his arms hanging down like an ape's, about to clasp his hands around a bird, too tight to let it go but not tight enough to hurt it. Pretty soon, he is swivelling to the right in the barrel and finds that his left arm has mysteriously fused into the line of the shaft, which he now uses to describe an arc. At the top of the back-swing, he tries to point his left thumb at his right ear, which is quite a trick since he is also intent on carrying a tray with his right hand. At last he swivels back, does a lateral shimmy with his hips and then attempts, according to taste, either to pull down on a bell rope, or thresh a field of wheat, or hit the ball with his wrist watch or plant the top of the shaft in the ground.

Most players have heard of these images and for most of us some of them transfer their meaning with great effect and others mean nothing at all. A good deal of the bickering that goes on among the great pros is not so much due to their differing on essentials as to the other guy's metaphor seeming forced or unreal.

It is the great gift of Bobby Jones that, in analysing all the motions from 'holding the club' to 'the competitive attitude', he is acutely aware that 'the words in our language that we must use to describe feel are necessarily vague and susceptible to varying inter-pretations among different persons . . . for this reason I think it is necessary in all forms of golf instruction to repeat over and over descriptions of the same movements, all the while altering the

[67]

modes of expression and terms of reference.' So there is no shibbo-
leth too familiar to escape his painstaking probe. He dislikes
'keeping your eye on the ball' and prefers 'staying behind it', or—
better—Abe Mitchell's saying that 'the player should move freely
beneath himself'. Many of the club clichés he takes apart with a
touch of grim, Lippmannesque humour. (On 'never up, never in':
'Of course, we never know but that the ball which is on line and
stops short would have holed out. But we *do* know that the ball
that ran past *did not* hole out.') He discovered, after many playing
years, that 'hitting from the inside' could be felt more vividly if he
thought of trying to swing the club 'through the ball outward
toward the right edge of the fairway'. For the first time, the universal misunderstanding implicit in the advice to establish the left arm
as a continuation of the shaft is exposed in this Aristotelian sentence: 'The teaching that the left arm and the club should lie in the
same vertical plane is all right, but no one in his wildest moments
ever conceived that they should lie in the same plane *in any other*
direction.'

Here is no Boomer testiness ('you are by no means trying to hit
the ball'), no Armour bullying, no 'tips', no dogma, and—thank
God—no locker-room humour. Here is the fruit of fifty years'
observation of golf by the wariest intelligence and the most attractive man who has ever played the game greatly. As such, it is the
classic manual and a boon to the learner and, I am told, the expert
alike.

In response to the publication of this piece, Jones dropped me a letter beginning:
'Offhand, I can't think of another contemporary author who has been compared, in
one piece, to Aristotle, Flaubert, John Donne and Walter Lippmann.'

[68]

16

The Heat on for
Arnie & Co.
[1968]

It was 102 degrees and the wet winds from the Gulf of Mexico were drenching everybody from the eyebrows to the balls of the feet, when Arnold Palmer pulled a long-iron into the small Sahara of a bunker on the eighteenth hole of the Pecan Valley Country Club in San Antonio, Texas.

A long, low groan fanned over this mangrove swamp, in which the Professional Golf Association of America chose, God knows why, to play its fiftieth annual tournament. The groan came from Arnie's panting army, which through the long summer of his discontent has made more agonized sounds than the French going home from Moscow.

But Arnold had birdied the seventeenth hole and on the previous two he had been within a whisker of sinking two birdie putts that would have evened his score for three rounds and put him in the lead for the only one of the big four championships (the Masters, the US Open, the British Open, and the PGA) he has never won.

Now he loped down the fairway with wet circles under the arms of his flypaper shirt, and smaller rings in the wrinkles of his forehead. He looked at the poached egg of his ball in the deep sand. Wearily he took a mid-iron.

It was 120 yards to the flag and offered the sort of preposterous recovery that Palmer in the old, audacious days would have gone for and got. He mimicked the necessary lazy swing and the quick break of the wrists. He dropped his head and took a bead on the invisible rim of the poached egg. And he blasted.

The egg ballooned into a glistening white ball and it shot from a barrage of white sand and took a low trajectory over the intervening rough and the concrete fairway and the coarse fringe and it bounced on the green and plopped into the hole against the flag and rebounded an inch beyond the rim.

The empty sky was filled with a roar, the like of which has not been heard since he birdied the ninth hole at San Francisco two years ago in the US Open, and was seven strokes up at the turn. Palmer was Arnie again, the duffer's idol who makes the kind of recovery the duffer makes in dreams.

It was enough to send him in to an ocean of cheering and put him at the start today only two strokes behind the taut little gorilla known as Marty Fleckman and Frank Beard, the spectacled swinger—the new generation to whom a long, hot summer is the name of the game and Palmer is an old hero about to be buried in the record books.

Nothing has been more obvious or more comfortable to forget, in the recent US Open at Rochester, and the current joust in the pecan country, than the muscular youngsters knocking on the door of the fortress where Palmer and Nicklaus and Casper live. Lee Trevino, the young Mexican, turned Rochester into a pop Waterloo, where the old guard with their long arcs and basic swings and all the panoply of the classic strategy were put to rout by an upstart with a baseball swing, a gabble of jokes and a ditch-digger's putting stroke.

Just behind Trevino was Bert Yancey, the last walking ghost of Bobby Jones, maintaining to the end the beautiful turn, the pause at the top, the falling right shoulder and the graceful sweep through that is now about to be anachronized before an onslaught of young guys with the forearms of apes who ram the ball into the air and rap it into the hole and know one thing and one thing well: that whether you slug or scramble, the low score takes the moneybag.

To this historic breakthrough there was added yesterday, and the day before, and again today, the needle of the heat. It turned the knife in the wound of the oldsters' humiliation. Julius Boros, looking like a whipped Arab general, missed a putt of three inches and almost slumped into the hole after it. Tall, calm Weiskopf blew up at a news photographer.

Palmer had a blinding headache on Friday and sent out for a hat: 'Not, for God's sake, a visor'—he still has some pride left and a baseball visor is for baseball players. Yesterday Palmer had 'puffy hands' and other veterans complained that in their greasy hands the club felt no firmer than a snake.

There was a general call for salt tablets, and Trevino, who thrives on sweat as a Scotsman on a keen east wind, grabbed a pill just for the heck of it. He threw up. Never heard such nonsense. He went back to his usual therapy of quick, short strides and incessant gags, and his usual tactic of missing the greens, shovelling up the short pitches, and ramming home the long putts.

And where does this get him against Palmer's graceful heroics? Identical score, that's where: 212, two strokes off the lead.

At the blistering end of the day when there was no wind at all, and the sun glowered like an approaching comet, the youngsters heaved and chuckled around the locker room, and the traditional heroes went for footbaths and their memories were of mellower days and a slower pace.

Today is Palmer's great chance to retrieve the game for the old guard. If he fails,* he might well imitate the memorable San Francisco millionaire, a dogged old golfer, who pulled his drive, topped his wood shot, fluffed in the bunker, and took a small divot on the putting green! He straightened up and looked at his towering companions in utter amazement.

'What am I doing?' he cried, 'I don't *have* to do this. I'm a rich man!'

*He did.

17

Pottermanship
[1968]

To say that this book (*The Complete Golf Gamesmanship* by Stephen Potter) is a landmark study in human sensibility comparable to the Old Testament or Freud's *Interpretation of Dreams* is, of course, obvious. But it is not yet obvious to the Establishment, whose members are uncomfortable with Potter's insights and tend to gather in corners and mumble about 'sportsmanship'. But no one has demonstrated better than Potter that sportsmanship is death to the spirit of gamesmanship. Sportsmanship produces nothing but decent, kindly, fair-minded, *petits bourgeois*.

The fact is that until Potter, laying aside his former preoccupations with D. H. Lawrence and Samuel Taylor Coleridge, published his pioneer work, *Gamesmanship*, so long ago as 1947, our knowledge of human hypocrisy and how it might be exploited for the well-being of the exploiter was haphazard at best. Dickens had done some rough experimental work in his—what is it?—fifteen novels. Alexander Pope was no slouch at celebrating the rich meanness of the human spirit. Machiavelli, of course, was the true forerunner of Potter, but his insights, and the technique of deception we can develop from them, were never systematized. It was left to Potter to throw a great light, in two modest monographs, on the wonderful possibilities of cheating under the guise of loving thy neighbour. It is Potter, not Freud or McLuhan or Marcuse, not Bertrand Russell or Isaiah Berlin, or any such simpleton, who has truly discovered the tough, tart root of human behaviour—*like it is*—and who, in his new book, shows us in no more than 177 cogent pages, the way to a fuller, more deceitful life.

Even the index to this book is a revelation. Other men's indexes, or indices, are stark guideposts to a sprawling terrain of births, marriages, deaths and other, if any, mortal statistics. Potter's index shows the range of his mastery of the continuing war between man and woman, man and man, pro and amateur, brother and brother-in-law, snob and counter-snob. For example: 'Cuffey, made to feel poor, 52'; 'Cornpetter, Major, fails to snub Tickler, 32'; 'Anti-anti-Semite play, 144'; 'Darwin, W. R., his indifference to innocent pride ploy, 74'; 'Woking, route to, how to argue about, 34'; 'Val-jean, Jean, misplaced remorse of, 160'; 'United States, clubhouse comforts of, how to counter, 103'.

It will be fussily argued by some readers that Potter is writing about golf. Nothing could be further from the truth. You might as well say that in *Othello* Shakespeare was writing about a handkerchief. Potter simply uses golf as his locale in which to tap the secret springs in all of us—well, in some of us—of Simon Legreemanship, Mata Harimanship, Lyndon Baines Johnsonmanship. If this were a mere history of golf, you would expect to read a great deal about Robert Tyre (Bobby) Jones, the greatest golfer of his time, some say of any time. But here, in Potter, there is only one brief, regretful paragraph about him, for the simple reason that Jones was a sportsman, in the anachronistic sense our grandfathers used: a genuinely good man. 'Many heads are shaken,' writes Potter 'when his name comes up.'

Potter chose golf, above all other games, through which to expound about life because, he once wrote (when he was under the influence of James Joyce) 'it is the gamesgame of gamesgames' for employing the human resources of pretence: pretended admiration, pretended courage, pretended hurt, stoicism, indifference and so on and on. He makes clear at the start that his prime concern is with life, for as he says, in brilliantly demolishing the oldest cliché, 'it is not golf that is a microcosm of life, but rather that life is golf in miniature.'

[73]

He begins with a penetrating history of the game that will replace once and for all the tedious chronicles that plod through all the boring progressions of the game from the feathery to the rubber-cored, from Holland to Scotland to South Carolina to Yonkers. His starting point is the usefulness of idiosyncrasy (bordering on hypocrisy) in the Scottish character, moves on to the growth of the Englishman's gift for exploiting 'one downmanship', and winds up with a brilliant and persuasive explanation of how the United States came to dominate the game in the 1920s. Like all great historical truths, it is very simple, and it is best expressed through the actions of one Great Man. The American conquest was due, we learn, to the appearance in Britain of 'the King Gamesman', Walter Hagen, and had little to do with 'his thread of skill'. He was the first American actually to intimidate the most confident Britons. He systematically overtipped his caddie. He hired a Rolls to take him to the *side door* of the clubs he was to play at (since, as a professional, he was not allowed in the main rooms). His great achievement, however, was to introduce and flaunt the two-tone shoe—soon to be known from Brighton to Cannes as the 'co-respondent's shoe'. He thus blithely transferred to the British his own inferiority complex, from which they have never recovered.

For precocious students of Potter there is the joy of discovering that the Master has greatly enlarged and developed his pioneering work. Here the diligent student of the ploy and counter ploy may may go on to practise the Secondary Hamper, the Pour, the Baltusrol and many another device for reducing one's partner (opponent?) in life, in golf, in business, in marriage, to dithering acquiescence or even frank surrender. It is a happy thing that the book appears at Christmas. Potter can be recommended wholeheartedly to those who prefer to believe that the Christian era is over, and that henceforth it is the bland and the sly who shall inherit the earth.

1 8

Walter Hagen
1892–1969
[1969]

Every golfer who has read the books or listened to the Oldest Member knows about Hagen's iron play, his incredible recoveries, the thrust of his right shoulder to the target, his dependable quota of atrocious shots, and how he arrived in Britain to win the Open and wound up fifty-fifth. But to recapture his stunning effect on Britain and British golf, you have paradoxically to forget about golf and see him strutting into the social scene of the 1920s. For—to the query of the young, 'What was so great about Hagen?'—the only possible answer is: his character, which was achieved without benefit of public relations releases or image-makers.

When Hagen arrived at Deal in 1920, there were no 'talkies' or television news roundups. And throughout the twenties, few Englishmen knew even what an American sounded like. He was a species of exotic. All the ordinary Englishman had to go on, unless he had billeted some doughboys in the First War, was Woodrow Wilson preaching soundless sermons in the newsreels and Gertrude Ederle, the Channel swimmer, grinning at ecstatic little men in bowlers as she sloshed ashore at Dover. Most of us in those days kept a file at the back of our minds of what we took to be the standard American types, compiled naturally from the silent movies. Wallace Reid was the clean-cut, sensitive young man, Warner Oland was an early prototype of the Mafia, William S. Hart was every rancher west of the Mississippi, Lew Cody was the boudoir villain, and Douglas Fairbanks was—Douglas Fairbanks.

So, who was this Hagen, with the head of a seal, the sleepy eyes, the peacock sweaters and co-respondent's shoes, and his much publicized love of the high life? He looked like the 'lounge lizard' all nice girls were warned against. He looked like a young associate of Warner Oland out after Pearl White's inheritance. The outrageous anecdotes supported this suspicion: a mere pro hiring a chauffeur and a champagne lunch, whamming golf balls into the Thames from the Savoy roof, calling the Prince of Wales 'David', indeed! Today we chuckle, but in the beginning the chuckles were punctuated by pained cries from the Old Guard whom the Lord sent Hagen to mock. His original, and imperishable, appeal was that he confounded all our preconceptions about the 'typical' American. He was a walking contradiction, a preposterous and engaging amalgam of types that were supposed to be poles apart. He could battle a golf course like Fairbanks, mutter snide remarks like W. C. Fields, and be as chivalrous as Bobby Jones. He was Lew Cody and Fairbanks and Wallace Reid all in one. And small boys like me, cricketing maniacs who had no interest in golf as such, dived on summer mornings for Tom Webster's cartoons of him to revel in what my father called 'a card and no mistake'.

There was a time in and around New York and Hollywood when almost any famous witty line was attributed to Dorothy Parker. Hagen had a similar gift for annexing any hilarious, anti-Establishment anecdote and making it his own. 'Who's going to be second?'. . . 'Your opponent's been in bed for two hours.'—'He may be in bed but he's not asleep.' . . . 'Hold the flag, David!' These are tag lines as familiar to golfers as 'Never . . . was so much owed by so many to so few' and 'Some chicken, some neck' are familiar to every free man who remembers how much of his freedom he owes to Winston Churchill.

When other great players will be remembered only by the photographs of their swing and the tournament statistics, Walter Hagen will be immortal for certain other records that recall not so much his prowess as his brash charm and his delight in the game:

[76]

the first man to give his caddie all the prize money; the first, and perhaps the only, first-class player who had the gall to have the flag removed for a long-iron approach from about 170 yards; the only professional who ever jerked a putt out of bounds; and always the only golfer who honestly and always forgot the last bad hole. For these things and also for the remark, practically a capsule philosophy, that does not dim by endless repetition and which would have made the perfect epitaph for his gravestone: 'Take time to smell the flowers.'

Make Way for the
Senior Golfer

[1970]

Do you want to hear about my 39 on the tough back nine at Noyac, a fairly new—but, as we oldsters like to say, a 'testing'—course at the end of Long Island? Well, you're going to.

I will make the account of this masterful round brief, but only out of consideration for those lobster-tanned veterans who took up the game at the age of eight, progressed by kangaroo stages to a 2 handicap and have deteriorated so alarmingly with each decade that when asked to exercise total recall and recount the history of some of their triumphs they reply, like Bing Crosby, 'Total recall? I can't even recall when I last broke 80.'

Well, sir, it was a glittering Sunday afternoon in the late fall. I was sitting out on our terrace on the North Fork of Long Island facing the deep blue waters of Peconic Bay and feeling pretty hot under the collar. We had had three people to lunch. We were still having them to lunch and it was twenty-five minutes to four, a whole hour past the time when I normally have bussed my wife with resounding gratitude, torn off to a links course twelve miles away and started to lace long drives and cunning little pitches—alone, of course—into the declining sun. I had already given rather gross notice to these dawdlers of my intentions by retreating to my bedroom and going through my normal medical routine as a senior golfer (we shall come to that a little later on).

Our guests—my lawyer, his wife and sister—would have been, at any other time, enchanting company. In fact, until they started on their third lobster at three p.m. I was convinced that no more amiable guests had ever wolfed our vodka or darkened our towels.

Far off, across the old Colonial meadows at our back, a church clock struck three-thirty. The old Colonial churches still have their uses, not the least of which is to toll the knell of parting guests. My lawyer turned to me and said: 'A beautiful time of day, this, especially in the fall.' In a flash, I saw my opportunity for a cliff-hanger's cry. 'Yes, indeed,' I said, 'you know, a friend of mine now pattering towards the grave told me that when he gets to Heaven —he is what they always call a *devout* Catholic and he has no anxiety whatsoever about his destination—and is asked by St Peter what, if he had lived longer, he would most wish to have prolonged, he will reply—"late afternoon golf".'

'That's right,' said my lawyer, 'you usually play around this time, don't you?'

I furtively leaned over to him while the ladies were still slurping up the repulsive butter and lemon sauce. '*Around* this time,' I said with a meaningful ogle. '*By* this time I am usually recording my first par on the very difficult fourth hole whose green recedes invisibly into Long Island Sound.'

He is a guileless man—except in all matters pertaining to residuals and cassette rights—and he started as a fox might start out of its burrow on our fast-eroding bank or bluff. 'Listen,' he whispered beseechingly, 'don't let us stop you . . .'

I stopped him right there and begged the ladies to round things off with a liqueur. 'A dram of cognac, a soupçon of kirsch?' I suggested. 'Goodness, no thanks,'—thank goodness—they said.

'Really,' he implored.

'I tell you what,' I said, now in complete control of a situation not even imagined by the late, great Stephen Potter, 'we are going to dinner on the South Shore not far from you. Why doesn't Jane drive your ladies over an hour or so from now, *when they are ready to leave?* You and I will take your car, whisk around a fast eighteen

[79]

holes at Island's End, and then we'll meet them all back at your place?'

I anticipated his next line, which was: 'You know, I'm ashamed to say I don't play, but I love to walk around. D'you think I could just amble along?'

The trajectory of our departure was never matched by Bugs Bunny. Fifteen seconds later we were on our way, leaving the women to surmise, 'Did they go for a swim? Irving doesn't really care for swimming.'

Island's End is a semi-public course, which means that at unpredictable times it is likely to be infested by a couple of bus-loads of the Associated Potato and Cauliflower Growers of Long Island. It was such a day. 'No way,' said the young pro, 'there are seventy-five of them out there and you wouldn't get through five holes before dark.'

'Too bad,' said my honest lawyer.

'I retain,' I said, 'an escape clause for just such emergencies. I am a member at Noyac on the South Shore, and on Sundays not even guests can play.'

We snorted off to the ferry, trundled across the Bay, roared the five miles to the North Haven ferry, made it, and thundered up to the pro-shop at Noyac on the stroke of five. To all such jocularities as 'trying out a little bit of night golf, eh, Mr Cooke?' I turned a contemptuous ear. We were in an electric cart in one minute flat. (I hasten to say to snobs from the Surrey pine-and-sand country that no invention since the corn plaster or the electric tooth-brush has brought greater balm to the extremities of the senior golfer than the golfmobile, a word that will have to do for want of a better.)

A natural and chronic modesty forbids my taking you stroke by flawless stroke through the following nine holes. ('I think we'll take the back nine,' I had muttered to my lawyer, 'it's a little more test-ing.') Suffice it to say that when we approached the dreaded

[80]

eleventh—an interminable par 5 with a blind second shot up to a plateau three yards wide between two Grand Canyon bunkers— my friend was already goggling in the car or cart stammering out such memorable asides as, 'I don't believe it, it looks so goddamn easy.'

An imperious drive had put me in the prescribed position for the perilous second shot. I was lining myself up, with the image of Nicklaus very vivid in my mind, when I noticed two large gorillas disturbing my peripheral vision. I paused and looked up in total, shivering control. Happily, on closer inspection, they turned out not to be gorillas but two typical young American golfers in their late twenties. They were about six feet three each, they carried the dark give-away tan that betokens the 4-handicapper, and they waved at me nonchalantly and said, 'Go ahead, grandpa, we've got all the time in the world.'

Again I went through my casual Nicklaus motions. My 3-wood followed the absolutely necessary arc and the ball came to rest pre- cisely midway between the two bunkers.

'Many thanks,' I said briskly and waved back at the aghast goril- las. They marched fifty yards or so to what I was crestfallen to real- ize were their drives. Gallantly I indicated that no matter what the humiliation to me they should proceed. They banged two stout shots, one into the right bunker, the other on the edge of the pine woods.

By the time I came up to my ball, I was sitting upright with a commanding expression worthy of Adolf Hitler arriving in Vienna in his hand-made Opel. The gorillas paused again, and waved again. 'Go ahead,' they said.

''Enks vemmuch,' I said. I took a 5-iron with all the slow calcu- lation of Geronimo Hogan. Ahead lay a great swale, another swirl of bunkers, a plateau and the bunkers guarding the sloping green. I heard in my ears the only sentence I have ever heard at the moment of address from George Heron, my old Scottish teacher of seventy-eight summers, springs and winters: 'Slow along the ground, big turn, hit out to me.'

It rose slowly like a gull sensing a reckless bluefish too close to the surface, and then it dived relentlessly for the green, kicked and stopped three feet short of the flag.

'Jesus!' cried one of the gorillas, 'd'you hit the ball this way all the time?'

'Not,' I replied, 'since I left the tour.'

We left them gasping. And, to be truthful, I left the ninth hole gasping.

'You never told me!' shouted my beloved friend and lawyer.

'I never knew,' I said.

It was the kind of round that I play every night on the pillow but never, at any other time, on a golf course. As the man said, 'it looks so goddamn easy'.

Every golfer who reads these historic words has played such a round. But few know the secret of a senior golfer's total relaxation. I am about to confide it to you. While other men change their slacks, down a Scotch and head for the first tee, the really thoughtful senior golfer knows that before he leaves his house he must follow a routine that will take a decade off his life and give him the illusion of careless youth.

First, then, the toenails in old age grow almost as fast as the ears and the nose. There is nothing you can do about *them* but you can spend a minute or two trimming the toenails. Next, swallow a couple of Bufferin against the old back injury. Next, a swift application of some mild anaesthetic for the bothersome scar tissue from that old hemorrhoidectomy. Don't forget the Tums, Bisodol or simply a packet of sodium bicarbonate as a precaution against indigestion. Clean the spectacles. Rub a little resin on the last three fingers of the left hand. Stand up straight—think of Raquel Welch. (On second thoughts, don't think of Raquel Welch.) Comb the hair smoothly and think of the swing of Dave Marr. Walk very slowly, masterfully, to the first tee. Put on the cap bought in Edinburgh and think of Hogan. Stand up straight.

That is all. Cypress? Pebble Beach? Pine Valley? The Old Course, anyone?

Nicklaus: Twenty-Two
Years at Hard Labour

[July 9, 1972]

Jack Nicklaus, thirty-two, of Columbus, Ohio, is the best golfer
in the world, and he means to improve.

That, in brief, is what sets him apart from the other giants of
the game, and perhaps from the giants of most other games also.
He first picked up a golf club when he was ten and for the past
twenty-two years has been labouring over his game, in the flesh by
day and in the mind by night. He is certainly the most cerebral
golfer since Ben Hogan, whose *The Fundamentals of Modern Golf* is
practically an advanced text on human anatomy and aerodynamics. And he is the coolest, the least fooled, analyst of his own game
since 'the immortal one' of golf, Robert Tyre Jones.

'The golf swing for me,' Nicklaus told Herbert Warren Wind,
who has written the best golfing biography that has appeared so
far, 'is a source of never-ending fascination. On the one hand, the
swings of all the outstanding golfers are decidedly individual but,
on the other, the champions all execute approximately the same
moves at the critical stages of the swing . . . there is still a lot about
the swing we don't know and probably never will . . . in any event,
scarcely a day goes by when I don't find myself thinking about it.'

These spells of monkish contemplation are given over to a
physical act that takes approximately two seconds to perform:
namely, the dispatching of a dimpled white ball 1.68 inches in
diameter towards a hole in the ground 4¼ inches wide. The
British, an enervated race, prefer to make the attempt on a ball
only 1.62 inches in diameter. The British ball balloons less alarm-

ingly downwind and bores more easily and accurately *into* the wind, but it compensates nastily for these advantages by nestling more snugly in the rough, in the sand of the bunkers, and in the lusher fringes of the putting greens. Nicklaus, at this moment, is bringing his powerful and finicky mind to bear on the problems of the British ball, since next Wednesday he will use it to tee off at Muirfield, one of the great strategical courses of Scotland, in the British Open championship.

It is very likely that the television audience for this joust will be larger, and more breathless, than any since the cathode tube turned golf into a weekend mass entertainment and Arnold Palmer into the first millionaire professional golfer. For, after Nicklaus's win in the US Open three weeks ago at Pebble Beach, on Carmel Bay, he will be on the third leg of a four-lap ambition that has never been achieved: to win in the same year the four main golf tournaments of the world—the Masters, the US Open, the British Open, and the American Professional Golfers' Association championship. In April, Nicklaus led the field from the first day to the last in the Masters. He did the same at Pebble Beach in the Open.

Because he is acknowledged to be the best golfer to have come along since Ben Hogan, and is thought (by himself among other experts) to be in his prime, he began to tempt himself last winter with the heady vision of performing in 1972 the so-called Grand Slam. The phrase is borrowed from the unique performance of Nicklaus's boyhood idol, Bob Jones, in sweeping in 1930 what a sports writer of the day called 'the impregnable quadrilateral'. This grandiose morsel of 1920s prose described what were in those days the four main world championships. It tells us something about the social shift of golf from 'a gentleman's game' to a money game that these four were then the US Amateur championship, the British Amateur, the US Open and the British Open. Jones's feat, done by a twenty-eight-year-old Atlanta lawyer as handsome

[85]

as Apollo and as engaging as Charlie Brown, earned him a ticker-tape parade up Broadway as impressive as Lindbergh's and made him the one golfer known and adored in countries that wouldn't know a bunker from a hole in the ground. He retired, still an amateur, from all competitive golf, and it is about as sure as anything can be that his Grand Slam will never be done again. Today, if any amateur should emerge of Jones's superlative quality, he would surely turn pro in a game which only twenty years ago rewarded the leading money-winner of the tour with $37,032 and today would guarantee him closer to $200,000.* Moreover, if a second such prodigy remained an amateur (Jones, for most of the year, was a weekend golfer), he could not possibly hone his game to the relentless modern standard of a hundred or so pros on the tour who follow the sun from January through October playing, on an average, about 150 days a year. The University of Houston alone scouts the country for promising lads, entices them with a golf scholarship, plants them on the practice tee in the dawn of their freshman year, has them hitting two or three hundred balls a day for four years and releases them at sunset on graduation day with the prospect of an early place on the professional tour (and the bonus of a highly 'relevant' degree, a Bachelor of Business Management).

It is against such an army of single-minded young warriors, dedicated from their teens to the glory of golf and one million bucks, that Jack Nicklaus is now waging his audacious, one-man war. Less than a decade ago it was safe to wager that the Masters or the US Open would be won either by Arnold Palmer, then at his peak, or by two or three other giants who were always pacing him, including the hulking young man from Ohio State who would soon match Palmer and eclipse him. Today, picking the winner of a given PGA tournament is about as rational as lining up in one

Now, 1994, it would be not less than two million dollars.

[86]

race every winning nag of the year between Belmont Park and Santa Anita and laying a hundred to one. There are at the least two dozen players on the golf tour capable of winning any tournament.

When the golf writers began to conjure with Nicklaus's vision and approached him to name the odds on his Grand Slam, he facetiously guessed 'a million to one'. When he came into the press tent at Augusta having won the Masters, the compulsive purple-prose writers pressed him again. 'Well, now,' he said, 'I guess they're down to a thousand to one.' Three weeks ago, two down and two to go, the racing touts were still at it.

'You name it,' sighed Nicklaus, 'fifty to one, a hundred to one.'

He has, by the way, developed since the early days of his modest fame as US Amateur champion an attitude to the press that reflects very sharply his uncalculating Midwestern assumption that everybody in sight, a President or a busboy, is his equal until proved otherwise. It is the custom at all the professional tournaments for the leaders of the day to retire to the press tent and go over their round hole by hole, club by club. It can be a dull, or funny or embarrassing ceremony. There are the anxious ones who crack the snappy chestnuts known to every Sunday foursome in the land. There are fine golfers who interminably unburden their woes, usually to convey the subtle point that they ought to be leading by four strokes. A few imperious ones, presuming—often correctly—that most of the reporting pack are golfing duffers, exercise the tolerance of Aristotle discussing philosophy with a convention of high-school prize essayists.

Nicklaus's golfing intelligence (a special endowment and one, like an actor's or banker's intelligence, quite unrelated to wisdom, horse sense or even a creditable IQ) used to make him brusque with neophytes. But he has matured in this, as in several other traits, and is now alert to the slightest hint of golfing know-how from any reporter, no matter how green. He warms to cub reporters with candid, often long and detailed answers. Only rarely does he glare in stupefied disbelief at the reporter-statisticians who, year in year out, think of golf as a bucolic variation on roulette. Five years ago, he came dripping in from the 100-degree heat of Baltusrol, New Jersey, having figured on a finishing 65, having made it, and having incidentally beaten the record four-round score for the US Open. (In a practice round early in the week, he had matched the infernal heat with a scorching 62. 'A freak,' he called it, 'it doesn't mean a thing.' 'Jack,' cried a palpitating reporter, 'if you hadn't bunkered your approach on the second, and three-putted the tenth, and you'd made that short putt on the sixth, my God you'd have had another 62.' Nicklaus looked at the man with stony compassion. In his incongruously squeaky tenor, he snapped, 'If, if, if—that's what the game is all about.')

What *his* game is all about is a question now absorbing many million golfers throughout the world, not to mention the captive wives and small fry huddled around the telly who are just learning to take the old man's word that the grim-jawed blond up there scrutinizing four feet of innocent grass, and whom the gee-whiz commentators keep calling 'The Golden Bear', is also the golden boy of contemporary golf.

Jack William Nicklaus (pronounced Nicklus, not Nick-louse) is the great-grandson of an immigrant boiler-maker from Alsace-Lorraine and the son of a prosperous Columbus, Ohio, pharmacist whose hobbies were Ohio State football, golf, fishing, and recounting to his son the miracles of St Robert Tyre Jones. Jack was born in 1940, the year of Dunkirk and the Fall of France, when the British were ploughing up their golf courses and planting land mines against the anticipated Nazi invasion. (Last month, one of them exploded under an oak tree on the ninth fairway at Knole, in Kent, causing an irritated Englishman to lose his stance and his ball; he was allowed, however, to drop another, two club's-lengths from the crater, no nearer the hole, without penalty.)

[88]

Considered as a modern type, Nicklaus's progress through school and college makes him sound like a throwback to a De Sylva, Brown and Henderson musical of 1927. A Midwestern boy so albino-blond that an early golfing teammate called him 'Snow White', he worked in his father's drug store after school, played basketball, baseball, football and track; never thought of going to any other college than good old Ohio State; made Phi Gamma Delta ('it was crucial to make a fraternity, for the undergraduate who had no social life at all'); met a pretty blonde, Barbara Bash, Pledge Princess of the campus in her freshman year, and married her in his senior year. In the intervals of playing basketball, competing in college or national amateur golf, or fly-casting with his father, he completed a pre-pharmacy course and majored in insurance. 'Corny?' he says, 'I loved it.'

He started to toddle and hack around a golf course after his father had an accident to his ankle. It required an operation and suggested to the doctor that henceforth Father Nicklaus had better forego volley ball and take to gentler exercise, 'the sort of movement you get when you walk on soft ground'. Soft ground recalled golf, which he had given up fifteen years before. But now, on taking it up again, he found he was something of a lagging invalid to his regular partners and he hauled in his ten-year-old as a walking companion. The youngster got his first set of cut-down clubs just as the Scioto golf club, to which Father Nicklaus belonged, acquired a new pro, a taut, tanned, shoe-black-haired forty-year-old named Jack Grout. Nicklaus, to this day, has had no other teacher except himself, who is probably the more exacting of the two.

So on a Friday morning in June 1950, the golden bear cub lined up on the practice tee with fifty other youngsters. It is clear from the record that the perfectionist strain in the Nicklaus character at once refined the normal, rollicking ambition of small boys to bang out a succession of rockets. The first time he played nine holes he had a creditable 51. 'My second time out I had a 61. Then, for weeks, I got worse and worse.' He supplemented the Friday morning regimental drill with private lessons from Grout. The knobbly-jointed stripling began to develop a golf swing. At the close of his tenth year, he went round the course in 95. The next year he shot an 81. During the third summer, he had a maddening run of eight 80s in a row, and suddenly a 74. At thirteen, he had a 69. At sixteen, he won the Ohio State Open.

At some point along this determined trajectory from hacking moppet to boy wonder he admits that he occasionally flexed his ego along with his muscles. And at such times his father deflated him with a regular recital of 'Bobby' Jones's boyhood record: junior champion of his Atlanta club at age nine, amateur champion of Georgia at fourteen, of the whole South at fifteen, at eighteen tied for fourth in the US Open. 'Whenever,' Nicklaus recalls, 'I was getting too big for my britches . . . that usually did the trick.'

Three weeks ago, Nicklaus became the only golfer to tie Jones's record of winning thirteen of the world's main titles.

The long trail, the making of the Nicklaus game, began on the practice tee at Scioto. What had he got to begin with? This is as good a place as any to introduce the bugaboo of 'a natural golfer'. According to the best players and teachers of their time—Harry Vardon, Bob Jones, Ernest Jones, Percy Boomer, Tommy Armour, Archie Compston, Ben Hogan, Henry Cotton, Bob Toski, and today John Jacobs—there is no such thing as a natural golfer. A boy may have an aptitude for sports. He may have, according to the chosen game, the required muscle or speed or grace or stamina. Assuredly, there are born 'unnatural' golfers, as there are men built like kangaroos or penguins who will never learn to dance or thread a needle. But given the best natural endowment, which in golf would be a fluid sense of timing and a temperament of relaxed concentration, the gifted one has then to learn a series of co-ordinated movements with his feet, ankles, knees, insteps, thighs, arms, shoulders, back muscles, hands and head; a series so unnatural that he will use it nowhere else in life. The golf swing is, if anything, more unnatural than classical ballet, and the training for it is as severe as anything known to the Bolshoi. Jack Nicklaus began the grind at ten and he is still working at it, even though he is the Nureyev of the links.

If there was any luck in the time and place of his initiation, it was in having Jack Grout newly arrived at Scioto. Grout was a teacher with some very firm convictions, one of which, however, was that every golfer is an individual. This runs counter to the insistence of many young pros and to most of the instruction text-books, that every pupil must be broken into the mould of a favourite dogma. For instance, ninety-eight golfers in a hundred use the so-called Vardon grip, which has the little finger of the right hand resting on top of the cleft between the clasped first and second fingers of the left. The ninety-ninth manages—don't ask me why—with a baseball grip, the two hands completely separated. Nicklaus was the hundredth oddity who was more comfortable with the interlocking grip: the index finger of the left hand securely planted between the third and fourth fingers of the right. Nicklaus has hands surprisingly weak in their grip. Grout let him stay with this eccentricity, and he uses it today.

But Grout's tolerance of idiosyncrasy had severe limits. He insisted from the start on two fundamentals. Since they apply to every golfer, young and old, they may help us all, if only we can absorb them well enough to let them pass over into what Ben Hogan called 'the muscle memory'. Nicklaus avows that his game is rooted in these two fundamentals. The first is that 'the head must be kept still' throughout the swing. Nicklaus figures it took him at least two years to master this simplicity, sometimes under the duress of Grout's assistant holding on to the hair of Snow White's head to make him, in J. H. Taylor's fine phrase, 'play beneath himself'. Anyone who has ever had his head gripped while trying to repeat a serviceable swing will have quickly learned the painful truth that we are all 'natural' jumping jacks. I once had an easy-going friend, a cheerful hacker, who refused to take any lessons on the down-to-earth assertion that 'I simply try to be a pendulum'. Unfortunately, the human body is constructed, with marvellous ingenuity, not to be a pendulum.

Much of the difficulty of teaching, and learning, golf has to do with the rich ambiguities of the simplest English words. Taking the club 'back' is not the same as taking it 'behind'. 'Pushing' the club back is a whole stage of development beyond 'lifting' it. To take an example that prolonged one habit of dufferdom for over twenty years, and mentally aggravated Nicklaus's trouble with his head, there is the routine injunction very popular in the 1920s to 'keep your eye on the ball'. It was a phrase deplored even then by Bob Jones, and it drove the irascible Tommy Armour to swear that it was 'the most abysmal advice ever given by the ignorant to the stupid'. The point these dissenters wished to make was that it is possible to lurch and sway all over the place, maybe even to lie down, while still keeping your eye on the ball. To keep watching the ball as it leaves the club, instead of the spot it lay on, is now said to be fatal. The famous phrase was later seen to mean no more, but no less, than to 'keep the head still'. Golf arguments, even between the best pros, often revolve not around a difference of insight but around an image that means one thing to one man and something else to another.

The second fundamental, which Nicklaus maintains gave his game its early solidity, was Grout's insistence that 'the key to balance is rolling the ankles inwards', the left towards the right on the backswing, the right in to the left on the downswing. Here again, the picture in the mind has been painted many ways. Some talk of keeping the left heel down while 'bracing the right leg'. Jones hit off a sharp poetic image when he said that golf is played 'between the knees'. Nicklaus more recently said, 'if you go over beyond your right instep on the backswing, if you relax the pressure there, you are dead.' And George Heron, the little eighty-year-old Scot who, as a boy, made clubs for Vardon, is still telling his pupils down in St Augustine, Florida: 'a knock-kneed man is going to be a better golfer than a bow-legged one.'

On these two fundamentals alone, Nicklaus calculates he spent four or five years, in the meantime working through the range of clubs for hours on end on the practice tee. He says that today 'whenever anything goes wrong', he goes out and hits a thousand balls 'flat-footed'. He was known, fairly recently, to feel he had played a short cut-shot poorly, so after the day's play he chipped four hundred balls in three hours.

There are about a half-dozen other fundamentals. And the later refinements, which can convert an average golfer into a good one, and then a good one into a great one, can be counted by the score, and by Ben Hogan into infinity. Nicklaus has wrestled with most of them though he still believes he is only an average player of short pitch-shots. The problem of mentally selecting which subtleties are applicable to any given golf situation is what explains that fixed stare and riveted jaw as he plods down the fairways oblivious of everything but the tactical cunning of the next shot.

So you put together years of daily practice, the putting and chipping and 'fading' and 'drawing' and 'punching' and 'cutting' of a million or two golf balls; the gift of total concentration; the sure knowledge that the only opponents that matter are the golf course—and yourself. You still do not get Nicklaus. These disciplines have been practised and earned by any twelve golfers you choose to call the best living dozen.

The overriding supremacy of Nicklaus is due to what you might call calculated gall, or generalship under pressure. When Jones retired from the neurological nightmare of championship golf, he explained: 'There are two kinds of golf, and they are the worlds apart. There is the game of golf, and there is tournament golf.'

[93]

(When Nicklaus won the Masters in 1965 by an unprecedented nine strokes, Jones said, in his typically chivalrous way: 'I have learned something about golf in the past fifty years or so, but Jack plays a game with which I am unfamiliar.')

Every fine player cracks at some point in the three to four hours of his chosen form of tension. Nicklaus appeared to collapse on the tenth at Pebble Beach with a double-bogey worthy of an average club player. He promptly forgot it. So it comes down in the end to extraordinary judgement, at the tensest times, of when to draw rein and when to cut loose. Palmer remained an idol because he 'went for' impossible retrieves all of us achieve only on our pillows at night. Not Nicklaus.

Standing in 1966 on the seventeenth tee at Muirfield, where he expects to stand four times again this week, he faced a par-5, 528-yard hole, rising for two hundred yards and then disappearing as it turns to the left. It takes Nicklaus four crisp and explicit pages of Wind's biography to explain exactly how he played the hole differently each day. Briefly, on Wednesday, he drove off against an east wind with a 3-wood. The next two days, with a west wind blowing right to left, he took a 1-iron. On the last day, approaching the seventeenth, he had to have a birdie and a par to win, a challenge that nobody but Nicklaus relishes. The wind was a little stronger behind him. He decided on a 3-iron and landed 290 yards away, precisely 2 feet short of the rough. 'That meant I was 238 yards from the centre of the green.' (Nicklaus paces everything out before the tournament, keeps a yardage chart and makes notes on odd trees, church spires, bushes, hillocks, swales, visible landmarks. And when he says 238 yards, he does not mean 235.) If he had been playing the bigger American ball with no wind, he would have instinctively reached for a 1-iron. But he paused and thought hard (always the most awesome sight in modern golf) and he decided to allow 'one club less for the small ball, one and a half clubs less for the following wind, one club less for the run on the

[94]

ball, and a half club for the extra distance you get when the adrenalin is flowing.' So he took—for a 238-yard approach shot that had to land on the fairway short of a bunker and bounce over it on to the green—a 5-iron! He stopped 16 feet from the flag, decided not to be a hero but to lag it close and tap it in for his birdie. The par on the eighteenth was, for Nicklaus, almost a yawn.

All of this, I am alarmed to realize, makes him come out a hero about as granity and lovable as a Viking invader. In spite of the journalistic tradition of tying up such Titans in pink ribbons at the end of the piece, a practice that would not in the least endear me to Nicklaus, something should be said about the noticeable ease with which he matured out of his twenties. He was not always 'The Golden Bear' to the crowds. In the days of Palmer's supremacy, he padded along behind Arnie and his howling 'army' stolid and unloved, and often applauded only when he barely missed a splendid putt. He bore these outrages with great grace, and occasional clenched teeth. He has only lately gained the affection, as well as the awe, of the following crowd. In a country that overrates the sporting swinger and the fairway comedian, he has refused, under considerable outside pressure, to improvise a public image. For his health's sake, and for his much improved appearance, he took off twenty pounds and is unlikely ever again to be jeered at, by some other idol's 'army', as 'the Kraut' or 'Fatso'. In a passing bow to the 1970s, he sprouted sideburns and acquired an extra tumble or two of Byronic locks.

Otherwise, he is simply a mature and relaxed version of what he always was: a Midwestern boy of remarkable candour, quick wits, a pleasant touch of self-deprecating humour, and an unflagging devotion to the traditions and courtesies of golf. All that is formidable about him is what has put him where he is. The unwavering industry to improve his game. His refusal to know that he knows. His iron self-discipline. And the really terrifying self-confidence, which rarely nowadays sharpens into cockiness, of

[95]

a golfer who is only uncomfortable when he is leading a tournament. He is probably the only great golfer alive, or dead, who could honestly have meant what he said to an English friend who casually asked him what was his idea of the most rousing prospect in golf: 'Three holes to go, and you need two pars and a birdie to win.'

Workers, Arise! Shout 'Fore!'

[1974]

A few weeks ago I was staying in San Francisco, and I had a call one morning asking me to lunch with the Russian Consul General and his deputy. The invitation came from an unlikely host, a friend, a lawyer, an affable and fastidious gent, and a first-rate golfer to whom the great game is not only a major exercise in military strategy and tactics but also a minor rehearsal of the Ten Commandments. He is, indeed, the chairman of the championship committee—and will without doubt soon become the president—of the United States Golf Association. His pairing with the Russian Consul General seemed improbable in the extreme. Where, I asked, shall we meet? 'At the golf club, of course,' was his mad reply. But why, why? 'It is very important,' he said, 'I should surmise that the Consul General is coming under orders, and the whole point of the lunch is to talk golf.' This was like being invited by a rabbi to lunch with the Pope to discuss stud poker. I accepted instantly.

The co-host was a young American, a boyish type, who is associated with his famous father in the most successful golf-architecture firm on earth. Golf architecture is the art and science of designing and building golf courses, and it involves much knowledge of landscape, soils, grasses, water drainage, engineering, meteorology, and sometimes—I feel—black magic. Let us call the young man Mr Jones, for that happily is his name.

It seems he had recently got back from Moscow, where he and his father had responded to what must have sounded like a joke more unlikely than the reason for our lunch: a call from the Mayor of Moscow to consider building the first Russian golf course. The impulse, apparently, had come from a Soviet diplomat who had been exposed to the decadent West and had become one maniacal golfer. This in itself should give us pause. I should have guessed that any Russian who had yielded to such a capitalist diversionary activity as golf would have been, on his first homecoming, bundled off to Siberia, where he'd have been condemned to play golf with a red ball and a snow sled. But he was a close friend of the Mayor of Moscow. When he returned from a foreign, Western, post, he came into the airport carrying a golf bag. The customs men—as also, I imagine, the military and the narcotics squad—examined the weaponry, but reluctantly gave him the benefit of his diplomatic passport. Somehow the man sold the Mayor of Moscow on the idea of a city—public, of course—golf course. I don't suppose things rested there. The matter went up to the Kremlin. And, from all I could gather, Mr Brezhnev gave the nod.

Well, we sat down to lunch, and the Consul General—a stocky man in the regulation Sears Roebuck suit—turned out to have a puckish humour. When we asked him if the Russians would take to golf, he said: 'I think, because, you see, the Russian people like quick games.' Somebody said, 'Like chess.' He came back on the hop: 'Yes, we like a quick win.' He plainly and admittedly knew nothing. But he asked everything. And to help him with the rudiments—of building rather than playing—young Mr Jones put on a lantern lecture, with colour slides showing rice paddies in Bangkok being transformed—slide by slide—into a bulldozed mess, then into terraced ground, then into ground being planted with gravel and soil and seed, and eventually emerging as a pastoral golf hole. Through a series of other slides we went to Hawaii and Florida and Scandinavia and, in the end, to the five sites around Moscow from which they will choose the one on which to build the course.

After that, the Consul General was given a lesson in weaponry.

We went off in electric carts, like a little motorized battalion, to the eleventh tee on the noble San Francisco Golf Club course, a swaying landscape of lush green meadows flanked with towering cypresses and pine and occasional stands of eucalyptus.

The eleventh hole is a par 3: that is to say, you are required to hit the green with your first shot and then sink the ball with two putts.

Our lawyer host, Mr Frank (Sandy) Tatum, straightened his waistcoat (all *ex officio* members of the United States Golf Association board are very sensitive to the ancient amenities and insist on playing in ties and waistcoats, like the respectable Scots in the old prints). Offhand, I would bet that this Tatum, on that hole, would hit the green ninety-nine times in every hundred. He hit about six inches behind the ball, which rose in an unsteady arc and landed about 150 yards away, well short of a cavernous bunker. 'Dear me,' he said with splendid restraint.

'So,' said the deputy consul (a pretty fresh type, I thought), 'the first pancake is never any good.' Ignoring this gem of Russian folk wisdom, Mr Tatum set up another ball, and this time was comfortably on the green. Now, with many open-handed gestures and facetious bows, the Consul General was motioned to 'have a go'. He took off his jacket, looked down at the ball, gripped the club with all ten fingers (the so-called baseball grip, which about one professional in a hundred uses). His two hands were far apart. He missed the ball at the first swipe, but at the second it fell just a little short of Tatum's first effort. There was general applause. 'A natural talent,' purred the gallant Mr Tatum. 'Please!' said the Consul General.

Then the deputy had a go, and he slithered the ball about thirty yards along the ground. 'That deputy,' one of our group whispered, 'he sure knows what he's doing.' Well, then we all departed for the clubhouse, had our pictures taken, and the Consul General was presented, by young Mr Jones, with a copy of an article I had once written on the origins of golf. Mysterious, this. 'Why?' I asked young Jones. He looked for a second over his shoulder. 'Don't you see,' he hissed, 'it supports the main argument?' And what would that be? 'What we kicked around at lunch.'

I realized then why I had been seated at lunch next to the Consul General. He had dropped several uncomfortable hints that he knew golf was a rich man's hobby, and I sensed that Moscow had asked him to check on this repulsive legend. I hastened to disabuse him with—young Jones later assured me—deeply moving eloquence. 'No, no,' I said, 'that used to be so long ago, even then only in England and America, never in Scotland.' I painted a picture, all the more poignant for being true, of poor little boys going off with their sticks and paying a few pennies to play some of the most hallowed courses on earth. 'In Scotland,' I said, 'the people learn to play golf as simply as they learn to drink tea. And St Andrews, which is the Vatican—pardon me, the Kremlin—of golf is a public course. On Sundays they close it so that little old ladies and dogs and babies can frolic—can walk around—for it is a public park *absolutely for the people.*' 'No?' said the Consul General. 'Yes,' I said.

'What,' he asked, 'will our people do, will they succeed at this sport?' No question, I said, 'ten years from now'—we were well along with the vodka martinis—'I swear to you the British or American Open champion'—('Open? What means this open?')—'the golf champion of Britain or America will be a Russian. After all, not so many years ago you sent over a Russian basketball team, and Americans shook with laughter. Until you wiped the floor with both the Americans and the Canadians.'

'Wiped?'

'Beat, trounced, massacred, defeated!'

'It is so,' said the Consul, looking gloomily into his vodka.

'Very well, then,' I went on, 'maybe the big switcheroo will come sooner than ten years. Maybe four, five years from now, there will be a match between the best player in the world, Jack Nicklaus, and Nicholas the Third.'

'There was never any Nicholas the Third,' said the knowing Deputy.

'But there will be,' I cried, 'and he will win!'

'Iss possible?'

'Is certain.'

I went back to town feeling I had done creditably on my first assignment as ambassador without portfolio. There were, of course, certain little nuisances: of having to learn to play the game (from whom?), to find courses to learn it on, pros willing to spend a couple of years teaching the first Russian golfer how, for God's sake, to hit a golf ball straight. I thought of Nicklaus, at the age of ten, going on the practice tee every day for a year to have his head gripped for an hour on end by the hand of an assistant pro so he could learn to keep his head still. Perhaps I should have stretched the apprenticeship period to ten or twenty years.

Still, if they get around to building the Jones course,* I like to imagine Mr Brezhnev or his successor, or *his* successor, standing on the first tee and approaching a ribbon with a mighty pair of shears. He will carry in his hand a note or two from our San Francisco Summit, and he will proclaim to a vast assembly of the peoples of all the Russias: 'So! I have the extremely great honour to say to the citizens of our Soviet Socialist Republics—let us begin to play Goalf! The pipple's sport!'

*Nine holes of the proposed course opened in the autumn of 1993.

[101]

Snow, Cholera, Lions and Other Distractions

[1975]

Just after dawn on a brisk but brilliant December day a couple of years ago, I was about to ask Raquel Welch if she was all set for a droll caper I had in mind, when the telephone went off like a fire alarm, and an eager voice shouted, 'All set?' It was, alas, not Raquel but my golf partner, a merry banker of indestructible cheerfulness who calls all stock-market recessions 'healthy shake-outs'. I climbed out of my promising dream and out of bed, and in no time I was washing the irons, downing the bufferin, rubbing resin on the last three fingers of the left hand, inserting the plastic heel cup, searching for my Hogan cap—performing the whole early morning routine of the senior golfer. This was the great day we had promised ourselves ever since I had suffered the shock of hearing Herbert Warren Wind confess he had never played Century, the tough and beautiful rolling course in Purchase, New York, where Ben Hogan had his first job as a teaching pro. It seemed ridiculous that the man who had helped Hogan lay down *The Fundamentals of Modern Golf* should never have played the course on which Ben laid them down. Another telephone call alerted Wind to get the hell out of his own variation on the Welch fantasy. An hour later we were on our way, up the West Side Highway and the Saw Mill River Parkway, and on to Purchase.

Century is the private domain of some very well-heeled gents from Wall Street, but they are so busy watching those healthy shake-outs that none of them has much time for weekday golf. Furthermore, in December, the caviar and hamburgers are stacked in the deep freeze. But, since it is very difficult to close a golf course, the course is open. The caddie master had been briefed about the signal honour that Wind was going to confer on one of the fifty toughest courses in America and he had obligingly mobilized two of his veteran caddies.

As we swung around White Plains and began to thread up through the country lanes of Purchase, we were puzzled to see strips of white cement smearing the grassy banks of the highway. They got thicker as we turned into the club driveway, and as we came out on the hill that overlooks the undulating terrain, we saw that the whole course was overlaid not with cement but with snow. The caddies were already there and looking pretty glum. They greeted us by stomping their feet and slapping their ears and otherwise conveying that, though our original idea was a brave one, it had obviously been aborted by the weather. 'You serious about this thing, Mr Manheim?' one of the caddies asked the banker. 'Sure,' said Manheim, who would play golf in a hammock if that's what the rules called for.

We started off with three reasonable drives, which scudded into the snow the way Hawaiian surfers skim under a tidal wave. The caddies went after them like ferrets and, after a lot of burrowing and signalling, retrieved them and stood there holding the balls and looking at us, as the song says, square down in the eye, as if to say, 'What are you going to do with these damn things?' We had to find little slivers of exposed ground (no nearer the hole) and drop them and swipe off once more. The greens were either iced over or had sheets of ice floating in little lakes. After several five-putts on the first two greens, we decided that anybody who could hold a green deserved the concession of two putts.

This went on for eight holes, at the end of which, however, Wind allowed that Hogan sure loved to set himself problems. Plodding up the long ninth fairway, with Cooke beginning to turn blue and the banker humming happily to himself (it was the two-putt rule that did it), Wind turned and said, 'Tell me, Manheim, do you do this because you're nuts or because your PR man says it's good for your image?' We three-putted the ninth green, which 'held' with the consistency of rice pudding, and that was it.

As I recall this Arctic expedition, there is a blustery wind bending the trees in Central Park and a steady rain, a combination of circumstances that fires many a Scotsman to rush out and play a round of golf in what one of them once told me are 'the only propair condeetions'. But, because this is America, they are conditions that immediately empty the golf courses from Maine to San Diego, forcing the sons of the pioneers to clean their clubs, putt on the bedroom carpet or sink into the torpor of watching a football game. We have it from the Mexican ambassador himself, His Excellency Lee Trevino, that there are Texans who will not play at all whenever the temperature toboggans below 80 degrees Fahrenheit. And there are by now many generations of Dutchmen who gave up the game once it moved off ice on to grass.

It is a wonderful tribute to the game or to the dottiness of the people who play it that for some people somewhere there is no such thing as an insurmountable obstacle, an unplayable course, the wrong time of the day or the year. Last year I took Manheim— whose idea of a beautiful golf course is a beautiful park—to play his first links course. It is the home course of the English golf writer Pat Ward-Thomas (Ward-Thomas's idea of the most beautiful golf course in the world is his home course). It is up in the bleak stretch of southeastern England known as Norfolk, a sort of miniature prairie exposed to the winds whistling out of Siberia. The course is called Brancaster, and you can drive up to the rude clubhouse, a kind of Charles Addams gabled shack, and start asking people where is the golf course. For ahead of you is nothing but flat marshland—which floods at the high tide—and beyond that the grey North Sea and a chorus of squawking gulls. The flags are about two feet high, so as to encourage the notion that

[104]

man has not been known to tamper with a masterpiece of nature.

When we went into lunch it was spitting rain and when we came out it was raining stairrods. The wind gauge at the clubhouse entrance registered forty-three knots. There was Ward-Thomas; a handsome and imperturbable Englishman named Tom Harvey; Manheim and I. There were also two caddies, aged about ten, already half-drowned and cowering in the whirling sand like two fugitives from Dotheboys Hall.

Nobody raised a question or lifted an eyebrow, so Manheim and I—remembering the good old White House slogan—soldiered on. By about the seventh, Manheim, who wears glasses, had to be guided to the proper tees. We were all so swollen with sweaters and raingear we looked like the man in the Michelin ads. Well, sir, they talked throughout in well-modulated tones about 'sharp doglegs' and 'a rather long carry' and 'it's normally an easy 5-iron, but maybe with this touch of wind you'd be safer with a 4-iron, even a 4-wood, I shouldn't wonder.' We were now all water-logged, from the toenails to the scalp, and Manheim came squelching over to me and said, 'Are these guys nuts?' I told him that on the contrary this was for them a regular outing: 'You know what the Scotsman said—"If there's nae wind, it's nae gawf."' Manheim shook his head like a drenched terrier and plodded on. The awful thing was that Harvey, a pretty formidable golfer, was drawing and fading the damn thing at will, thus proving the sad truth that if you hit it right, even a tornado is not much of a factor.

Outward bound, we'd been carried downwind. But as we were bouncing like tumbleweed down to the ninth green, Ward-Thomas came staggering over. I should tell you that he is a gaunt and a very engaging gent and he has a vocabulary that would have qualified him for an absolutely top advisory post in the last Republican administration. He came at me with his spiky hair plastered against his forehead and water blobbing off his nose and chin. He screamed confidentially into the gale: 'If you think this (expletive

[105]

deleted) nine is a (expletive deleted) picnic, wait till we come to the (expletive deleted) turn!'

He was right. We could just about stand in the teeth of the gale, but the balls kept toppling off the tees. It was a time to make you yearn for the old sandbox. Manheim's glasses now looked like the flooded windshield of a gangster escaping through a hurricane in an old Warner Brothers movie. Moreover, his tweed hat kept swivelling around, making him stand to the ball like a guy who'd been taught about his master eye by a one-eyed pirate. At this point, Ward-Thomas offered up the supreme sacrifice. He is a long-time idolater of Arnold Palmer and he cried, 'Hold it!' and plunged into his bag. He came up with a faded sunhat and tendered it to Manheim with the reverent remark: 'It was given to me by Palmer. Try it.' As everybody knows, Palmer's head is on the same scale as his forearms, and this one blotted out Manheim's forehead, nose, glasses, master eye and all. What we did from then on was to slop our way down the last nine, pity the trembling caddies and throw murderous glances at Harvey, who was firing beautiful woods into the hurricane.

Very little was said as we retired to Harvey's home, fed every strip of clothing into a basement stove and stewed in baths that would have scalded a Turk. At dinner it came out. All through the first nine, Harvey and Ward-Thomas had been muttering to each other just as Manheim and I had been doing: 'They must be out of their minds, but if this is what they're used to . . .' Harvey said, 'We decided that since you were our guests, the only thing to do was to stick it out.'

If these are fair samples of maniacal golfers, how about crazy golf courses?

You would not think, looking at the stony rampart of the mountain face behind Monte Carlo, that anyone could plant a one-hole putting green between those slabs of granite. But when you get to the top, there the indomitable British have somehow con- trived a course that lurches all around the Maritime Alps. There is rarely a straightaway drive. On the very first tee, you jump up in the air and see the flag fluttering in a depression way to the left. You ask the caddie for the line. He points with a Napoleonic ges- ture to a mountain far to the right. 'La ligne!' he commands. And if you believe him and bang away at the mountain top, you than see the ball come toppling about a hundred yards to the left and going out of sight. Which is the proper trajectory to the green.

The golf 'clubu' at Istanbul is, if anything, more improbable still. The banks of the Bosporus are studded with more boulders than Vermont. But when the Scots took Constantinople at the end of World War I and laid in an adequate supply of their *vin du pays*, what else was there to do but build a golf course? The original rude layout is still there in the 'clubu' house, and on paper it looks like a golf course. In fact, it is simply a collection of flags stuck at random on a mountainside of boulders. Every ball comes to rest against a rock. The local rule is a free drop on every stroke. You drop it and drop it till it stops, and never mind the fussy business of 'no nearer the hole'.

In Bangkok, before the natives took to cement and the auto- mobile, the canals looked like irrigation ditches slicing every fair- way. Forecaddies, as nimble as grasshoppers, spent the day diving into the canals and surfacing with an ear-to-ear grin while they held aloft a ball drenched with cholera. Once they'd wiped it and dropped it, you were on your way again, and free to enjoy the great game in a dripping temperature of 110 degrees.

A lion, you might guess, is not a normal item of wildlife on your course or mine. But in Nairobi once, a tawny monster strolled out of the woods, sniffed at my ball and padded off again, while my partner, a British native of the place, tweaked his moustache and drawled: 'You're away, I think.' At about the third hole I pushed my drive into the woods, and when I started after it, the host

[107]

screamed at me to cease and desist. 'Snakes, man, snakes!' he hissed; 'leave it to the forecaddies.' They plunged into shoulder-high underbrush, and I meekly muttered, 'How about *them?*' 'Them?' the man said, 'Good God, they're marvellous. Splendid chaps; lost only two this year.' That round, I recall, was something of a nightmare, what with my pushed drives and the caddies (the ones who survived) chattering away in Swahili. The whole place was so exotic that I began to wonder if any of the normal rules of golf applied. One time, we came on a sign which read, 'GUR'. I gave it the full Swahili treatment. 'What,' I said, 'does GHOOOR mean?' He gave a slight start, as if some hippo were pounding in from the shade. Then he saw the sign. 'That,' he said firmly, 'means Ground Under Repair.' And he sighed and started to hum a Sousa march. After all, you must expect anything in golf. A stranger comes through; he's keen for a game; he seems affable enough, and on the eighth fairway he turns out to be an idiot. It's the rub of the green, isn't it?

Well, it takes more sorts than you and I have dreamed of to make up the world of golf. In Japan, they take a ski lift up to the tee of a famous par 3. In Cannes, the club members never bat an eyelid as they board a ferry from one green to the next tee.

But for sheer systematic nuttiness, nothing can compare with an annual ceremony put on by the Oxford and Cambridge Golfing Society, a collection of leather-elbowed oldsters and shaggy-haired youngsters who play for the President's Putter, no less, every year in the first week of January at Rye, on the coast of Sussex, another treeless links course fronting on a marsh which gives out into the English Channel. This tournament is intended to prove the English boast that 'we can play golf every day of the year'. If they can do it at Rye in January, they can do it at the South Pole, which in some sharp ways Rye resembles. At any rate, under the supervision of Gerald Micklem, a peppery stockbroker in his sixties who is the Genghis Khan of British amateur golf, these maniacs go through with this tournament on the scheduled date no matter what. Snow, hail, wind, torrents—nothing can keep them from the swift completion of their Micklem-appointed rounds.

I was there four years ago. On the first morning, the small town and the course were completely obliterated in a fog denser than anything in Dickens. It seeped into the hotels so you needed a links boy to light your way to your plate of bacon, baps and bangers. I assumed the whole thing was off, till a telephone call warned a few dallying competitors that their tee-off time was about to strike. We crawled out to the course, and the first person I ran into, marching around the clubhouse, was Micklem. I asked him if anyone was out there, and if so, why. 'Nonsense,' he barked. 'They're all out there. Haven't lost a ball yet.' He motioned towards the great grey nothingness outside, not fog, not landscape, but what John Milton (13 handicap) once called 'not light but darkness visible'. I hopped off into what might very well have been the edge of the world, as it was conceived by those Portuguese mariners who would have liked very much to discover America but who were afraid to sail out into the Atlantic, beyond sight of land, for fear of falling off. The word, God knows how it got through, was that Donald Steel was doing niceiy towards repeating his win of the previous year. He had just teed off on the second nine. I ran into a swirl of nothingness and, sure enough, there emerged, like a zombie on the heath in a horror film, a plumpish, confident figure recognizable at three yards as Steel. He took out an iron for his approach shot, though what he thought he was approaching I have no idea—San Salvador, no doubt. He hit it low and clean, and a sizeable divot sailed away from him and vanished. He went off after it and vanished too. I kept following in the gloom, and from time to time a wraith swinging a golf club would loom up, take two steps and be gone.

It was true! They all finished, and nobody lost a ball. I felt my way back to the clubhouse, and at the end the last ghost was in.

Within five minutes they were up against the bar, chests out, faces like lobsters, beer mugs high, slapping thighs, yokking it up. Queer fish, the Oxford and Cambridge Golfing Society. They behave just as if they'd been out for a round of golf. What they play every year on that barren fork of Sussex that reaches out to the Channel, and Holland, and eventually to the Bering Strait, is a wholly new game: Invisible Golf.

Movers and Shakers of
the Earth

[1976]

On the opening day of a recent Masters tournament, *The Times* (of London, as we say in these parts) carried a dispatch from a correspondent in Augusta, Georgia, sketching out the memorable history of the course. Among the many splendid, even original, things in that perceptive article was the information that in transforming a tree nursery and former plantation into what is surely the most beautiful inland course in America, Robert Tyre Jones was assisted at every turn 'by Dr Alister Cooke'.

This is not strictly accurate, as Mr Jones and a couple of generations of nurserymen and greenkeepers will testify. For some psychological reason not too hard to fathom, I have never bothered to write to *The Times* and refute this clanger. But at the time I was agreeably pestered night and day with invitations to—oh, I don't know—redesign Sunningdale, convert Hyde Park into a pitch and putt, abolish Pine Valley. The most embarrassing of these bids came from Pat Ward-Thomas in the present instance: namely, to write a preface to this formidable work.* I must say I should have thought that Ward-Thomas knew as well as anyone that Jones's co-worker in the creation of Augusta National was none other than Dr Alister Mackenzie, the Scottish doctor who put his indelible imprint also on Cypress Point and Royal Melbourne.

The scabrous truth had better be revealed here for the first time. I have never designed anything, not even a Christmas card.

The World Atlas of Golf.

While I'm at it, I had better make what they rather rudely used to call a clean breast of it: until a dozen years ago, I thought of Bermuda as an island, and Fescue I should have guessed to be a Shakespearean clown. Nevertheless, I accepted the invitation of Pat Ward-Thomas with alacrity and a large dollop of vanity. For it offered a duffer the opportunity to write about golf architecture, something that I believe has not been done before in the history of the game. Indeed, few duffers have ever thought much about golf architecture, but every duffer willingly carries on about the wonders of his own course. Ask the average golfer to explain the principles of strategic design and he will humbly disavow all such knowledge; tell him that he doesn't know the difference between a good course and a bad one, and he will knock your block off. In other words, in a variation on the duffer's platitude about art, we don't know much about 'architecture' but we know what's good.

It was quite by luck that I became wary of this cliché soon after I took up the game. Being a journalist, I naturally fell in with golf writers, and it was soon my good fortune to make lasting friendships with two distinguished writers, and one fine amateur golfer, who wrote or talked better, and seemed to know more, about the mysteries of golf architecture than anyone else I met. Playing some great course in England with Pat Ward-Thomas, or with Herbert Warren Wind in the eastern states, or in California with Frank Tatum, Jr I had the feeling that I was being taken over a Handel score by the late Sir Thomas Beecham. (Often, of course, and especially with the eloquent Tatum, I had the feeling that I was simply being taken.) I discovered to my enjoyable relief that a great golf course, like a supreme piece of music, does not reveal its splendours at a first or second reading; nor, for most of us, ever. Its subtleties will always be beyond us. I don't mean beyond our performance but beyond our recognition.

That is where Pat Ward-Thomas, Peter Thomson, Charles Price and Herbert Warren Wind come in. If you are willing to follow them closely, and to forget for the moment your resentment that your own club course has been carelessly omitted from this selection, you can begin to see the differences between the good, the better, and the best. This coaching will not only enhance your pleasure if you have the luck to play any of these famous battlegrounds, but it will, I do believe, sharpen your feel for the alternative shots offered by a good hole anywhere. To the common objection that 'taking things apart' spoils one's pleasure in the assembled object, I can only retort that the most enlightened criticism of poetry has been written by the best poets, and that it takes a watchmaker to be truly moved by the best Swiss watches.

This book is, of course, meant for consumption in every country that plays golf, most of all in Britain and the United States. This reminder exposes a famous bone of contention that is gnawed on periodically on both sides of the Atlantic. It has to do with the rooted prejudice, which the duffer retreats into more than anybody, about the two different orders of golf course. At the latest count, there are roughly thirteen million golfers in the United States and something like two million in the British Isles.

Most Britons, of whatever skill, have been brought up to regard a links course as the ideal playground, on which the standard hazards of the game are the wind, bumpy treeless fairways, deep bunkers and knee-high rough. Most Americans think of a golf course as a park with well-cropped fairways marching, like parade grounds, between groves of trees down to velvety greens. Along the way there will be vistas of other woods, a decorative pond or two, some token fairway bunkers and a ring of shallow bunkers guarding greens so predictably well watered that they will receive a full pitch from any angle like a horseshoe thrown into a marsh.

There is a marked element of national character in these opposing preferences: the British taking strength through joy in the belief that discomfort is good for the character, the Americans believing that games are meant for pleasure and should not be

[113]

played out in moral gymnasiums (unless you are going to make money at them, in which case they become the whole of life).

The Scots say that Nature itself dictated that golf should be played by the seashore. Rather, the Scots saw in the eroded sea-coasts a cheap battleground on which they could whip their fellow-men in a game based on the Calvinist doctrine that man is meant to suffer here below and never more than when he goes out to enjoy himself. The Scots, indeed, ascribe the origins of golf to nothing less than the divine purpose working through geology. Sir Guy Campbell's classic account of the formation of the links, beginning with Genesis and moving step by step to the thrilling arrival of 'tilth' on the fingers of coastal land, suggests that such notable features of our planet as dinosaurs, the prairies, the Himalayas, the seagull, the female of the species herself, were accidental by-products of the Almighty's preoccupation with the creation of the Old Course at St Andrews.

Americans are less mystical about what produced their inland or meadow courses: they are the product of the bulldozer, rotary ploughs, mowers, sprinkler systems and alarmingly generous wads of folding money. And often very splendid, too. It seems to me that only a British puritan on one side of the Atlantic, and an American sybarite on the other, will deny the separate beauties and challenges of the links and the inland course.

Pasture, meadowland, links, oceanside, whatever its type, a fine golf course will obey certain elementary rules best stated forty years ago by Bobby Jones: 'The first purpose of any golf course should be to give pleasure, and that to the greatest number of players . . . because it will offer problems a man may attempt according to his ability. It will never become hopeless for the duffer nor fail to concern and interest the expert; and it will be found, like Old St Andrews, to become more delightful the more it is studied and played.' In a word, the fine golf course offers rewards for the duffer's limited skill; the moderate player senses exciting possibilities;

[114]

the good player a constant challenge; and the great player knows that only when he is consistently at his best can he hope to conquer it.

Begging the pardon of our authors, I must say that this famous prescription is not exactly filled by all of these awesome seventy. Among the experts there will be furious debates—as, for instance, why should Medinah, a claustrophobia of woods, be in, and the lovely, cunning Inverness of Ohio be out? The members of Maidstone will no doubt mount a civic protest against their exclusion from what the late Al Wright has called 'the three best unplayed courses in America', meaning the three old cheek-by-jowl links courses at the end of Long Island: National, Shinnecock and Maidstone. (My own private conviction is that Shinnecock was designed by Lady Macbeth.)

But all such doctors' disagreements aside, it is probable that a committee of international golfers of the first chop would agree with seventy-five per cent of these choices. For the rest of us, this colossal book comes along, none too soon, to review the history of great golf architecture from its invention by Willie Park, Jr just before the turn of one century to its likely demise just before the end of the next. For in the United States at any rate, an amendment to the federal tax law, allowing the states to reassess land taxes according to the doctrine of 'best possible use', could soon tax golf courses at either the real-estate or public rate and doom once and for all the private playground. In the interim period—between God's rude links and Mammon's foreclosure—there is the consolation for us duffers that the population explosion and public housing campaigns together will drastically arrest the movement of the 1960s towards 7,000-yard courses and holes made only for Nicklaus. Even so astute a team of architects as that of Robert Trent Jones & Sons foresees only a shaky future for the traditional layout; rather, there will be appendages to housing estates having short holes and a par of 60. This should usher in the golden age of the senior golfer with the arthritic pivot but the cagey short game.

[115]

While there is yet time, then, let us turn these pages and read and weep. Here are the power and the glory, the fine flower of many landscapes preserved in the microcosm of the golf course. Here are the masterpieces carved out in the eighty years that saw the dawn, the high noon and possibly the twilight of golf architecture. This book may well be, whether the authors knew it or not, a memorial tribute to the game before Nader's Raiders, followed by the Supreme Court, decide that the private ownership of land for the diversion of the few is a monstrous denial of the Constitution under the Fourteenth ('the equal protection of the laws') Amendment.

When that happens, old men will furtively beckon to their sons and, like fugitives from the guillotine recalling the elegant orgies at the court of Louis XV, will recite the glories of Portmarnock and Merion, of the Road Hole at St Andrews, the sixth at Seminole, the eighteenth at Pebble Beach. They will take out this volume from its secret hiding place and they will say: 'There is no question, son, that these were unholy places in an evil age. Unfortunately, I had a whale of a time.'

The Money Game
[1977]

'Half the world,' it says here, 'will have watched or listened to Wimbledon before the hundredth anniversary of tennis is over.' I fancy I hear the high protesting voice of Muhammad Ali crying: 'No way, brother. Not one tenth, not one thousandth, of the world is gonna watch that tennis, but the whole world watches me, because I am the best, the prettiest.'

Well, never mind the percentages, Let's hope that many more thousands saw Chris Evert correct the umpire's ruling in her favour than saw Connors snub the anniversary parade of champions and spend the time of the ceremony practising fifty yards away with his partner in boorishness, the inimitable if not unspeakable Nastase. Miss Evert reached to lob a return of Miss Wade and was awarded the point. But she shook her head and pointed out that she had not reached the ball before its second bounce. It is a small thing and would have gone unremarked ten or twenty years ago. But today, in the money jungle of professional sports, it shone like a candle in a naughty world.

I remember the time when Bill Tilden, about fifty years ago, threw his racket at Wimbledon. The game was stopped. He was warned at once that one more tantrum like that and he would be thrown out of the tournament. He didn't do it again. But no more than two years ago I saw one of the most famous women tennis players reel with shock at a linesman's call. She was the one who stopped play. She walked over to her chair, gathered her five or six rackets, tucked them under arm, and as she walked off she poked her forefinger up at the umpire in what the spectators applauded as an obscene invitation. (If the Supreme Court came to divide on the question of obscenity, it would only be because the dissenters had led a sheltered life.)

She hadn't quit. She was just biding her time, and temper, till the officials came running, or kneeling, begging her to return. Which, about three minutes later, she graciously consented to do, as thousands of spectators came to their feet to pay tribute to an act of bravery in giving the umpire his come-uppance. The umpire had not taken her out and paddy-whacked her. He didn't fume or shout. He blushed. He cowered. He knew he had behaved badly. He seemed truly sorry. And the crowd cheered their heroine again and forgave him. The terrifying touch here was not the sluttish-ness of the—er—lady but the attitude of the crowd.

I am told by Mr Herbert Warren Wind, one of the most distin-guished of American sports writers, that a few years ago, when he was watching the Davis Cup matches being played in Romania, he got the ghoulish impression that this reversal of values—this upside-down courtesy which George Orwell might have anticipat-ed—was not only common among tennis crowds in Romania but was organized by the state as a required exercise in patriotism. The crowd was expected to boo or hiss every point won by the Ameri-cans and to cheer every gesture—whether skilful or rude—of their idol, Nastase. Mr Wind, who has been writing about tennis and golf for forty years or so, said the Romanian experience was the most frightening thing he had seen in his professional life. He came away with the uncomfortable feeling that he had been brain-washed, or morally washed, or whatever.

It is this sort of thing that led an American political columnist at the end of last year to offer some pointed advice to Mr Carter, who was then about to begin his term as President. The columnist laid down twenty numbered tips for the new President, most of them, of course, having to do with prudent political tactics. But the last

[118]

three were about sports. Don't, he urged, use football lingo by way
of encouraging your party. Don't talk about team play, or coming
through in the last quarter, or giving it that old one-two. Don't
invite athletes to the White House for dinner. Don't invite athletes
ever. Have the courage to decide with Harry Truman that 'sports
is a lot of damn nonsense'.

This attack of bile, I don't doubt, must have been brought on
by unpleasant memories of Mr Nixon's occupation of the White
House, for nobody in American history, I dare say, has given the
language of sport such a bad name by using it to recommend a
strategy of deceit.

At the end of last year, too, Jim Murray, of the *Los Angeles Times*,
the raciest, the most gifted of American sports writers, wrote a
piece called 'Whatever Happened to Frank Merriwell?' For the
more tender readers, may I say that a couple of generations
ago Frank Merriwell was the fictional hero of all American small
boys. Today he would provoke salvos of raucous laughter as a
square and a sissy. Because—to use the quaint old phrases—he
played fair, he gave his all and lost with a smile, he held to the
naïve delusion that sport is synonymous with what we used to call
sportsmanship.

I was mentioning these odious comparisons to a sports official
the other day. He was not greatly moved. He said: 'Well, sure.
You're talking about the days before sports was a billion-dollar
industry. Today we've got the Commies on our back. We teach the
youngsters to develop competitive bite. We feed 'em money. The
Russians draft 'em.' It is true. Most nations now train a picked
quota of their young to devote their lives exclusively to excelling in
some single sport. In the so-called Free World we do this voluntar-
ily or by the pressure of parents and the expectation of a million
dollars. In the Communist world they do it by compulsion, isolat-
ing promising babies, like so many blood strains, from their fel-
lows. In all countries the process intensifies, to the greater glory of

the Fatherland, and no doubt also to the development of a ragged nervous system and a blank ignorance of the variety and values of human society.

This is nothing new. It happened more than two thousand years ago. But it was not looked on, by the generations that came after, as the high point of their civilization. The Greeks, when they developed competitive games, divided them into two categories. Neither offered money prizes. One, practised by inferior athletes, rewarded the winners with gifts of olive oil. Which would be, I imagine, the equivalent of presenting the local tennis champion with a gallon of one of those 'arthritic' rubs that don't cure anything but set up a secondary irritant to make you forget the first.

The great games, the spectator sports, were those competed for by the best, and to the victor went only a wreath. The Olympic Games, throughout their early history, were managed by officials whose title was a literal synonym for fairness. And the ground, the territory, on which the games were held, was regarded as a holy place, so much so that it was held—even by the country's enemies—to be sacrosanct from invasion (Middle Eastern papers please copy). This great age of Greek sport was the fifth century BC. After that, the most learned of their historians says all too cryptically: 'Later, athletics degenerated into professionalism, and experts in various sports spent their whole time going from one contest to another, sometimes winning them all and styling themselves *periodonikai* or "leading money winners".'

In Rome the decline from sport as an enjoyable end in itself to a spectacle designed to satisfy the blood lust of the spectators was very much more rapid. In the early days Rome took over from her Etrurian invaders the practice of a gladiatorial combat as the last ceremony of a funeral. Pretty soon they added contests with wild beasts, bred and fattened for the purpose. By the time of the emperors the Romans were the supreme military power of the world, and though Augustus decided that enough foreign conquest was enough, the games were used as precautionary military exercises. To make the events at once more realistic and more satisfying to the mob's love of cruelty, the losers now faced defeat in the form of death. In the beginning, even in contests to the death, the contestants were the sons of noble families. To lose a son in the games was as honourable as losing him on a foreign battlefield. But when you have a large army permanently on hand whose military and naval games are much like the real thing, there is bound to develop a corps of performers who are better than others. They too, ordinary legionnaires, prisoners of war, even slaves, became an elite corps of gladiators and were trained severely and lavishly paid.

There is a passage in Robert Graves's *I, Claudius* in which the gladiators are assembled in their underground locker room for a pep talk by Livia, the wife of Augustus and as wily an entrepreneur as the manager of any baseball club. She spent huge monies on the games, and at this point in the story she feels she is not getting her money's worth. At the end of her harangue she says: 'The games are being degraded by more and more professional tricks to stay alive. I won't have it. So put on a good show, and there'll be plenty of money for the living, and a decent burial for the dead. If you let me down, I'll break this guild, and I'll send the lot of you to the mines in New Media. That's all I've got to say to you.'

Well, we've not quite come to that. But the true tone of sports in the 1970s is set by the elite corps, the best of the pros—that is to say, by the richest gamesmen: the baseball, basketball, football, and now tennis stars who have sweated their way up to prodigious incomes, are admiringly interviewed by cynical sycophants, and receive the same adoring space as rock stars about their lavish pads, their king-size beds with sable quilts, their hand-made automobiles, their sleek girls in every port.

Money has got to be the reason, a primary reason anyway, why the insulted umpire sent his officials to beg the tennis star to return to the court and go on with the game. She earns a fortune. The fans pay to subsidize that fortune. The fans come not merely to see a game superlatively played. They have learned to expect high jinks and low jinks as part of the show. Any sports promoter will tell you that a sports crowd spurned is a dangerous social animal. In other words, the officials, who sometimes seem so cowed, must have in mind the maintenance of public order, which has come to have little to do with public courtesy. In America we have much rough play and some furious spectators, but—for no good reason I can see—we do not yet have basketball and baseball crowds tearing up the grounds or breaking up trains and ripping underground stations apart. I don't know why this hasn't happened—it no doubt will—since those of us brought up on the legend of British courtesy read with dismay of the hooliganism, bordering on criminal assault, of British football crowds, and of such desperate proposals to meet it as building ten-foot concrete walls around the inner ring of the stadiums and surrounding each playing field with a hundred cops.

I may have seemed to be reacting so far in the old man's standard fashion to the disappearance of amateurism in first-class sport. And, of course, it is true that—in tennis, particularly—much of the genteel air of the sport in the old days has been drowned out by the roar of the cash register. But I must say that genteelism, with its pleasant manners, was due to the comfortable fact that most players at Wimbledon and Forest Hills were upper-middle-class offspring who didn't have to work for a living. The same, at one time, was true of international golf. But plainly—it ought to be plain today—it is not only absurd, it is unjust to expect people who earn a living at a game to have the same nonchalant code of behaviour as the loitering heirs of company directors who could afford to travel to France or Britain or America to play a game while professionals (footballers as a gross example) were being paid at the going rate of plumbers' assistants. I applaud the fact that games

[122]

can now be a career, and a profitable one, and that the expert should be considered like any other star entertainer and be paid accordingly.

But there has come a point where the impulse to take up a game is very often the impulse to earn a million dollars, and so far, in the rush of a whole generation to make the million, there has not yet evolved a decent ethic that can discipline the game for the audience that has its mind more on the game than the million.

Six figures, I suggest, is some sort of turning point in the career, and too often the character, of the very young. A twenty-year-old who earns $100,000 or £100,000—and nowadays it's more likely to be half a million—is encouraged by the media to see himself/herself as a movie star entitled to adoration, the pamperings of luxury, and no questions asked about behaviour on or off the course, the rink, the court, the field. I suppose the television satellite has had a world to do with it. The best boxers know that—by virtue of worldwide exposure—the organizers will take in twenty millions or more, so the boxer doesn't pause for long before saying, 'Some of those millions should be mine.' And if the difference between winning forty thousand and twenty thousand turns on a linesman's call, it takes considerable character not to blow up. I heard a young fan say it would take a superman.

Well, it doesn't take a superman. It takes simply a type of human being who was taught when young the definition of a brat. I like to think that in one sport, at least, the type is still extant. Golf remains an oasis in a desert of gold and scruffy manners. Maybe it's because it doesn't allow for team-play in-fighting. It's you and the ball and the course. And the rules. Even so, a man missing a three-foot putt today can lose in the instant $20,000. He looks wretched or very forlorn. He does not batter the marshals with his putter or refuse to play next week. A few years ago two acts of cheating—of slightly moving the ball into a better lie—caused a well-known pro to be suspended from the tour for good. Three years ago Jack Nicklaus, the reigning star of the game, and—it seemed then—his heir apparent, Johnny Miller, were offered one million dollars to the winner of a head-to-head eighteen-hole game. One million dollars in one afternoon. They promptly turned it down as being, in Nicklaus's words, 'not in the best interests of the game'. May their tribe increase.*

*By now (1994) this scruple has been overwhelmed by an avalanche of dollars.

2 5

Pat Ward-Thomas*
[1978]

It is always hot inside an American telephone booth in summer, and the caller often pumps the split-hinged door like a concertina in the hope of wafting in gusts of bearable air.

That's what the man was doing. But it wasn't summer. It was spring in Georgia, which can be as intolerable as any Northern summer. And he wasn't making a social call, he was dictating copy to some cool girl at the Manchester end. He was pumping the door all right, but not just for relief. On the outside, close at hand, was a henchman or legman, clutching a bit of paper that bore hasty hieroglyphics, up-to-the-minute notes on what was going on outside.

What was going on outside was the annual Masters Tournament in Augusta, and the legman—name of Cooke—was trying to feed the latest birdies and bogeys, especially if they were being performed by an English golfer, to the desperate man inside the booth: a hawk-like figure with the exact profile of Goya's Duke of Wellington. This distinguished image was a little roughed up at the time, because the man's steel-grey hair had recently been subjected to a trim by a one-armed barber with blunt scissors, and from the poky strands of it rivulets of sweat were coursing through the clefts and canyons of a face that just then looked more like that of an impoverished Mexican farmer with twenty acres in beans and not doing very well.

No wonder. It was 98 degrees outside, out along the rolling

*Written for the Guardian the weekend he retired from the paper.

[125]

fairways and under the towering Georgia pines of the most beautiful inland course on earth. Inside the press building, it must have
been 110. And inside the man's booth, you could name any figure
that might suggest a sauna on the blink or the inner rim of the
crater of Vesuvius.

Imprisoned in this inferno the man was shouting, against the
clatter of a hundred typewriters, the squawking amplification of
the relayed television commentary, and the hullabaloo of other
maniacs in other booths. He would shout out a phrase, glance at a
paper, drop it, curse, bend over and crash his head, curse again,
swing the door open and pant—'Was Jacklin's birdie on the twelfth
or—blast it!—the eleventh?' He'd get the legman's word, swing the
door shut again, sweat some more and shout out the cadence of
the sentence he was writhing through.

I say cadence deliberately, because even in the bowels of hell
this is not a man to toss out unkempt sentences or sloppy sub-
sidiary clauses. When the stuff was in print, you would always
assume it had been written by some imperturbable oldster brought
up on Hazlitt and Bernard Darwin: always the loving delineation
of the landscape, the knowing adjective, the touch of Edwardian
grace, and the meditative close.

He was coming to the close now. He was hunched against the
door and I could see him mouthing the words with exaggerated
articulation, like a goldfish waiting for the water to be renewed. I
saw him chew on a word, wring his free hand, and glare at the
mouthpiece with Max Wall's Bela Lugosi face. I opened the door
to give him a breath. He was screaming: 'In the serenity of the
Georgia twilight . . . Ser-en-ity! SER-ENN-IT-TEE!!' He covered
the mouthpiece and hissed at me: 'Bloody idiot! She can't get it.'
Then back again and saying to the girl: 'That's it, yes, serenity,
thnksvermuch. Goodbye.'

He emerges, the rivulets having now formed spreading lakes
beneath his armpits. 'This goddamn time-zone business!' he says.

[126]

(For the further exasperation of the British correspondents, the Masters is always played during that brief interval between British and American (Eastern seaboard) summer time, so that the time difference is not the usual five but six hours. Since the climax of any day's play tends to happen around 6 p.m., the impossible assignment is that of describing the finest hour to that cool girl transcribing it at Manchester's midnight.)

The reader may be puzzled to recognize in this raw slice of life the lineaments of his favourite golf writer. The alert *Guardian* subscriber might be expected to guess that there has to be some agile hole-hopping, some frantic checking of the leader board, behind the smooth account of a tournament and the planted hints of why it was inevitable that the victory should go to Watson's iron discipline or Nicklaus's competitive stamina. But the reader of Ward-Thomas's weekly musings in *Country Life* must believe that he is reading the oldest member, a gentle sifter of hot memories cooled by age and tolerance.

Well, the man in the booth is nobody but Pat Ward-Thomas on active service, from which he is now retiring, full of honour, fond memories and troops of friends. He is one and the same with the *Guardian*'s austere reporter and *Country Life*'s weaver of stately prose in the twilight. I must say that if there is a regret obtrudes about his talent, it must be that in print he always distilled his disgust at some idiotic rule, some passing vulgarity, into a mannerly sigh, leaving only those who know him well the relish of having seen the splendour of his original indignation.

That, in its raging pristine form, was reserved for nobody but himself. I see him now, the top of his spiky head rather, banging away in a bunker at Maidstone, with the sand flying and the seagulls wheeling away in dismay from the obscenities that were rocketing out at them. Any true account of a round of golf with him would require, before publication, more 'expletives deleted' than all the Nixon tapes.

[127]

The Masters at Augusta seemed more serene than usual because—the crack circulated—Pat was not there, for the first time in fourteen years. Augusta was also considerably less fun than usual. In the press building, there were lots of the familiar cronies. But way down there, on the eighth row, there was an empty chair and a silent typewriter. No more the blacksmith's back bent over, the elbow leaning a millimetre away from a smouldering cigarette, the index finger poised for just the right verb. No more the smothered curses, but no more the quick smile, the bottle-blue eyes greeting chums and bores with equal good nature.

There were two things about his golf reports that set him apart from all the others. He tramped the courses, when most were settled in the press building scanning the big scoreboard and—on the basis of a figure change—tapping out 'he fired a birdie on the ninth'.

And he loved the landscape, all the landscapes of golf, from the ocean beauties of California's Pebble Beach to the Siberian wastes of Rye, from the pine and sand undulations of Swinley Forest to the yawning bunkers of Pine Valley and the cathedral aisles of Augusta. He knew the terrain, and made you know it, and how it shaped its peculiar form of golf, of every county of England and Scotland.

When others settled for 'this magnificent course', he pictured the beeches and copses, distinguished an upland from a weald, weighed the comparative hazards of a cypress tree or a swale. Nobody has ever conveyed so easily the sense of being in Wiltshire or County Down or Fife or Arizona.

He will be greatly missed, but not by everybody. Only by those who care about the good earth and its cunning conversion into golf strategy, about the unsleeping conflict between character and talent, about the courtesies as well as the joys of the game, about many small favours, and about unfailing geniality to man, woman (especially) and beast.

[128]

2 6

No One Like Henry
[1979]

Everyone knows the special pleasure of discovering a new writer, even though the 'new' man may have been mouldering in his grave for centuries. The joy of discovering a new columnist is rarer. A columnist is of our own time and is not likely to have a point of view so far removed from the standard attitudes as to provide us—like, say, Sir Thomas Browne or Max Beerbohm—with an unexpected brand of common sense, quaintness or indignation.

But from time to time it happens. Some years ago, in San Francisco, I had just finished riffling through the two more or less compulsory New York magazines (the *New Yorker* and *New York*) and turned to the San Francisco *Chronicle* and came on a column by an unknown—unknown to me. His name was Charles McCabe. His piece was called 'The Good and the Chic'. He, too, by some fluke of extrasensory perception, had in his hands the same two magazines. The *New Yorker* issue was eighteen months out of date but there were things in it that were permanently good. The *New York* issue was only two weeks old, but McCabe was already gripped by the fear that he was dangerously behind in knowing where to eat, what to read, what to think. The *New Yorker*, he concluded, was a good magazine; *New York* was chic, the epitome, he wrote, of 'boutique journalism'. Since then, McCabe is the first item I turn to whenever I am out there.

It is so with Longhurst. When I took up golf, lamentably late in life, I plunged into the golfing literature for instruction and into golf journalism for entertainment. I was not entertained. Most of the reporting I would later recognize as the best required much more technical knowledge than I then possessed. Herbert Warren Wind impressed me with his subtle and accurate knowledge, which plainly I must try to acquire; but in the meantime, I was a kindergarten arithmetic student stumbling around in a text on astrophysics. Pat Ward-Thomas, too, offered tantalizing hints that in a year or two I might hope to appreciate why clover might require a hooded 5-iron or an innocent swale a lay-up. Of the others, Dan Jenkins was obviously having a lot of racy fun with locker-room know-how that was beyond me, and the American newspaper reporters seemed to be assembling and reassembling, week by week, a jigsaw puzzle of statistics.

But Longhurst wrote about the game as an entirely familiar exercise in human vanity. It is why, of all sports writers, he had for so many years the highest proportion of non-sporting readers. Izaak Walton on fishing, Dickens on lawyers, Mark Twain on steam-boating, Cardus on cricket: they have appealed for generations to people who know nothing about baiting a hook, filing a suit, taking a sounding or flighting a googly. Longhurst is of their breed. He is recognizable in the first few sentences as a sly, wry, rheumy-eyed observer of human beings who happened to choose golf to illustrate their fusses and follies. He might just as well have chosen oil-drilling, toboggan racing, military service, being a member of parliament or the motives that propelled an old lady over Niagara in a barrel. That, in fact, he wrote about all these things only went to prove his particular virtue: a curiosity that centred not on a game but zoomed in on whatever was bold, charming, idiotic or eccentric about human behaviour. After due meditation, he decided early on that as a weekly exercise of this curiosity, golf would do as well as anything.

In the beginning he served me, though he never knew it, as a canny uncle who was on my side against the commandments and prohibitions of my teachers. I was advised I must buy a 'matched' set of clubs. Longhurst said you'd do better with whatever you picked up that felt right. A tiger of a young pro in Los Angeles told me it was 'vital' to keep the right elbow practically knotted to the right waist. Longhurst said nothing was 'vital' except delivering the clubhead to the ball at a right angle. I was solemnly told to memorize the entire book of rules. Longhurst said you mustn't blow your nose when your partner was addressing the ball, but otherwise the book of rules was mostly nonsense.

Very many of his readers, I should guess, never got so far with the actual dogma of this or any other game. They were wooed and won by Longhurst's reminiscences of caddies who ranged 'from enchanting children to out-and-out brigands', by his affection for the praying mantis, by the boxing coach with 'traditional black cigar stub, unlit, who would have been ruled out of the average Hollywood film as a caricature', by the Dublin woman singing in the gutter and carrying a baby in her arms, 'possibly her own'. While his conscientious colleagues were calculating the yardage of the drives on the eighteenth at Augusta, Longhurst saw Weiskopf missing a tie by an inch and imagined him muttering, 'We was robbed.' It is the Hazlitt touch. Nobody remembers anything about the performance of the Italian jugglers who thrilled London in his day. But everybody remembers Hazlitt's remark that when anything at all is done so perfectly, you don't cheer, you cry.

From such an affable and sharp-eyed cynic, you must not expect starry-eyed tributes to the great ones of golf, or of any other game. Longhurst was as capable as any fan of a 'Hear, hear!' or 'Right on!' But there have been few sports writers so unfooled by the motives and the sought rewards of professional sportsmen. He could write with relish about cunning, skill, ingenuity, physical prowess, but he did not mistake games for the Battle of Britain or *The Pilgrim's Progress*. You must look elsewhere for rhapsodies about the courage, heroism, endurance or bravery of even the best of their time. I suspect he always knew that these words are better

[131]

reserved for Scott at the Pole, Solzhenitsyn in prison or the long marches of Martin Luther King Jr. As for the heroes of golf, he inclined to the scamps and the droll ones.

All these oddities, these agreeable and hilarious occasions, are written about in a prose style as effortless as falling out of bed: a more adroit achievement than some of his wordier rivals will ever appreciate. There are very few wasted words in Longhurst.

Enough. No tribute—to an artist, writer, musician, golfer or character, come to that—can equal the simple remark that 'there is no one like him'. Of course, each of us is unique. But the ability to put that uniqueness—however engaging or obnoxious—on to paper or over the box is totally beyond the multitude of people who would like to have a go at television or muse that one day they must 'write a book'. Let them bow before the fact that—there was no one like Henry.

The Written Record
[1980]

Every sport pretends to a literature, but people don't believe it of any sport but their own. Ask Herbert Warren Wind or Ben Crenshaw to guess who is writing about what in the following passage, and he might cite Horace Hutchinson writing in 1903 on the never-ending problem of the swing: 'The art, though difficult, may be acquired by imitation of a good practitioner, and, once it is mastered, constitutes one of those delightful combinations of strength and delicacy in which is found the chief charm of the higher athletics.' The real author, however, had probably never heard of the golf swing, though he is or was—I am told—the revered master of the grilse, the gilaroo, the finnock, the sewin and every other guise of salmon. He is Sir Herbert Maxwell talking about the art of 'casting the fly'. Indeed, as I was settling to write the piece, my doctor was dangling before me the improbable dream of a million-dollar market for an anthology of fishing literature. All I could think of was Izaak Walton, Hemingway, and Red Smith (for that matter, Red Smith can create a literature of any sport he cares to write about). But, the doc insists, there is an enormous literature of fishing. I take his word for it and leave him to it.

I *know* there is a cricket literature, beginning—as far as I'm concerned (which is not very far)—with 'a deathless hush in the Close tonight' and ending with Neville Cardus. And for the sake of peace at any price, we had better assume that there is an impressive literature also of curling, gin rummy and table tennis. But, now, golf. Does anybody—except the entire world of non-golfers—deny that 'the gowf' has produced the richest literature of any known sport?

Granted that to get any pleasure from golf reporting (i.e., 'fired a 3-iron to the tenth . . . sank a fifteen-footer at the twelfth . . . fashioned four birdies, two bogeys and two long par-saving putts for a third-round 68') it helps to know the difference between a 3-iron and a branding iron; although it is debatable whether, since the invention of the transistorized edit terminal, any pleasure at all is to be had from news-agency reporting. But this daily drone bears about as much relationship to the literature of golf as the stock market index does to the romance of money, as revealed in, say, a biography of J.P. Morgan or the novels of Balzac. Every Sunday for forty years, the late lamented Henry Longhurst kept a devoted following, at least thirty per cent of whom had never lifted a golf club or were likely to. He saw golf as an ample outdoor stage on which a cast of Dickensian characters was compelled by the firm etiquette of the game to act out a script by Jane Austen. The unique, the furtive pleasure that golf offers to the inveterate spectator—whether on the ground or on the box—is something that is not required of the ecstatic goal scorer or the tennis player in a tantrum: the tension of restraint. Once in a while, Johnny Miller may groan at the skies, Trevino may bark at his ball as at an errant puppy. But in moments of crushing disappointment, not even Sam Snead and Tom Weiskopf browbeat a marshal: they explode in a sigh. One great opportunity of tournament reporting, variously seized by such as Dan Jenkins, Bernard Darwin and Michael Williams, is to sense the turmoil or the ruefulness going on inside the placid exterior of a possible winner two strokes back with five holes to play. In short, character, and the tracing of its foibles, is only one of the things that the game is about. It has been enough to make memorable the entire golfing output of P.G. Wodehouse, Stephen Leacock, and Jim Murray.

But the game is complex enough, and beautiful and leisurely

enough, to open up all sorts of specialties for all sorts of writers. Unlike, shall we say, tennis or chess, golf has an incomparable range of landscape, which encourages Pat Ward-Thomas to delineate the different pains and pleasures of the chase in Scotland and France and the California desert; John Updike to peel off the social layers from the artichoke of Augusta, Georgia; and Charles Price to enlarge on his lifelong feud with practically any course that gets the better of him.

There is the fantasy, indulged by every hacker on his pillow, of playing with Nicklaus or Palmer—and George Plimpton actually did it and put the experience into humiliating prose.

There is even—as with no other game—a fascinating detective literature, a wry commentary on the human comedy, implicit in the book of rules. I must say that for a game whose aim is to get a little ball in a hole in as few strokes as possible, the book of rules would seem to offer, at first glance, less excitement than the propositions of Euclid. In fact, and precisely because golf is played on a board of 120 acres or more, the vagaries of weather and topography, not to mention the unpredictable whimsies and prejudices of the human animal at play, have produced shelves of legal commentaries on the rules that suggest to the imaginative reader as many subtle and hilarious interpretations as the Constitution of the United States. Anyone who doubts this should run, not walk, to procure the entertaining gloss on the rules recently written by Frank Hannigan, with Tom Watson standing watchfully at his elbow.

I suppose that the least satisfactory prose in the whole body of the literature (it is also true of the literature of any other game) is that devoted to describing the technique of how it is done or ought to be done. This is a nearly inevitable failing, since God decreed that the doers of this world are seldom, if ever, writers. Nobody has yet written a *Sudden Death in the Afternoon* to compare with Hemingway's bone-clear exposition of how a bull is fought. But pending this masterpiece, several famous players and their ghosts

[135]

have made a brave stab at it. And the great one who never needed a ghost, Robert Tyre Jones, has left us an incomparable file of lucid and literate commentaries (see p. 65).

More than anything else, though, to anyone who would write about it, golf offers a four-hour drama in two acts, which becomes memorable even in the tape-recorded reminiscences of old champs, and which—in the hands of someone like Herb Wind— can become a piece of war correspondence as artfully controlled as Alan Morehead's account of Gallipoli.

The Making of the
Masters
[1986]

'This is the place!' It is a famous phrase in American history, and well-tutored students will at once, and correctly, ascribe it to Brigham Young, looking down on the immense white sand flats of the Salt Lake Valley and choosing it as the final haven for his band of Mormons after seventeen years of hounding and persecution and a trek on foot of over two thousand miles.

But golfers, to whom Brigham Young is the name of a university in Utah where Johnny Miller tuned up his golf, are more apt to think of Georgia, and call up a picture of Robert Tyre Jones, the immortal 'Bobby', standing in 1931 on rising ground, his back to a graceful pre-Civil War plantation house, and looking out over small hills, spacious meadows edged with pine, and a long, winding creek banked in April with bushes of pink and white dogwood, with redbud, azaleas, magnolia, the flowering peach, the yellow jasmine, and many other blazing native flowers. 'This,' he said, 'is the place,' where the Augusta National golf course would be built.

Jones was twenty-eight, not the age for a first-rate golfer to retire. But he had won more than sixty per cent of all the national championships he had entered. He had done what nobody else has done before or since: he had in one year won the Open and the Amateur championships of Britain and the United States. He wanted to remain an amateur. The nervous tension of the tournaments was pressing too hard. He wanted to return to the law and to an unhampered private life. First, though, he hankered after one more golfing ambition: to design his dream course.

His fame at the time was unique in the golfing, perhaps in the sporting, world. Not just because he was the best living golfer but because, as a modest man of extraordinary charm and grace, he had attracted the admiration of millions of Britons and Americans who would not have known a mid-iron from a midwife. Once it was known he was looking for a golfing site, 'somewhere in the South', the offers came hustling in from near and far. Near was best. Augusta had connections with his wife's family. It was a small, old country town (Thackeray lectured there and was enchanted by it, not least because the fee was many times his usual honorarium). It was a winter resort for comfortably-off Georgians. The clincher was Jones's luck in running into a foxy New York financier, one Clifford Roberts, who knew many things, including the potential value of pieces of obscure real estate in places far removed from Wall Street.

Roberts had heard of a stretch of land, just west of Augusta, that was up for sale. It had been a fruit and vegetable farm supplying the Confederate armies. For seventy-three years, it had been the property of a Belgian baron, one Berkmans, whose horticulturist son had developed it into the South's first great nursery. The baron was long gone now, and what Jones and Roberts purchased, with the help of the 'men of some means' who would form the nucleus of a private club, was a beautiful, abandoned botanical garden of 365 rolling acres. You need about 130 acres for an eighteen-hole course, and 365 acres was God's plenty.

Jones knew more about shot-making than anybody, but he did not see himself as a one-man school of golf architecture. He at once brought in Dr Alister Mackenzie, the Scot who had sensibly forsaken medicine for golf and whose incomparable links course at Cypress Point, on the coast of northern California, Jones greatly admired. Jones was firm on one point. He wanted to run against the current of the 1920s, which had multiplied courses with anything up to two hundred bunkers that penalized shots good, bad and indifferent. Jones wanted a strategic course, one which—while having only forty-four bunkers, no rough to speak of, very wide fairways, fast undulating greens—would offer 'a way round' to the high-handicap golfer, a challenge to the middle man, yet a supreme test of a great player's ability to think out the placement of every shot. Placement is everything at Augusta. You do not automatically bang a driver from every tee. There are boundless fairways which yet require the approach shot to be played from a stretch of grass not many yards wide. The tournament has often been won or lost from the eleventh through the thirteenth, the dreaded 'Amen Corner', where a rambling creek imperils all approaches. The par-5 thirteenth especially, invites the 'hot' player to fire his second shot at the green over the creek, into which last year's very hot Curtis Strange dumped his ball and lost the tournament. Nicklaus calls the short (155-yard) twelfth 'the most demanding par-3 in tournament golf', for a break in the trees can permit an unfelt wind to seize a fine ball and drop it into the fronting water like a diving kingfisher (the eminent Tom Weiskopf once landed there eight times in two rounds). The great, long fifteenth dares the best players to carry 245 yards over a lake to the flag, which Nicklaus did, in 1975, with what he has since called 'the best 2-iron I have ever shot'. When the early days are rainless, the switchback greens are like ice rinks. And so on and on.

Jones intended the course to be the private enclave of close and distant friends who would join him once a year for an invitational four rounds. But such was the swift-rising fame of the course that Jones extended the invitations to the best living golfers and they were soon heading for Georgia every April. Some news reporter dubbed it the Masters tournament. It is the only one of the four majors (the British and US Opens, the American PGA, and the Masters) that is played on the same course, by now for the past fifty-two years.

Throughout that half century, those 365 acres have burgeoned, in many natural and disciplined ways. Discipline was Roberts's obsession. A born dictator, he roped off the fairways, invented the modern scoreboard, forbade all signs and hoardings, appointed a retired brigadier general, a major general and a lieutenant colonel to organize about a hundred roaming stick-jabbers who spear every paper cup, shred of cellophane, hot dog discard and other trash. Nature has done the rest. The flowering bushes are luxuriant. The ordered forests of pines are now so towering that several fairways look like cathedral naves, down which two or three midgets tread lightly on hallowed ground. The majestic fairways are cut finer than most putting greens. The place looks much like a royal park, so that the spectator has the agreeable sensation of being a privileged guest at an Edwardian garden party. There is little dispute that Augusta is one of the dozen best courses in the world. There is none at all that it is the most beautiful inland course.

The Inauguration of
President Grant*
[January 1990]

You may well wonder what are my credentials for standing up
and addressing the Politburo and Central Committee of the ruling
body of golf.

I have two credentials. The first is, that I am the President of a
world-wide organization: I am the President of HOW—Hackers of
the World. As such, I am invited by the Chairman of (the) Augusta
National (Golf Club) every April to attend the amateur dinner
(which is held the evening before the Masters tournament begins)
and talk to the amateurs—usually from Britain and the United
States—who are about to play in the tournament. I tell them two
things.

First: Do not slight the hackers. Pay attention to them. Be kind
to them. It's because of them—of us—that you can earn $800,000 a
year for merely hitting a small ball across country into a small hole.

The second thing I tell them is: Don't do it! Don't turn pro! Be
like Bobby Jones. Stay an amateur for life. Yield not to temptation!
Be like General George Marshall, when Mr Henry Luce, the
founder of *Time* and *Life* (the magazines, that is) came to him and
said: 'General, I want to publish your memoirs.' To which, Marshall said: 'I am not going to write my memoirs, because there are
too many people who were involved in the Second World War who
are still alive and who might be hurt by what I write.' Mr Luce

*Speech given to inaugurate Grant C. Spaeth at the annual meeting of the
United States Golf Association at San Diego, California, January 1990.*

said: 'General, I don't think you understand. I am offering you one million dollars.' And General Marshall replied: 'Mr Luce, I'm afraid *you* don't understand: I am not interested in one million dollars.' Well, I tell this story to these pink-cheeked nineteen-year-olds, and add: 'Don't lust after a million dollars. There is more in life than golf.' I always notice from their expressions—and from yours—that they can't imagine what that possibly could be.

So, they are very polite and pay absolutely no attention. I'd say that of the forty or fifty amateurs I've preached to in the past ten, dozen, years, maybe three have made their way on the American tour. The rest slog away on the European tour, if they're lucky, on the New Zealand tour, on the Fiji Tour, the Tibetan tour. By which time, they decide to change teachers. They line up with some exotic instructor in southern Florida or the Carmel Valley, and from him they learn that the backswing has fifteen 'accumulated' positions, which must be fused into a single action. If they master this procedure, it does guarantee that they will become the club pro in Four Corners, Colorado, or Little Piddletrenthide and secure the local franchise in sweaters and jock straps.

My second credential far outweighs the first: it is the express invitation of—how can I say *Mr* Spaeth? Who for so many years, at the San Francisco Golf Club, was pointed out to me striding through the grill room, striding down the fairways, striding out of the woods. And they would say: 'That is Mr Big.' Then came the time, only a year or two ago, when he won the—wait for it!—Senior—Amateur—Championship—of—the—municipality—of Palo Alto! Since when, he has been universally known as Big Muni. We thought at the time that that was as high as a man would want to go. But no. He has gone up and up to improbable heights, and now—against all the predictions—he is the President of the United States Golf Association! El Presidente, no less. (Incidentally, I asked a Spanish friend of mine how would they address him if he came to play Sotogrande, or El Prat, in Barcelona. He said: 'Well, you would call *heem* El Presidente Ess-pah-ate.' [*Dead silence.*] Let me put it another way. The same Spaniard told me years ago [this will ease your way into that last joke]—when I asked him who was the most popular movie star in Spain—he said, 'No question! Ham-ace Ess-tay-art. It's true: James Stewart. Hence—President Ess-pah-ate.)

Some of you may be curious to know how it comes about that I am not only a good friend of President Ess-pah-ate and of his great friend—Francisco Tatoom—but that I am also a golfing partner of both of them. An absurdity made possible by what to me is the most magical thing about the game of golf: the handicapping system.

Does the name Ellsworth Vines mean anything to you? (*One clap.*) Very good. A great tennis player—of the first chop—Wimbledon champ, US Open champ. Came the time, as it must to all tennis players, to retire—in his thirties. He took up golf (indeed, he was on the tour for a time). A few years ago, he said to a friend of mine: 'Golf is the most marvellous game. When I was at my tennis peak, there were half a dozen, say a dozen, guys who could give me a game. In golf, I can play against all but the most abject hacker and have a tough time.'

And it's because of that magical system that I am a member of a foursome that engages in a periodical joust at the San Francisco Golf Club. The foursome consists of your new President—Big Muni; Frank Tatum, known as Sandy. I am known—because of the striking resemblance of my swing to a famous Latino—as Alistairos. The fourth member, I greatly regret to say, is not a member of the San Francisco Golf Club. But he's a dear friend, and we forgive him for belonging to—what the humble members of San Francisco call—the Bloomingdales of golf and country clubs. It is also known as Olympic. He is a man named Carl Borders. A 1 handicap! Even a shade lower, on the index, or slope. In his spare time, he's an orthopaedic surgeon. Least, he *says* he is. If you call his office, his wife answers the phone. I suspect she is the orthopaedic surgeon. It's the only way you can explain how he manages to play golf six days a week and practise eight days a week.

What I'm saying is: in what other game can a 1 handicap and a 3 and a 5 even pretend to enjoy playing with an octogenarian who gets a stroke a hole and two strokes on the par 5s? You laugh! Let me tell you that the winning side is rarely more than one up. Which Dr Borders and I were in our last joust, and when also on the back nine, *I beat Tatum!* That required him to disgorge four dollars—to me, an event unique in the history of the club. So much so, I understand there is to be a plaque installed up against the only other golf picture or memento in the men's locker room. That is an immense blow-up of Harvie Ward taken at a split second after he has hit the ball. If you ever see it, you'll notice to your astonishment that at that moment, as he is going or has just gone through the ball, he is—like Bobby Jones!—on the tips of all his ten toes. A position which today, I suppose, would be thought freakish if not downright incompetent.

It only goes to show that in spite of *Golf Digest's*—I think it's now 1,942—tips, on what is *fundamental* about the golf swing— nobody knows what is fundamental about the golf swing. And so the writers and the critics have to fall back on colourful prose. Thus, a fine English writer, the late Pat Ward-Thomas, loved to quote an immortal sentence about Bobby Jones: 'His swing had all the drowsy beauty of an English summer's day.' (Just for the record, I ought to mention that the swing of the late, beloved, Pat Ward-Thomas, had all the drowsy beauty of a pneumatic drill.)

These bizarre facts only prove again that you don't have to be a great golfer to be a great golf critic. Look at me! Whatever I had in golf—or never had in golf—has gone. But I retain my uncanny ability to say what's wrong with the other guy's swing.

Of course, you must realize that for this expert trio to play with me and pretend it's a great pleasure, they have to observe certain precautions. And the first one they observe is precisely the first thing I was taught by my old Scottish golf teacher, George Heron. He was about four feet eight. A wonderful man, one of that generation sent over after the First World War to teach the Colonials how to play golf. Soon after he took me on, a middle-aged simpleton who didn't know which end you held, I became a maniac and read all the books. One book came out called *Square to Square*. I asked George about it: 'What is this Squ---'? 'Mr Cooke,' he said, 'forget it! Since the days of Vardon and Braid, nothing has evair been added to this game excaipt an aixtra slice of baloney.'

Well, his first bit of advice was to make a point of watching a good swing and trying to copy it. But never look at a bad swing, because it will pass over into what Ben Hogan called 'your muscle maimory'. So the first golf tournament I ever attended—twenty-five years ago, the Masters—I hurried off to the first tee to await the arrival of the heroes. Pretty soon, one obvious hero was on his way, because there was a wave of applause coming with him from the clubhouse. By the time he'd teed up his ball, you'd have thought, from the applause, it was VJ Day. Clearly, a man to watch. He teed up the ball, he swung (golf commentators say 'swang') and he hit the ball. At the finish of the swing, I noticed that his right shoulder was practically on the ground, as if he'd tossed the caber underhand. His right arm and hand were outstretched into the sky, like Adam reaching for God's touch in the well-known Vatican painting. I said to myself: 'He will *never* be a golfer. If that's what's going to pass over into my muscle memory, I'll be muscle bound for life.' He was a fellah named Palmer, I believe. (Considering what Palmer has done with that swing, you had better repeat twenty times on waking: 'There are many ways to skin a cat.')

From this memorable scene, you can probably deduce the sort of precautions my three companions take, in order to protect the purity of their own swings. I've noticed that whenever I address the ball—on the tee, in the fairway, in a bunker, anywhere—these splendid partners look meditatively down the fairway or are suddenly concerned for the condition of their spikes.

Now, you ought to get a picture of what they're trying not to look at. For many years I had an impression of my golf swing, which was: that I vividly resembled Tom Weiskopf in the takeaway, and Dave Marr on the downswing. Unfortunately, there came a day when I was invited to have my golf swing filmed by a video camera. Something I will never do again. When it was played back, what I saw—what *you* would have seen—was not Weiskopf and Marr but a man simultaneously climbing into a sweater and falling out of a tree.

However, in spite of all these precautions and safeguards and secret vows to give Cooke a wide berth when he has a club in his hand, we all know that the great, the overriding, thing about golf is—companionship, right? They look away, but when I'm through with my stroke they come over, sometimes, and talk to me. 'Didn't see that,' they say, or 'Hit a good shot?'

Well, in pursuing this relationship down the years (that's to say in simply playing golf with the same people) you pick up certain secrets about them. I've picked up some observing your President, and there are two secrets I'd like to convey to you. On the understanding (as I once heard Secretary of State John F. Dulles say to an audience of about 250 reporters) that 'this will not go outside the four walls of this room'.

The first secret takes us back into the mists of time. And what I'm going to give you is a true account of the distorted and sentimental version—of a meeting between a man and a boy—you have just heard from Frank D. Tatum. Let me tell you what really happened.

What Sandy was too modest to tell you was that when he'd been out of college six or eight years, he was the all-American college

[146]

champ, the idol of Los Angeles's golfers (he is an Angeleno—pretends to be a San Franciscan). And back then, maybe forty years ago, he did have this close friend. And the close friend had a son, a little boy. And the little boy worshipped—St Francis Tatum. One day, he said to his father: 'Father, do you think that I might ever caddie for St Francis?' And the father said: 'Of course, my son.' Came the day, and the little boy stomped around in the ecstasy of being altar boy to St Francis.

Now, we flip, as they do in the movies: we flip through the calendar—through the fifties, sixties, seventies, eighties. And we come to November, 1989. Four men are standing on the first tee at the San Francisco Golf Club. My partner, the wizard doctor (who calls himself, anyway, a doctor)—Dr Borders—turns and says, 'Sandy, what's your handicap?' Sandy truthfully replies: 'Five.' The doc now turns to the little boy, who is now a very big boy, and says 'Grant, handicap?' And Grant says: 'Three.' I want to tell you: Tatum is such a gentleman that the spasm of pain, the wince he emitted from his lips, was no more audible than an approaching hurricane. This might have been a short story by Maugham, or—better—by Thomas Hardy. It would have been called: *The Revenges of Time*.

The second secret. When I took up this game, at an age about five years beyond the age of anyone present, I soon deduced that most golfers were—Midwestern, decent, upstanding, buddy-boy, knee-jerk Republicans. A suspicion that was confirmed several years later when I found myself in the locker room at Augusta (I was just there hailing my peers—'Hullo, Gene, Hi Jack, Arnie') and I ran into two journalists who were interviewing the leading money winner of the year. Just then, Tom Watson had won his first tournament, I believe. One of the reporters said to the pro (who shall be unmentionable): 'Frank,' he said, 'is this Watson a comer-good?' And Frank the Unmentionable said: 'Sure, he's good. He may be very good. Of course, he's a kook.' 'A what?' 'A kook.' 'How so?' 'Well,' said Frank, 'first of all, he's a Democrat. How kooky can you get!?'

Well, the word I have to pass on to you is that your new President, El Presidente Ess-pah-ate, is a kook. And as for his friend Tatum, *he* once voted for John Anderson! He is a Super Kook. As for me, in spite of my having, for fifty years, watched American presidents and American politics, as a foreign correspondent, and being renowned (I'm told) for my amazing ironclad objectivity, at the same time, when I find myself in the privacy, I may say the closet, of the polling booth, I tend, from time to time, to be a closet kook.

So, it's a personal pleasure and privilege for me to pay tribute to not only the second member of the San Francisco Golf Club to become your President but also the second kook. I leave you, though, with the assurance, which I'm sure Grant will confirm, that *nevertheless*—some of our best friends are Republicans.

Marching Orders
[1993]

Once every year, the San Francisco Golf Club holds what it calls 'A Day of British Golf'. The idea is to reproduce as faithfully as memory can recall the procedures, prohibitions, quirks and folk-ways that were peculiar to amateur golf in Britain in its heyday. Not all these prescriptions have been filled in the past, but the hope is that they will provide an ideal which the club will strive to realize in all future battles of Britain. (I ought to say that in the matter of dress, the younger generation of British golfers has by now shamelessly violated the traditions of their fathers—the baggy grey flannels, the rumpled shirt—and gone berserk in puce slacks, canary-yellow shirts and grossly patterned sweaters in many colours; even, I'm afraid, sometimes flaunting baseball caps worn backwards, in the lamentable manner of William Jefferson Clinton, 42nd President of the United States.)

Handicaps:

Two weeks before the tournament, each participant shall be required to post his three best scores of the preceding year. The average of these shall be deemed to be his true handicap. The handicaps of club members posted on the board shall be declared inoperative for the Day of British Golf.

Before the Day:

1. The showers must be locked. The adjoining washroom must be swept clean of all its hair lotions, unguents, perfumes, deodorants, toiletries, brushes and combs.

2. All clean towels must be removed.

3. One lavatory may be left open. Behind the door, a nail (preferably rusty) should be installed, and on it a hand towel should be hung. To get the right atmosphere, it would be well to have the towel hang there, and be freely used, for about a week.

4. A well-worn nail brush should be chained to the faucet of the wash basin.

On the Day:

5. The Practice Range must be closed.

6. All caddies must be given the day off.

7. No carts (motor carts) will be allowed. Players must either drag a handcart (which will be called, as loudly as possible, a trolley) or carry their clubs in a canvas bag.

8. Matched sets of clubs are prohibited.

9. Baseball caps and visors are prohibited (*see above*).

10. Any member arriving in a suit and changing at the club into golfing clothes shall be disqualified. He may, however, use the locker room to change from his regular shoes into golf shoes (sneakers would be preferable). And, of course, he may drop his jacket on to a bench.

11. Club ties, however greasy, must be worn in the grill room, but not at the bar. If a club tie has to be purchased, a smear of egg yolk before leaving home will suffice.

12. The player's dress should be conservative and suitably dingy. Folded turnups on the trousers are not essential but add an authentic touch. Bicycle clips—worn as if from forgetfulness—tap many a mellow memory. Headgear may be either a cap or a fedora ('trilby') with the brim turned down. Tam-o'-shanters are strictly prohibited: they are worn only by Americans visiting Scotland.

13. The pro shop shall provide (for a fee) wax tees instead of wooden ones.

[150]

The Game:

14. The fairways will not have been cut for a week. The rough will have been allowed to grow waist-high (measured by the waist of the tallest member).

15. No four balls will be allowed. The game of golf will be played (i.e. foursomes, sometimes whimsically known in the United States as 'Scotch foursomes'.)

16. Putts closer than six feet shall be defined as 'gimmes' or—'This one all right?'

17. Marshals posted at suitable intervals shall reprimand all players crying: 'Go, ball, go!'—'Cut!'—and 'Come round, baby!'

NOTE: Expletives and blasphemies of every sort are, however, allowed.

18. Score cards need not be carried. Each player is put on his honour to announce his final score, however surprising the figure may be to the opposing team.

The Lunch:

19. Many bottles of kümmel should have been added to the bar stock. The choice of any other liquor between nines is permissible but is apt to raise eyebrows.

All American beers should be locked up in the refrigerator, along with American beer manufactured in Europe and labelled with the names of famous Danish, German and Dutch brewers. For the British Day of Golf, beer should be defined as Bass's Ale, Watney's, Whitbread's, Carlsberg Special, Dos Equis, Tecate and Foster's.

20. No great pains should be taken over the provision of a suitable lunch. Since the peculiarly British combination of ingredients (sausage rolls, bubble and squeak, shepherd's pie, etc., etc.) are difficult to come by—or even to imagine—the best thing would be simply to offer a choice of lamb, beef or ham sandwiches, served on white bread

[151]

(English, but not French, mustard should be available). The chef need purchase only the minimum order of the meats, remembering the American Jane Walmsley's comment on first encountering a British luncheon sandwich: 'I see the bread but where's the filling?'

English club coffee (which reminds the sharp-witted of the last time they drank—er—coffee) should be no problem, since it is standard in American and compulsory on the West Coast.

If the above conditions are met, something very close to a Day of British Golf may be enjoyed, or endured.

My Life with Gabriela Sabatini*

[1994]

It has been my privilege for many years, during the first week in April, to go down to Georgia to that marvellous botanical garden that masquerades as a golf course, and address the amateur dinner given by the Augusta National Golf Club to honour the reigning British and American amateur champions in the name of the greatest amateur of them all who founded the Masters tournament, Robert Tyre Jones.

At that dinner, everyone except me is or was an amateur golfer of deafening fame. Not quite as deafening as the fame of the humblest pro on the American tour, for the simple bleak reason that amateurs do not appear every weekend on national television. (By the way, the amateur champions of Britain and America are not always Britons or Americans. Last year, I recall, the British champ was a Dutchman. You will appreciate this embarrassment, I'm sure: you have been appreciating it in gentleman's tennis for— what is it?—fifty-eight years!)**

Now these champions, however far flung their native land, are uniformly very young and very pink-cheeked. And I am there— you may have been wondering—to address them because I am the President of a world-wide organization: HOW—Hackers of the World. I tell them two things. One: do not mock or disdain us

---

Given before the annual dinner of the All-England Lawn Tennis and Croquet Club, April 14, 1994.

**The last British Wimbledon singles champion was Fred Perry, in 1936.*

hackers, who are riveted to the box every Saturday and Sunday pathetically buying everything that's urged on us to improve our game (a new rubber grip, different balls, magical metal woods). It is we who make it possible for you to tap a very small ball into (as Winston Churchill put it) 'an even smaller hole' in order, on Sunday evening, to pick up a quarter of a million dollars. Secondly, I beg them not to turn pro, to resist the lust for a million dollars. There is more to life, I tell them, than golf. They haven't the faintest notion what I'm talking about.

This leisurely introduction is, you may have guessed, a way of postponing an answer to the awkward question: What am *I* doing here? I am not a 22-handicap tennis player. I can't quite imagine what that would be. I am not, indeed, a tennis player at all. I gave up the game forty years ago. I am too vain, I suppose, to share G. K. Chesterton's splendid philosophy, so simply expressed: 'If a thing's worth doing, it's worth doing badly.'

It must be, I decided, simply because I am an amateur, a lover. To be truthful, I am a lover (John Barrett is the only person here who knows this) of Gabriela Beatriz Sabatini! But I mean in the larger, purer sense. I love her tennis. (She is only the latest of the very many women of whom I have been an amateur.) I have been watching tennis, and watching the best, longer than most people here. That is not, believe me, a foolish or tasteless boast. It's just the unfortunate accident of the calendar. It's a dread reminder of something Mr Justice Blackmun said last week when a reporter, a very pink reporter (couldn't have been a day over fifty) asked him why he was retiring. He said: 'My goodness! Eighty-five is very old.' So it is. The first tennis player I fell in love with was Mrs Lambert Chambers. The fact that I was only six at the time is no reason why you should smirk at my passion.

But I have gathered that you mean simply to honour me as a symbolic amateur, and if so I am touched and very grateful.

Now, John Barrett—in, I imagine, a sort of mild panic—fearing

I might forget myself and talk exclusively about golf, phoned me to say he was sending by express mail two weighty volumes. The lighter one—Alan Little's *Wimbledon Compendium*, and his own 3-lb 4-oz tome (I took it with me on my bathroom scale). He apologized for imposing these encyclopaedias on me. And then he said a very sinister sentence: 'You'll be *needing them*, won't you?'

So that's what this was to be! I thought it was going to be a jolly dinner. But he made it clear with his meaningful stresses: it was to be also an examination! Well, I can tell you, and him, that I have done my homework. I have swatted away. I have boned up. *I* know who was the British general who said what he enjoyed most about Wimbledon was 'the man-to-man combat'. (He couldn't apparently bear the thought of the woman-to-woman combat and went home.) I don't need to be told about the mind-shattering third set of the 1937 men's singles semi-final, between Bunny Austin and the Baron von Cramm: 12–14! I was there. I know why the American champion, May Sutton, was born in Plymouth. The same reason, the same answer to a very puzzling question put to me when I was a very small boy: Why was the Welshman Lloyd George born in Manchester? The answer was: His mother happened to be there at the time! Same with May Sutton. How many veterans here know the name of the Sleeping Lineswoman? If you don't you'd better get John to send you his book. Better, buy it. The name? Of course, it was none other than Dorothy Cavis Brown. First round, 1964, court No. 3.

But, in this great work, I don't see a picture of Mr Tilden banging his racket on the ground. Rebukes, penalty. Conference of umpire, referee, officials. Play suspended, headlines in all the papers, it was in all the newsreels. As Othello said at the time: 'Chaos is come again.' John, will you please correct this in the second edition?

To be fair, I ought to say that John is to be applauded for his really staggering scholarship: diligent, unflagging, meticulous with minuscule details—splendid. And he bends over backwards to be objective. I think the most back-breaking sentence in the book is about the ladies' singles champion of 1961.* About her, he writes: 'She was sound more than spectacular.' (I'll bet he's never heard the last of that.)

I have been immensely fortunate to spend my life in the observation of two nations, two cultures. The main reward has been to double my interest in, my curiosity about, the human being. And, in a small way, I like to think that coming to tennis from golf lets you see some things in the game that the people preoccupied with it may not see. For instance, whenever I come, as I do, more or less directly from the United States Open (golf) championship to Wimbledon, I am always struck in the first days by the innocence, the naïvety, of tennis players considered as gamesmen. I was a good friend of Stephen Potter and associated with him in the furtherance of his mission: How to Win at Games Without Actually Cheating. That's the way we put it in the early days. It was later refined into the business of helping games players to lead a fuller, more deceitful, life. I expected that tennis players would know all about the Double Ploy, the Secondary Hamper, the Pour. But from my observation, gamesmanship in tennis is in its infancy.

Mary Carillo, watching Steffi Graf bounce the ball nine times instead of six, says: 'She's taking her time, *she's* going to dictate the tempo.' Pretty crude. Ivan Lendl has never got beyond examining his strings as he if he was playing with a harp. Though I have to recall that he once managed what Potter called an Oblique Huff, which put paid to Monica Seles's grunt for a week or two. Lendl didn't object to *her* grunt but to the grunt of the Las Vegas Lollipop—Andre Agassi.

Time out for the paramedics: the bandaging of non-existent injuries. That's good, though the question arises whether watching

Angela Mortimer—Mrs John Barrett.

[156]

the clock doesn't generate more anxiety in the one being bandaged than in the opponent counting his strings. Boris Becker, I have to say, is the best gamesman alive at lounging in slow motion through 24¾ seconds.*

But so far, the only first-rate tennis gamesman I've seen is a gameswoman: Mary Pierce. I saw her a couple of weeks ago win the first set. She did something extraordinary, something she'd never done before. She lifted those heavy eyelids and smiled! In disbelief, suggesting it was a freak. Then she appeared to have lost her nerve. She lost five games in a row, and the second set. She was shattered. She shook her head. She paced the baseline. She tapped her left toe and her right in rhythm. She was plainly doomed and bedraggled. Which gave the cue for her opponent, Sanchez-Vicario, to go into her well-known Bouncing Midget act. Which immediately gave Mary Pierce *her* cue to abandon her masquerade and slaughter Sanchez-Vicario 6–love! Of course, Pierce does have the advantage of a cruel father. She invites sympathy, the crowd on her side, the moment she steps on to the court.

I do wish somebody would give Sabatini a kindergarten course in gamesmanship. I think that in the hands of a good gamesman coach, that second serve could become a great weapon. Time and again, I've thought—if only she'd read Potter and just make a point, at unpredictable times, of seeing that her second serve was no faster than twelve miles an hour! Imagine the effect on the opponent. Martina!—'You kidding or something.' Could be as effective as Michael Chang's serving underhand to Ivan Lendl. Result: bewilderment, outrage and, of course, defeat. That, by the way, was the only masterful bit of tennismanship I've seen in the past few years.

Of course, you've noticed, I talk as a critic, a commentator, a

At Wimbledon in 1994 he proved—with one or two crude ploys—that he didn't know the difference between gamesmanship and cheating.

never-challenged outsider. That's because most of my time watching golf or tennis is spent with critics and not with players. But I hope it's as true of tennis as it is of golf, that you don't need to be a great player to be a great critic or, for that matter, a great teacher. Look at John, again. I've never seen *him* play. I understand he *can* play. I don't care. He's a great teacher—he says.

But I have a cautionary tale for critics, either amateur or professional. Beware! Speak too often out of turn and you may be invited to demonstrate your expertise before experts. My tale is of a Lancashire and Yorkshire match in the long ago, in the late 1920s, I believe. Certainly, in those days, the Wars of the Roses had not ended. Whenever Yorkshire came to Old Trafford, the grounds could not contain the seething mob of Lancastrians come to see the Yorkshire snout rubbed in the mud. (Since the match was played in Manchester in midsummer there was every chance of actual mud.) Unfortunately, during most of that decade, it was Yorkshire that did the rubbing. But whether at their best or their worst, they were fair game for the Lancashire critics. Not least for the best cricket writer of his day, some say of any day: Neville Cardus.

Well, Lancashire had won the toss and gone in first, and were out at the end of the day with a modest score, thanks to the impressive bowling of Yorkshire's slow bowler, Emmott Robinson. Next morning, as always, Cardus had a long, eloquent and glowing piece, at the end of which he analysed the fine work of Emmott Robinson. While allowing him all due praise, he did suggest that if he paid closer attention to the flight of the ball, a touch more flexible with the wrist at the top, he'd be not just a very good bowler but a great one.

In mid-morning of that second day, an old friend spotted Robinson sitting on a bench in the pavilion watching his side bat. The man moved down and sat next to him. He said: 'Did you see what Cardus wrote about ya this mornin'?' Robinson said:

'Aye'—(*long pause*)—'Ah'd lahk t' bowl at bugger.'

All fun and gamesmanship aside, I can't end without telling you of my one brave effort to cure a very sore spot in championship tennis. It happened, oh, maybe ten, a dozen years ago, at a time anyway when the tennis world alternated between marvelling at McEnroe's magical skill and shuddering at his loutish manners. I had a head-shaking session about this with a very famous golfer— well, since it won't go beyond these four walls—it was Jack Nick- laus. He said at once: 'The guy to blame is the father. When I was about eleven years old, I threw a club. My father said: "Jack, if you do that again, you won't play golf for another six months." I sulked and went off to my room. He came after me, opened the door and said: "What would Mr Jones think?"—Bobby Jones was my dad's idol. I never threw another club.'

Well, it gave me an idea. I remembered a sentence. I wrote to Mr McEnroe, Senior. I said: 'Here is a sentence once written by the immortal Bobby Jones. I thought you might like to have it done in needlepoint and mounted in a suitable frame to hang over Little John's bed.' It says: 'The rewards of golf—and of life, too, I expect—are worth very little if you don't play the game by the etiquette as well as by the rules.' I never heard from Mr McEnroe, Senior. I can only conclude that the letter went astray.

Golf: The American Conquest

[March 31, 1985]

The first time I played the Old Course, at St Andrews, I had one of those inimitable Scottish caddies who—if Dickens had played golf—would have been immortalized in a character with some such name as Sloppy MacSod. A frayed cap. A rumpled topcoat, green with age. Pants that drooped like an expiring concertina over his wrinkled shoes. His left shoulder was permanently depressed from all the bags he'd carried. He re-lighted the stub of a cigarette that was already disappearing between his lips and tramped off at a crippled angle. A straight drive produced the tribute: 'We're rait doon the meddle.' The first slice evoked: 'You're way awf in the gorrse.' (Scottish caddies, like nurses, alternate between the first person plural and the second person singular as a handy method of distributing praise and blame.) From then on, he said very little, rarely nodding in approval, more often wiping his nose with the back of his hand by way of noting, without comment, my general ineptness. The fact is, all questions of skill aside, the wind had risen to a blasting thirty-odd miles an hour. 'I hate wind,' I said. He squinnied his bloodshot eyes and sniffed: 'If there's nae wind, it's nae gowf.'

Such a remark is inconceivable anywhere in the United States, though it is an idiom as hackneyed in Scotland as 'biting the bullet' in America. Not that Scotland is unique as a wind-blown country. Throughout the Southwest, in Texas as much as anywhere, the wind rides free, but golfers must learn to cope with it; they do not consider it—like the fences in show-jumping—an essential element of the game. The simplest explanation, and it is quite possibly a true one, of why the Scots look with disdain on such things as calm sunny days, winter rules, cleaning the ball on the green, and—God save us!—electric carts is that these devices are thought of as comfortable evasions of a game handed down by the Old Testament God as a penance for original sin.

Certainly, it is well established that the earliest courses were designed by nobody but God, and the most unquestioned authority on their history, Sir Guy Campbell, maintains that 'almost all (the courses) created after the advent of the gutta (percha) ball, around 1848, outrage nature in every respect, and they are best forgotten'. This veto would dispose of every championship course we know anywhere on earth, excepting only the Old Course and—just in time—the incomparable Dornoch, to the north, which this year will receive its first British Amateur championship.

Nature, then, according to the Scots, and to many Britons and some Americans still extant, is the only true golf course architect. In other words, the modern game, which originated on the coastal shelf of eastern Scotland, was seen from the start as a challenge, on stretches of terrain that to most other humans were plainly not meant for a game at all. The attested origin of golf might well have come from Genesis; it is at once fascinating and ridiculous.

The tides, receding from cliffs and bluffs down the millennia, left long fingers of headlands that in time were thus separated by wastes of sand; no doubt, way back there in the Palaeolithic period, some Scots tried lofting a ball from one link to another. In time, they found life easier, but not much, banging a ball along the coastal flats. By then, rabbits and foxes had messed up the smooth grasses, and swales burrowed by sheep huddling against the wind made what came to be called bunkers. At some unrecorded date, when the game had retreated to the meadows far beyond the headlands, sand was deposited in these swales as a sentimental reminder of the sand wastes between the links. Little holes were now scooped out by knives, for by now (we are already in the four-teenth century) an idea had dawned on the Scots that had never occurred to the Dutch during their national pastime of banging a ball across a frozen pond at an adjoining post. The Scottish brain-wave? That the ball might be hit into a hole.

So a golf course was never planned. It emerged. And consid-ered as the proper setting for a game, a golf course—compared with a tennis court, a pool table, a chess board—is an absurdity. Considered as a move in the Ascent of Man, it is hard to conceive of a smaller, more laboured, step. For by the time the game really took hold, in the fifteenth century, the land it was played on was thoroughly beaten up by the nibbling rabbits, the darting foxes, the burrowing sheep, not to mention the ploughmen, tramping farmers, and the ruts left by their cartwheels. It struck the Scots, as it would not have struck any other race, that here was the Calvin-ists' ideal testing ground. The bunkers, the scrubby gorse, the heather and broom, the hillocks and innumerable undulations of the land itself, were all seen not as nuisances but as natural obsta-cles, as reminders to all original sinners that in competition with the Almighty they surely would not overcome.

But the grim Scots went on trying, using first the old Roman ball stuffed with feathers and then inventing one made of gutta-percha, which bore into the wind straighter and farther. It was left to an American, at the turn of our century, to come up with the modern rubber-cored ball, which the British with surprising promptness allowed as the 'accepted missile'. But from then on, the American influence, in this as in many other departments of British life (cocktails, bobbed hair, paper napkins, frozen foods, supermarkets, parking meters, etc., etc.), has been looked on at first with horror, then with suspicion, then with curiosity, then with compliance, eventually with pride by later generations that assume the invention was home-grown.

Until the end of the First World War, the Americans appeared to have had little influence on the game. They had been playing it for a bare quarter-century, beginning by obediently fashioning links courses on the coasts of Rhode Island and Long Island. However, two of the five clubs that set up what was soon to be known as the United States Golf Association were incorporated on inland courses: at Brookline, Mass., and, a thousand miles from the sea, near Chicago. The best American professional players went to Britain rarely; in fact, the best of them were immigrant Scots. If they made the trip, it was to pay tribute to the ancestral home, as a parish priest might want sometime to visit the Vatican. But, in the 1920s, the Americans—in the persons of Walter Hagen and Bobby Jones—went to Britain not as acolytes but as conquerors. It was an appalling shock to the generation that pictured the regular visits to the United States of Harry Vardon and other established British pros as missionary expeditions to teach the Colonials. Evidently, there was something about American golf that had escaped the British.

There were many things. The Scots assumed that since it was their game, they must be the natural masters of it. The English, south of the border, had come to look on it as an agreeable, if sometimes an infuriating, pastime. The Americans, it was learned, prepared for it as if for a tour of duty with the Marines. The British were taught to acquire a graceful swing; the Americans learned to bang the ball 250 yards and pick up the niceties of the short game later on.

The British retained their loving prejudice in favour of a links course, and to this day the British Open is played on nothing else. But since only a fraction of the American population lived by the sea, the Americans were forced to be less mystical about the creation of their inland courses. They initiated what Guy Campbell deplored as 'The Mechanical Age' by building in our time a great variety of splendid courses, in every sort of landscape, that owed very little to the Creation and everything to machines and money.

[163]

Also, long before Americans were regarded as a threat to the British dominance of the game, they had been busy in secret, adapting the golf club itself to their damnably ingenious factory processes. The perforated steel shaft, the aluminium-headed putter with a centre-shaft, the pitching wedge with a slotted face, the sand wedge. In turn they were banned by the British, and in turn they were reluctantly allowed.

A typical progression, from hugging the characteristics of the primitive game to accepting the American century, is that of the size of the ball. For as long as any living golfer can remember— back to 1921, anyway—the British have played with a ball 1.62 inches in diameter, while the Americans came to standardize at 1.68 inches. When, in 1951, the world's ruling body of golf, the Royal and Ancient Golf Club of St Andrews, publicly acknowledged that in the United States the ruling body (self-proclaimed as such in the 1890s) was something called the United States Golf Association, a period of *détente* was triumphantly initiated by the decision of the two bodies to standardize the rules of the game (in everything except the size of the ball).

It became slowly but painfully apparent that playing a different-sized ball in the championship matches of each country would present a problem, if not an ultimatum. The R & A followed the usual practice of British diplomacy. They thought a sensible compromise was possible, in the shape of a ball somewhere in between. They manufactured two experimental balls, 1.65 and 1.66 inches in diameter, respectively. They were offered to the Americans as a proud solution. The Americans, however, remembering Jefferson and the Louisiana Purchase (which was unconstitutional, and sneaky, but worked), had a better idea. Why not compromise, they suggested, by using *our* ball? And so it was. The bigger American ball is now compulsory in all R & A championships and in British professional tournaments.

The British manufacturers maintain, against alarming evidence to the contrary, that the ordinary club player in Britain prefers his little ball. Naturally, they want to believe that a monopoly they have held for so long is the consumer's preference. But their day—like that of the builders of the hansom cab—is done.

And so with many other traditions and practices of the heyday of British golf: 1457–1956 (1457 was the date when King James II of Scotland published his famous interdict against the game, which was running rampant throughout his kingdom, threatening the national security by seducing the young from their archery practice). I pick 1956 as a watershed, tilting the game once and for all towards the American shore, because it was the year when a Chicago advertising man, one Walter Schwimmer, being pressed by friends to polish up his escutcheon by getting into 'cultural' television, mortified them by dismissing ballet and drama as fringe benefits. He voiced the odd opinion that most people 'want to see somebody doing expertly what they do badly'. He thought bowling and/or golf would be just the thing. He set up a golf game between Sam Snead and Cary Middlecoff and sold it to ABC.

After Schwimmer, the deluge. A surge in the game's popularity, not least among non-players. A greatly expanded pro tour. The emergence of golf heroes as recognizable as film stars, dogged immediately by lawyers and ten-percenters able to coax a troop of sponsors into disbursing undreamed-of monetary rewards. In 1947, Jimmy Demaret topped the pros' money list at $28,000. In 1984, Tom Watson's take on the tour was $476,260, a useful supplement to the larger income to be derived from his television commercials. Inevitably, the potential pro, who once learned his game in the caddie shack, now learns it on a university golf scholarship. And the first-rate amateur, once he has picked up his degree (appropriately in Business Management), is determined to turn into a millionaire pro as soon as possible.

In the running, and financial exploitation, of their own pro tour, the British, in concert with the Europeans, are not far behind. But we are talking mainly about the changes in the amateur game, as it is played in Britain by something like 2.5 million, in the United States by fourteen million and still rising.

Well, much has changed but much remains. The most noticeable departure from the old British game has to do with its surrender to the watering of the putting greens. As long ago as the 1940s Bobby Jones lamented that the British adoption of what he called 'the soggy American green' would see the end of the necessary run-up shot, whereby the ball is punched to run almost as far along the ground and on the green as it had flown through the air. And it is true that today, except on the wind-skimmed greens of Scotland, the American 'target' golfer can hit a high long-iron approach on a British course with the near-certainty that the greens will receive the ball from any angle and hold it, if not quite like a horseshoe tossed into a marsh. (Still, the British Open has never been won by a high-flying American who has not mastered the run-up shot.)

There are, however, three immemorial characteristics of British golf that amaze Americans and pass unnoticed by Britons, since they are accepted as ordinary facts of life: the clubhouse; the Secretary; the foursome. The sturdiest of these relics is the British clubhouse, which nowhere remotely resembles the Intercontinental Hotel look of, say, the Westchester Country Club or the Spanish grandee's castle of Seminole. Except on Johnny-come-lately courses, the British clubhouse is a lumbering Edwardian structure, hallowed with wicker or worn, lumpy leather chairs, a rug installed before the Boer War, and a locker room, with no lockers, that Americans are apt to confuse with a cell in a maximum-security prison.

The stone floors, the scuffed benches, the leaky faucet, the pre-war nail brush (on a chain) so upset British golfers with much experience of America that the late Stephen Potter suggested, as a ploy of 'Transatlantic Guest Play', that the British host, off-handedly

[166]

apologizing for the simplicity of it all, should say: 'At least, no danger here of what happened to me at your club: getting lost between the sauna and the cinema.'

Lately, I am told, there has been a brisk increase in proposals to remedy these rude amenities, and in some places the stuffed leather and wicker furnishings have been replaced by airport plastic. But no American wishing to help in the modernization programme should dare to enquire the whereabouts of the 'Suggestion Box' unless he is ready to face the glowering eye of the Secretary and cower before the immortal line: '*I* am the Suggestion Box!*' The Secretary, indeed, is a character quite unlike any official known to an American club. He is at once the manager, the senior starter, the rules administrator, the supervising treasurer, the *de facto* chairman of the board, and the Führer. His only counterpart in the United States was the late Clifford Roberts, the unchallenged dictator of Augusta National.

Finally, there is the game itself. There are middle-aged Englishmen, and Scots of all ages, who contend that foursomes (called but rarely played in America, Scotch foursomes) is 'the only game of golf and nae other'. Four players, as two teams, use two balls only, driving alternately and then playing alternate shots. The dwindling number of its advocates say that foursomes is the best team game, and the most rousingly competitive, ever devised by a golfer. It does, of course, bypass any handicap system. And the British, apeing Americans in their native competitive frenzy and their itch to flaunt an improbable low handicap, are succumbing in droves to the four-ball, five-hour match, and soon will be feeding their scores into the downtown computer that disgorges, once a month, a ream of handicap statistics on stock tickertape.

And, too, the British play golf everywhere on Sundays, a blasphemy long prohibited in Scotland. They have abandoned their old flannels and cricket shirts and, to the distress of the older members, the young now mimic the fine flower of the all-American dresser, even down—or up—to the baseball cap, or visor. They use fluffy or leather or polyester covers for their woods, where once they allowed them to clank and jangle in a canvas drainpipe bag slung over the left shoulder. They are losing caddies (to welfare) as rapidly as we are, and pull their clubs along in what they call trolleys and we call handcarts. Electric carts are all but unknown. There are two at the oldest of British clubs, that of the Honourable Company of Edinburgh Golfers. But the vast majority of Britons have never seen one. The only one I ever saw in England was imported by the late Earl of Leicester from Germany, an armoured monster that looked as if it had been designed by a veteran of the Afrika Corps who had heard about a golf cart but had never seen one.

So the British, of all ages, still walk the course. On trips to Florida or the American desert, they still marvel, or shudder, at the fleets of electric carts going off in the morning like the first assault wave of the Battle of El Alamein. It is unlikely, for some time, that a Briton will come across in his native land such a scorecard as Henry Longhurst rescued from a California club and cherished till the day he died. The last on its list of local rules printed the firm warning: 'A Player on Foot Has No Standing on the Course.'

PART TWO

Night People

1

Oasis in Baltimore
[1940]

The worst and most profitable nightclub in the United States is located on the corner of Frederick and East Baltimore streets, and is known as the Oasis, or Max's. In a section of town that is variously described as the tenderloin, or 'tainted', and which still looks like an old *Police Gazette* engraving, the Oasis is about the only place from which a stranger can expect to emerge unclipped by human hand. This is due in part to the raging, almost offensive, honesty with which it is conducted, more probably to a screwball formula for night life that its proprietor, Max Cohen, thought up during the winter of 1925. Some of the ingredients—such as guest-insulting, strip acts, and overall daffiness—have been tried elsewhere and once helped one Fifty-second Street club over a hard winter. But these are the more obvious items in a recipe, known only to Max Cohen, that adds up to that rare product, a truly bad idea come to beautiful and lucrative fruition.

Max keeps his private standard constantly before him inscribed on his writing paper. At the top it says, 'Oasis Cabaret: Entertainment of the Worst Kind'. And below his signature, 'You can teach a parrot to say "just as good" but he don't know what you are talking about.'

Max Cohen is a large heavy man around fifty with an expression of genial determination in front of his glasses and a restless one behind them. Seen from in front he looks like your best friend, from the side like a man waiting for a train bearing precious serum. He opened the Oasis late in March 1926 in a cellar and has been doing business down there every night since with no cover, no minimum, no peace, and nothing resembling talent. The capital for this venture came originally from an idea that occurred to Max shortly after the end of the First World War. He wondered what soldiers would do with their old uniforms. He invested a few hundred dollars in this mystery, buying up as many uniforms as he could lay his hands on. By a logical step, he then wondered what *he* was going to do with them. Before very long, the forestry service, and all sorts of transport firms, started to beg for army overcoats and boots. Max sold his stock for 8,000 dollars, in those days a goodly sum. What to do with it? (Max was feeling his way, step by eccentric step, into an original and profitable line of business.) He obeyed an undefined urge and bought a bathing beach. The following spring and summer were the coldest in twenty years. Without any change of facial expression, he donated two thousand swimsuits he had acquired to a Catholic church.

But what, during these experiments, was his livelihood? 'From 1924 to 1929,' he says, giving a theatrical stress to the dates (in the deep pit of Prohibition), 'I was in the whiskey business.' He looks you, as the song says, square down in the eye, defying you to pronounce the word bootlegger. He didn't like the profession. It was hazardous, and the competition was rough. 'My principle,' he says intensely, 'is to do what the other guys ain't doin'.' After long cogitation, he had the idea for a nightclub 'you could operate on a shoe-string: no food, no liquor, just a pack of nice, friendly girls, strippers'. Throughout the first sixteen weeks he lost 250 dollars a week. Max was in deep despair and sent a man along to the Gaiety, a burlesque house that never wanted for patrons. 'What are they doing that I ain't doing?' asked Max. 'Nothing,' said the man. 'Are they selling whiskey?' The man said of course they weren't. Next night, Max had a trucker he knew deliver the stuff directly to the club. He has never lost a dime since. Within a few weeks of this inspiration, the Oasis took on the lurid shape it has maintained to

[172]

this day. Max wasn't interested in anybody's eating there, but, just in case, he hired two cooks to sit in the furnace room and surprise the occasionally hungry with a remarkable steak. He refused to hire showgirls who had any hope of going into vaudeville or the legitimate theatre. Instead, he rescued them from burlesque, from failing vaudeville units and from a retirement institution he calls his 'talent factory'. The result has been a full house for fourteen years, the patronage of everybody from college boys and long-shoremen to Congressmen who come in under a false name and go out under false pretences. A clear profit of 85,000 dollars for Max was invested in the surrounding real estate.

The main room is a large, square, low-ceilinged cellar with tables packed like a jigsaw puzzle around a tiny dance floor. A partition at one end separates the band from what amounts to a combination kitchen, stage wing, and backroom where privileged customers may mingle with the performers and play the pin games. The inside wall of this partition is decorated with pictures of Oasis alumnae, noteworthy framed documents such as a regal endorsement from Boake Carter, the English radio commentator, and one magnificent sampler which, hung directly in the path of strippers exiting *au naturel* from the floor to their dressing room, looms hazily out of a gin-and-smoke barrage and bears the warning—'Virtue is the Foremost Beauty of the Mind'.

Up to two years ago, Max had been worried about the blank walls of the main room, until one Saturday night a sailor got high as heaven and ran up a bill of thirty-six dollars. When they roused him next morning, sprawled accurately between the legs of six piled chairs, he swore he was a born artist and offered to paint his way out of the red. Max asked him what brushes and colours he needed and the sailor stayed two weeks, knocking off every day at 10 p.m., when the place started to fill up. By that time, every available inch of plaster sported some part of an enormous nude, maidens strode and knelt and sprawled round corners, asserting in every nook and cranny tanned and bosomy visions possible only to a man long deprived of shore leave. According to Max, liquor salesmen from New York to Mobile have judged them to be 'the best murals now extant in these United States'. They were described for all time by a drunken actor who, being assisted out, loudly insisted Rubens had been in there. 'Rubens,' he shouted, 'painted those things with his foot.' In this subterranean mirror of flesh, the ceiling looks strangely flat and empty. When asked about this, Max said it would be a tough job painting on a ceiling. 'You'd have to lie on your back,' was his objection. He was reminded that Michelangelo had done it. Always on the alert, Max looked hard at his critic. 'Yeah?' he said. 'One of them New York painters? Maybe we couldn't afford his prices.'

The sailor's dilemma is, incidentally, a regular solution open to over-eager patrons of the Oasis. Once a man couldn't pay the cheque and left his girl in hock. She worked off the debt in two weeks but stayed for eight months, on her own account. 'It was a terrible bill,' comments Max. This casual labour is the basis of Max's employment system. He scorns to advertise for help. The showgirls are originally hired for two weeks and most of them last, out of sheer forgetfulness, for four or five years. He stopped a weary brunette and said, 'Hey, you! How long were you hired for?' 'Three weeks,' she replied. 'How long you been here?' 'Eight months.' Max waved her away. The only understanding they are given is that they take a salary and ply the customers with drinks. For any impropriety they may be fired Saturday night without notice by Alma, the captain, who has been singing the bawdiest songs imaginable three times a night for many years now. This is about the only disciplinary check that the girls need fear, and according to the cops who patrol the block it is strictly enforced. In return, their plans for tomorrow are their own. 'If they don't show up,' Max explains, 'well, maybe they figured they'd take a little rest. Or maybe they jumped in the river.' If a girl is missing when her act is introduced to the audience, 'who cares?' asks Max, 'forget it, it's a break for the audience.' There is more truth than gallantry in this, for the wildly surrealist schedule of the Oasis makes it impossible to recognize an accident. There are, for instance, twenty-four waitresses, an indefinite half-dozen of whom are supposed to serve drinks. The others sit around, sometimes occupying the best tables and having a fine time till they are bawled into action by a worn little master of ceremonies, one Willie Gray, who twelve years ago came in as a guest. He was snapped up by an admiring Max and has stayed on his feet ever since as an employee, announcing the floor show three times nightly as something beneath contempt and helping to prove it.

When a show begins, the general disorder becomes a little more intense, but certainly not more deliberate. From the crowd of dancers, Willie Gray suddenly bobs up and brushes everybody back to the tables. At this sign, women in evening gowns who have been drinking calmly at ringside tables seize their pocket books and dash to portside of the bandstand. They hurriedly rip off yards of tulle and climb into fluffy step-ins. They are, in fact, the showgirls and this corner over by the band is the only dressing room they use after they have once appeared in public. Regular patrons enjoy helping the girls along with their dressing. Then the band starts to play, and that too is something an out-of-towner would not expect. (A few years ago, an appreciative Congressman told a stunned Max that it was a fine band. This oversight was instantly corrected and since then it has kept up a standard of unflagging tunelessness.) Willie Gray walks on to the floor and tells the audience there's going to be a show and there's nothing they can do about it. He introduces a girl with 'the worst voice in Maryland'. Somebody applauds and she quits. None of the girls can sing a note, so they are nearly all allowed to warble a few bars. A plump little girl is introduced as the country's ranking tap-dancer. She clacks her heels for eight bars and gives up from fatigue or boredom. The same thing has been done in New York but with deadly earnestness. At the Oasis, it is the triumph of spontaneous lack of talent. Max Cohen had the ambition to ease showgirls into the grave, to prove that nobody can call herself down and out until she has made the Oasis. Though the requirements are exacting, considering the competition of the surviving burlesque wheel shows, Max has fulfilled his aim. He has to apologize occasionally for the two or three quite pretty girls who are still in their twenties, 'just to keep the continuity', but he hastens to explain that their present appearances are a sort of grooming for their heyday in the late 1950s.

When the singing and tapping are over, the show settles into a routine that can go on for thirty minutes or two hours. Willie begins to call the turns of a seemingly endless reserve of strippers who, when the corner stock is used up, appear from the kitchen and the bar. One or two of them have occasionally given their all for a favoured guest but, considering Max's delicate relations with the police department, they strip rather less than they would like to. Willie introduces them sometimes by their own name but more often glimpses over his shoulder a tremendous 250-pound blonde and announces 'direct from 1161½ Crescent Boulevard, the Bronx, the celebrated Milky Bottle. Miss-Milky Bottle!'

Professional actors, oblivious to all but the vain pride of their trade, have sometimes mistaken the general coma of the patrons for lack of interest. This is now a traditional breach of the local ethic. John Barrymore once surveyed the listless proceedings and strutted on to the floor to recite from Hamlet. He had soliloquized for about four minutes when the mounting Baltimore wrath broke with the loud enquiry, 'Have you ever played the Bronx?' The profile stood puzzled for a moment. 'Never heard of it, my good fellow,' he replied in his warmest manner. The answer came back clear, 'Then you don't know how big tomatoes are,' and it sounded, says Max, 'like the password for the French Revolution'. It is still a remembered evening by people who have never been within two blocks of the Oasis. Barrymore never went back.

The wonder is that in fifteen years, the nightly orgy has never turned into a brawl. Max talks darkly about keeping performers and audience 'toeing the line', but the line, like his success formula, remains his own secret. Regularly twice a year his bouncers, Machine Gun Butch and Tiny Jack Horner (who goes around in a perpetual Karloff stoop on account of the ceiling) come and complain to him about the lack of opposition. He reminds them that their attitude is his chief pride, attributing the Oasis' habit of keeping good-fellowship trembling on the brink of mayhem to 'our now well recognized principle that human nature can be tolerated, short of violence'.

Max expounds his philosophy generously to the thirty or forty tables he sits at each evening while his roving eye watches the girls, the kitchen, the bar and the check-room. He admits to being a born moralist, but his gift for coining slogans he attributes to the time he went into politics, and his proudest experience was his appointment as a Baltimore justice of the peace. He keeps the certificate in his office, alongside a portrait of Franklin Roosevelt and a snapshot of his small daughter. It extols 'your knowledge, integrity, and love of justice'. A lot of Baltimoreans didn't see Max quite that way, and he resigned. Next he ran for city council on a straightforward platform: 'the support of orphans and children and the protection of women'. There was another uproar and he withdrew in a classic statement to the press that he keeps framed over his desk: 'I sought election in accordance with the age-old desire of man to achieve ambition, dignity and further respectability.' However, he had to confess 'regretfully that I have learned something and am returning to my customary business'. He renounced politics forever and decided to go on doing good in the way he knew best: running the Oasis.

2

Recollections of a
Pudding Head
[1986]

Hasty Pudding, corn (maize) meal stirred in boiling water to make a thick
batter and eaten with butter or molasses, was a favourite dish in Colonial
America since the early eighteenth century. In 1795, twenty-one Harvard
students, swearing to eat hasty pudding at every meeting, formed the Hasty
Pudding Club, which is the oldest theatrical institution in the country.
Every spring, the members put on a musical, the hilarious attraction of
which was, for countless decades, the all-male hairy chorus. Today, of
course, Harvard is co-educational, and the raucous joke of the 1934 show
(which I was asked to direct) is a joke no longer.

On a butler's table in my living room there is a handsome silver
cigarette box, touchingly inscribed to me by 'The Cast of Hades,
The Ladies!' I leave the glittering, and unused, object there not as
a reminder of the Pudding show of 1934 (about which my memories are lively enough not to require constant nudging) but as an
artefact of a vanished civilization, along with an eighteenth-century
snuff box and a locked tea caddy. Pretty soon, I imagine, I shall
have to add my Royal portable typewriter, which is already an
object of curiosity and barely suppressed ridicule to my grandsons.

Fifty years are no big deal once you've come safely through
them, and I have no trouble recalling the sequence of the things I
did in the spring of 1934: the dates—in both senses; the very rare
expensive dinners at Lock-Ober's ($1.10, imagine!); the night they
raided the Old Howard burlesque (I was there); the parties, the
girls, the important professors whose thunderous fame is now
hardly an echo down the corridors of time. They are all more vivid

than the things I did in the spring of 1986. (Which is nothing to boast about since, I believe, it is a common symptom of oncoming senility. For instance, I am under the alarming impression that in the second week of April this year, I was down in Augusta, Georgia, watching Jack Nicklaus win the Masters. Nicklaus? He is forty-six, in the sere and yellow, and he won there first when he was a fat and sassy twenty-three. Obviously there's something very wrong there. My mind, if not blown, is already palsied.)

But 1934 is as bright and sharp and funny as a 'Bush For President' button once was. I had better explain how I got there, and what I was doing—a visiting limey—being called on to direct the Pudding. It was the second, and last, year of my Commonwealth Fellowship, a sinecure so lavishly funded by the late Edward S. Harkness that I and the other twenty-four British graduate students must have been, in that pit of the Great Depression, the richest students in America. My fellowship had been awarded for 'theatrical direction', a daring break with the fund's tradition of subsidizing nothing but research of the most academic respectability. I had directed plays at Cambridge (England) and spent a summer looking at the German Volksbühne (folk theatre) in Silesia. By the time the Yale Drama School took me in, I was ready to direct a season of Strindberg, Shakespeare, O'Neill, Coward, take your choice.

However, the director of the school at the time, a dim character who spelled out the name of S-O-P-H-O-C-L-E-S to the first class I attended, announced that if I worked very hard in his spelling classes I might possibly be allowed to direct a play at the end of my two-year stay. Thenks offly, and goodbye! The rest of the year I spent reading theatre criticism in the library stacks, flitting to New York to see all the plays, and learning to add juniper drops to distilled water and wood alcohol to manufacture a gallon or so of illegal stimulants for my Saturday night guests. By the spring of 1933, I had whipped up to Cambridge (Massachusetts), been accepted by the graduate school, and acquired an apartment on Garden Street opposite the Commander Hotel, which had two comely waitresses and a nifty piano. In the fall, I was a new-found Harvard man.

Within a week or two I was invited to direct the Harvard Dramatic Society in a play by Lennox Robinson. Great fun. After that, I started a dramatic group of my own called—don't ask me why—the Unnamed Players, and we put on a Japanese No play, a piece by W. H. Auden, and a version of *Cymbeline* in modern dress, which so enraged the eminent critic of the Boston *Evening Transcript* that he wrote his damning review one day and died the next (the *Transcript* itself expired shortly thereafter).

But the big thing, the real challenge, came from the President of the Pudding, one Robert Breckinridge. He brought along the composer of the show they had already put together: a gangling, bow-legged, heel-scuffing Midwesterner (subsequently a surgeon of slashing distinction), name of Franny Moore. Would I direct this opus tentatively, and then positively, called *Hades, The Ladies!* Two considerations made me grab it. I had never directed a musical. And the theme of this production was so neat and outrageous that it appealed to me at once. It was about some far-off, inconceivable, time when Harvard had gone—wait for it!—co-ed! We knew we had a hit right there. Moreover, instead of the usual rehearsal pianist (a sophomore roommate of the producer who 'plays swell piano') we had a pro, soon to be replaced by Ruby Newman and his Band, the debs' delight. We had an actual professional dance director, not that he was to help much with an elephantine chorus. We had the music of Francis D. Moore. (As I understand it, the enormous royalities he earned from his hit song—'I'm Outside and Looking In'—enabled him to pay his way through medical school and eventually make the cover of *Time*.) We had eight pairs of dinosaur kneecaps, one of them, I recall, surmounted by a face which in make-up bore the most startling resemblance to Katharine Hepburn. No wonder. His name was Bob Hepburn.

We worked our tails off when we weren't shaking with laughter over the thought of a co-ed Harvard, and after the ovation at the club, and the customary declarations by old codgers that this was probably the best show in the Pudding's history, we caught our breath and started off on a spring tour: Hot Springs, Richmond, Washington (a White House party at which Moore and I played a piano duet under the gaunt and stony gaze of Mr Justice Holmes), then on to Providence and the wind-up in Boston. Moore's wind-up was a mastoid operation with him as victim, not assailant. This required a substitute for the Boston theatre performance, for Moore was the leading man. Since the only person who knew all his lines was yours truly, I had to bow my legs and attempt to represent a heel-scuffing Midwesterner. It must remain an unforgettable sight and sound to anyone who was there, for at that time my unreconstructed Cambridge accent would have made John Gielgud sound like John Wayne.

Well, after that triumph, I expected to get back to England and revolutionize the London theatre. It turned out that *Hades, The Ladies!* was the last show of any sort I would ever direct. In the previous summer I had bought a second-hand Ford ($60) and driven through many, if not most, of the (then) forty-eight states. The landscape and the people, and what the Depression was doing to them, and how Roosevelt was rousing them to hang on by their ragged bootstraps: this was far more dramatic, and moving, and—to be cold-blooded about it—more sheerly interesting than anything that was happening on Broadway. That trip, and the undimmed memory of it, were to mark the end of my theatrical life and the dawn of the idea that a foreign correspondent's was a better trade for me.

The college year was over. Boston's on-again, off-again spring came haltingly in. There was a last get-together, a last bawling of Franny Moore's imperishable songs. We parted. We swore eternal friendship and saw each other rarely, if ever. But the memory of those guys, of the knobbly-kneed ones especially, remains green and tender.

[181]

3

Garbo
[1936]

When you start to write about Garbo, you are reminded more forcibly than ever that there is no aesthetic of criticism that has got beyond the age of puberty, whenever the subject under discussion is an actress; since to most men an actress is a woman first, and they have been affected on the left side of the chest before their heads can get busy rationalizing their instinctive liking or dislike. So if these notes seem over-ponderous, and stress with suspicious high-mindedness the maturity of Garbo's new performance, you can comfort yourself with the reflection that they are just professional periphrasis for a yen.

An actress is usually said to be mature just when her daughters threaten to take over the parts she made her name in. But Garbo's maturity, as revealed in *Anna Karenina*, is not the maturing of her career, it's a noticeable ageing of her outlook. The old, bold, slick disdain has given way to a sort of amused grandeur. Physically (to her I suppose this means technically) there is a new balance between two features—a softening of the eyes, a hardening of the mouth. Garbo's 'appeal' was always the commonest of romantic conventions: the world-wide convention of the come-hither look. Because she is a supremely beautiful woman, she could make this look like her way of greeting the love of a lifetime. In *Anna Karenina*, she has moved beyond such enchanting nonsense. She has learned that between men and women there are very few plots. She has acted them out and has survived. Before she has even chosen her lover, her look tells you it doesn't much matter who he is, they all go the same way home. The new Garbo grandeur wraps everybody in the film round in a protective tenderness. She sees not only her own life, but everybody else's, before it has been lived. And since the plot is now (or perhaps always was) high hokum, the chief fascination is to watch how touchingly she now sees backwards, like a perpetually drowning woman, not only her life but her part: the way, at one point, she takes Frederic March's arm in the box; the way she looks down at the baby of a young friend; the way she picks up the field glasses to watch March fall from his horse; the way—years ahead of the acting textbooks—she hides a spasm of grief not with a cute nose-dive into cupped palms but with the five inadequate fingers of one bony hand. Her gestures, too, therefore have the same tender calculation, the same desire to treat people with perhaps too much concern at the moment, because she knows what's going to happen to them in a year or two. Tenderness, I guess, is the prickly word I've been reaching for, an all-embracing tenderness, a quality of gentle tolerance usually found in life in women over sixty, but an overwhelming thing here when it goes with the appearance of a beautiful woman of thirty.

It's little use to talk about the others, for they are not so much independent characters as inmates in Garbo's rest home for the troubled and the forlorn. Basil Rathbone does stand apart and keeps up a steady electric hum as a refrigerator, chilling us all with his clockwork unconcern for other people's moods. But when anybody else looks up or down, laughs, asserts, boasts, or begs a favour, their well-meaning acting gets referred back to the way Garbo looks at people these days, the way she implies that the least you can do for people in this stupid, brawling world is to keep them warm and give them a share of comfort before the end comes.

4

'My Fair Lady'
[March 16, 1956]

In the theatre and arts supplements of the Sunday papers, where dying plays receive the last injection of desperate publicity and new-born plays are hailed like comets, a two-line advertisement reads like the obituary of a pauper. But one appeared yesterday that is quite possibly unique in the history of American publicity. It is a piece of self-assurance as remarkable as the one hidden pearl in a boatload of oysters. It simply says, without quotes, adjectives, or any explanation: 'Rex Harrison and Julie Andrews in a new musical, *My Fair Lady*'.

This is the show that stunned a knowing first-night audience like nothing since *Oklahoma!* twelve years ago; that had sophisticates crowding to the orchestra pit on Thursday night for thirteen slow curtains; that started a continuous queue shuffling for eight hours through Friday's flailing snowstorm. It is, to come down to banal details, the musical version of Shaw's *Pygmalion*, done by Alan Jay Lerner and Frederick Loewe. And it needs no bush, no braying tributes. It opened on Thursday, and this morning the word went out that seats were now available for the middle of August. Miss Andrews's contract runs only until 1958, which now looks like a blundering oversight.

It would be bathetic to say that on every theatrical count it is superior to the original. The original is one of the most agreeable, if tendentious, works of a great man; it was cherished in its time and its revival will be welcome as long as there is a popular taste for Shaw. But this is one of those occasions in the theatre that get out of the hands of the critics after the first act and pass into folk-lore before the final curtain: the first night of *The Merry Widow*, say. Two cunning New Yorkers, the authors incidentally of *Brigadoon* and *Paint Your Wagon*, have taken the raw material of a great and garrulous playwright, pared down all the fat, grafted on it some funny and tender songs and lyrics, and trimmed the whole thing into the fleet-footed shape of an exquisite Broadway musical.

They have respected the master only where he deserves respect: the novelty of the theme, the originality of Alfred Doolittle, the preservation of dialogue and sustained speeches that have wit and pace and a cynical sharpness. All the Fabian preaching, the spinster's repetitiveness, the chronic unscrewing of a screw to screw it back in again—these have been banished. Whenever Shaw is about to turn from a sprite into a bore, the conductor's baton is raised like a head-master's cane. There is a rattle of timpani in the orchestra, and the deleted sermon is paraphrased in a pointed song and dance.

Is the phonetic tutelage of Eliza about to bore the audience as much as it does her? Then the whole ordeal is reduced to a succession of shadow scenes, with Higgins mercilessly dictating to his for-lorn pupil the phrase 'The rain in Spain stays mainly in the plain.' The months dissolve as smoothly as the lighting until Eliza sudden-ly looks up, like Saint Joan about to report her voices. She opens her mouth and says it simply and truly. Pickering starts out of a long hibernation under a spread handkerchief, the ice-pack drops from Higgins's head, and the trio leaps into a grateful tango. The lyric, naturally, is 'The rain in Spain stays mainly in the plain.'

Does Shaw underplay the charm of Higgins's naïvety about his own cantankerousness? Then Messrs Lerner and Loewe point it up in a masterly lyric of protesting innocence: 'I am an ordinary man.' Did Shaw fail to plumb the more rollicking possibilities of the bach-elor household of Pickering and Higgins? Then, in this version, they must turn into Holmes and Watson, and Pickering is refash-ioned into an American image of the lovable, silly ass Englishman.

[185]

Perhaps the original occasion for Eliza's historic gaffe (a mere six people in Mrs Higgins's flat) was a little too cosy and incognito, rather like having Sam Small drop his musket in the barrack yard instead of in front of the Duke of Wellington. Then here Eliza shall drop the famous brick at Ascot: a Cecil Beaton blaze of whites and blacks and greys that consigns Mrs Higgins's taste for William Morris wallpaper to the sewing circles of yesteryear. And, since Eliza's vulgar word would today hardly shock a Girl Guide, the one whose first awful syllable she totters into is common to both countries, and learned by little boys at the age of four. Nevertheless, it might well throw the Lord Chamberlain when it comes to be done in England.

In short, the authors are just about as reverent towards the Shavian original as Shaw was to *Don Giovanni*. It is a nice fantasy to picture Shaw now, trimming his perpetual vegetable garden, bawling with celestial pain over the substitution in this Broadway version of the only end to his play that he declared to be 'unbearable': the firm hint that Eliza will marry Higgins and fetch his slippers to the end of his querulous days.

Rex Harrison at last emerges as the marvellous light comedian heralded in his earliest days by his snapdragon features and jaunty body. Miss Andrews, known to New York as the plaster saint of *The Boy Friend*, suddenly achieves a transformation into womanhood as enchanting as Eliza's own. And Stanley Holloway distils into the body of Doolittle the taste and smell of every pub in England. The Oliver Smith–Cecil Beaton stage picture has dukes and duchesses at embassy balls switching between curtains into costermongers in an Italianate Covent Garden: the perfect American view of London, heightened by an opulence that matches the Edwardian opulence of New York today.

For this reason, if for no other, it is possible that the whole show has an exotic appeal here that *Oklahoma!* had in London. No matter. London should count itself lucky to be known abroad as the inspiration and capital city of this delicious day-dream.

[186]

5

The Legend of
Gary Cooper
[May 18, 1961]

When the word got out that Gary Cooper (who died on Saturday, aged sixty) was mortally ill, a spontaneous process arose in high places not unlike the first moves to sanctify a remote peasant. The Queen of England dispatched a sympathetic cable. The President of the United States called him on the telephone. A cardinal ordered public prayers. Messages came to his house in Beverly Hills from the unlikeliest fans, from foreign ministers and retired soldiers who never knew him, as also from Ernest Hemingway, his old Pygmalion who had kept him in mind, through at least two novels, as the archetype of the Hemingway hero: the self-sufficient male animal, the best kind of hunter, the silent infantryman padding dutifully forward to perform the soldier's most poignant ritual in 'the ultimate loneliness of contact'.

It did not happen to Ronald Colman, or Clark Gable, or—heaven knows—John Barrymore. Why, we may well ask, should it have happened to Frank James Cooper, the rather untypical American type of the son of a Bedfordshire lawyer, a boy brought up in the Rockies among horses and cattle to be sure, but only as they compose the unavoidable backdrop of life in those parts; a schoolboy in Dunstable, England, a college boy in Iowa, a middling student, then a failing cartoonist, failed salesman, an 'extra' in Hollywood who in time had his break and mooned in a lanky, handsome way through a score or more of 'horse operas'? Well, his friends most certainly mourn the gentle, shambling 'Coop', but what the world mourns is the death of Mr Longfellow Deeds, who resisted and defeated the corruption of the big city; and the snuffing out of the sheriff, in *High Noon*, heading back to duty along the railroad tracks with that precise mince of the cowboy's tread and that rancher's squint that sniffs mischief in a creosote bush, sees through suns, and is never fooled. What the world mourns is its lost innocence, or a favourite fantasy of it fleshed out in the most durable and heroic of American myths: that of the taut but merciful plainsman, who dispenses justice with a worried conscience, a single syllable, a blurred reflex action to the hip, and who must face death in the afternoon as regularly as the matador, but on Main Street and for no pay.

Mr Deeds Goes to Town marks the first jelling of this fame, and *The Plainsman* the best delineation of the character that fixed his legend. These two films retrieved Cooper from a run of agreeable and handsome parts, some of them (in the Lubitsch films for instance) too chic and metropolitan for his own good. At the time of *Mr Deeds*, an English critic wrote that 'the conception of the wise underdog, the shrewd hick, is probably too western, too American in its fusion of irony and sentimentality, to travel far.' He was as wrong as could be, for the film was a sensation in Poland, the Middle East, and other barbaric regions whose sense of what is elementary in human goodness is something we are just discovering, perhaps a little late.

It is easy to forget now, as always with artists who have matured a recognizable style, that for at least the first dozen years of his film career Gary Cooper was the lowbrow's comfort and the highbrow's butt. However, he lasted long enough, as all great talents do, to weather the four stages of the highbrow treatment: first, he was derided, then ignored, then accepted, then discovered. We had seen this happen many times before; and looking back, one is always shocked to recognize the people it has happened to. Today the intellectual would deny, for instance, that Katharine Hepburn was ever anything but a lovely if haggard exotic, with a personal

[188]

style which might enchant some people and grate on others, but would insist she was at all times what we call a 'serious' talent. This opinion was in fact a highly sophisticated second thought, one which took about a decade to ripen and squelch the memory of Dorothy Parker's little tribute to Miss Hepburn's first starring appearance on Broadway: 'Miss Hepburn ran the gamut of human emotions from A to B.'

Marilyn Monroe is a grosser example still. Universally accepted as a candy bar or cream puff, she presented a galling challenge to the intelligentsia when she married Arthur Miller, a very sombre playwright and indubitably *un homme sérieux*. The question arose whether there had been serious miscalculation about a girly calendar that could marry a man who defied the House Un-American Activities Committee. The doubt was decided in Miss Monroe's favour when she delivered pointed ripostes to dumb questions at a London press conference.

At least until the mid-thirties there was no debate about Gary Cooper because he presented no issue. He belonged to the reveries of the middle-class woman. He reminded grieving mothers of the upright son shot down on the Somme; devoted sisters, of the brother sheep-ranching in Australia; the New York divorcee, of the handsome ranch hand with whom she is so often tempted to contract a ruinous second marriage in the process of dissolving her first. To the movie-goer, Cooper was the matinée idol toughened and tanned, in the era of the outdoors, into something at once glamorous and primitive. He was notoriously known as the actor who couldn't act. Only the directors who handled him had daily proof of the theory that the irresistible 'stars' are simply behaviourists who, by some nervous immunity to the basilisk glare and hiss of the camera, appear to be nobody but themselves. Very soon the box-offices, from Tokyo to Carlisle, confirmed this theory in hard cash. Then the intellectuals sat up and took notice. Then the Cooper legend took over.

[189]

For the past quarter-century, Cooper's world-wide image had grown so rounded, so heroically elongated rather, that only some very crass public behaviour could have smudged it. There was none. After a short separation he was happily reunited with his only wife. He spoke out, during the McCarthy obscenity, with resounding pointlessness and flourished the banner of 'Americanism' in a heated way. Most recently, there has been a low-pressure debate in progress in fan magazines and newspaper columns about whether his 'yup-nope' approach was his own or a press agent's inspiration, like the malapropisms of Sam Goldwyn, another happy device for blinding mockers to the knowledge that they were losing their shirts. This was decided a week or two ago by the New York *Post*, which concluded after a series of exclusive interviews with his friends, that Cooper's inarticulateness was natural when he was in the presence of gabby strangers, that gabbiness was his natural bent with close friends.

He could probably have transcended, or dimmed, bigger scandals or more public foolishness than he was capable of, because he was of the company of Chaplin, Groucho Marx, W. C. Fields, Bogart, Louis Jouvet, two or three others, give or take a personal favourite. He filled an empty niche in the world pantheon of essential gods. If no cowboy was ever like him, so much the worse for the cattle kingdom. He was Eisenhower's glowing, and glowingly false, picture of Wyatt Earp. He was one of Walt Whitman's troop of democratic knights, 'bright eyed as hawks with their swarthy complexions and their broad-brimmed hats, with loose arms slightly raised and swinging as they ride'. He represented every man's best secret image of himself: the honourable man slicing clean through the broiling world of morals and machines. He isolated and enlarged to six-feet-three an untainted strain of goodness in a very male specimen of the male of the species.

6

Shakespeare in Loafers
[March 26, 1964]

Richard Burton's Hamlet descended on the United States on Tuesday and the Yankee burghers of Boston who once put the British to rout surrendered *en masse*, possibly before the conqueror's grace and passion, certainly before the rumour, magnified by a two-year Hollywood exile, that Napoleon was back from Elba.

Not the least of Sir John Gielgud's problems has been to create a serious production around a matinée idol who is now going to be applauded at his every exit like a toreador who regularly departs with a tail and two ears. Last night's audience was the artistic match of the thousand or so Boston hooligans who tore Mr Burton and his wife apart when they arrived the other day in the city that once housed Emerson and Justice Holmes. The more fatuous puns and sallies were hailed as gold coins in a pudding, the frequent 'quotations' like arias spotted by an army of Beatlemaniacs at their first opera.

There is a larger and more continuous distraction. Since it is nothing less than Sir John's conception of how the play ought to be staged and dressed today, it had better be gone into at once, before what threatens to be an ordeal can be praised as a feast, or at least as two fine courses of a heavy meal.

The stage is as bare and grim as all stages are between plays, when the sets are stored away and the janitor has dimmed the lights to a working bulb. The walls are the structural walls of any theatre. There are two rickety platforms. The only chandelier is composed of the sandbags weighting the pulleys. Enter the janitor with a window pole and two beatniks with swords. They are, amazingly, looking for a ghost. From this original perversity, masquerading as 'simplicity', follows Sir John's disastrous premise, in a programme note, that if the play is 'acted in rehearsal clothes, stripped of all extraneous trappings . . . the beauty of the language and imagery may shine through, unencumbered by an elaborate reconstruction of any particular historical period'. This familiar but naïve theory presupposes that our own period is bare of associations. On the contrary, all the players looked like everything in our lives that they are not in the play. Unfortunately our reactions to blue jeans, corduroy jackets, pullovers, canary yellow sweaters, and coats with patched elbows are much more personal and vivid than they are to doublets and hose. Once Sir John puts swords and goblets in the hands of these undergraduates, GI veterans, television cameramen, and delinquents, the confusion is so compounded as to scream for some simple, unpretentious correction: putting the actors in Elizabethan costume, say, so that the Elizabethan richness of the language may 'shine through, unencumbered by an elaborate reconstruction of any particular historical period'.

Under these maddening circumstances, what are we to say about the playing? The best of it is Richard Burton's best, and against these odds it manages to reveal what two years' abandonment to the fleshpots has made us forget: his unsleeping intelligence so exquisitely articulated in his hands and eyes, his marvellous low-key cunning, his capacity, which out-Oliviers Olivier, for the wildest Oedipus agonies. His fatal fault is that he cannot husband these powers for the difficult last third of the play. By the time he has wrenched his mother from floor to chair and spat obscenities at her, and murdered Polonius, he has spent his whole allowance of passion. Thereafter, he is a peevish son with a hangover, and the noblest of all the soliloquies, which should give the final goad to his horrible intent, is petulantly tossed off, almost as if it began 'How all occasions do inform against me, damn it!'

There is also present one other tremendous pro, and since he is allowed to dress as a Chancellor of the Exchequer might, we can accept him whole as a contemporary and a character in Hamlet. He is Hume Cronyn and he offers, none too soon I must say, a quite new view of Polonius: as an honest, probably an expert, administrator who manfully puts up with the knowledge that his precision of thought, his irresistible instinct to keep the accounts straight, is universally regarded as pedantry. This central idea, paraded with Mr Cronyn's own great good humour and snapdragon style, makes him the most intelligent, even tender, Polonius I can remember.

Among the rest, who are not distinguished enough to rise as identifiable kings, ambassadors, and young princes from a crowd of college boys in sweaters brought in from the streets, there are some palpably unhappy castings. Ophelia is a forlorn Newnham girl slightly over her quota of two martinis. Alfred Drake, as the King, speaks with elaborate precision but cannot fail to convey that he arrived without his music for *Kiss Me Kate*.

The plight of this unhappy Elizabethan crew, marooned in Boston in 1964, takes us back to the root of the trouble: Sir John's untenable belief that a boy in loafers and a pullover sets us free for the beauty of the English language in its golden age. What it does is to maintain the glaring reminder that our own age is spastic and loose-limbed, inarticulate and blasphemous, dull and garish, callow and deeply troubled in its own quite separate ways.

[193]

7

The Coronation of Miss Oklahoma

[September 15, 1966]

Although the Jeffersonian Law ('All men are created equal') is the first article of the American faith, the facts of American life have demonstrated for some time now that it is an irksome faith to live by. The Robber Barons, especially the ones who started out as office boys or ferry captains, made no bones about transplanting Norman castles to Chicago and to Fifth Avenue, in the hope of being mistaken for eighteenth earls. Today the inequality principle flourishes in such studied insults to the plebs as automobile licence plates bearing the owner's initials and airline lounges reserved for the VIP (that is, a man who can afford to travel first on the company's money, carry a black pigskin brief-case, and wear coat-sleeve buttons that are actually unbuttoned).

But it is a universal itch, nagging most at the three countries which most profess their equality and fraternity. The Russians, once they got the hang of the quality syndrome, developed a blue book for the behaviour of the military that would not shame the Brigade of Guards; de Gaulle talks of himself in the third person as a Supreme Being indistinguishable from La France. America bespangles the breasts of her soldiers, whether of the combat or quartermaster supply divisions, with more ribbons and medals than Napoleon wore to his coronation.

For the female, America preserves a crown. It was balanced at midnight last night on the high beehive hairdo of Jane Jayroe, and Miss Oklahoma began the national reign that millions of American girls covet far more than they would hope to become

Miss Truman or even Jackie Kennedy.

It all started in 1921 in a naïve and fumbling way as a 'bathing beauty' contest. By now the process of succession has become as complicated as the rights to the Spanish throne. The civic fathers of every county of every state choose a comely girl, who must be certified as a practising spinster, a high school graduate, and an idealist who ignores her smashing beauty in the search for some admirable 'goal': to be a nurse, a sociologist, a concert pianist, or an archbishop.

Miss New Hampshire, who appeared to be cast by nature for a king's boudoir, insisted last night that she wanted to be a graduate student in international affairs, which, after all, was Madame Pompadour's specialty. Miss California, a nifty mermaid in a one-piece bathing suit, rattled off a Chopin *étude* with more aplomb than most festival finalists.

The coronation ritual itself is by this time as formal as a Greek tragedy. The stand-in for the Archbishop of Canterbury is a breezy, glossy-haired MC in white tie and tails known, in all humbleness, as Bert Parks. He carries white cards from which he reads uplifting prose. His minister is the forever regal Bess Myerson, the queen in 1945. From time to time she tries to explain the magic that creates a natural queen ('she must be compassionate and concerned about others, in the American tradition') and this chore leads easily into a series of television catechisms which suggest that a hair rinse, a cola drink, and an automobile have something to do with it.

Just before the witching hour itself, the judges announced themselves satisfied, or at least in public agreement. The five finalists are now called and sit, a blaze of teeth, heads held high, white gloves shimmering way above their delicious elbows. They are not to change expression by an eyelash until one of them is allowed to crumble on to the bosom of the runner-up.

The fourth runner-up is announced: New Hampshire's International Affairs Specialist. The third: Miss Ohio, whose 'goal' is, shamelessly, a husband. The second, Miss Tennessee, a ravishing, graceful blonde who sent the audience into a tumult of obvious dissatisfaction with the judges. Now the two heirs-apparent take a refined breath, gently undulating their adorable bosoms, and try to look as apparent as possible.

'Remember,' warned Archbishop Parks, 'that if for any reason Miss America is unable to fulfil her duties, this girl will be her true successor.' It is Miss California, the trim mermaid, and she duly receives the speechless bowed head of the lonely Miss Oklahoma, the Queen herself. The four losers sweep into minuet positions as a court of honour. Archbishop Parks lets loose a tenor aria: 'There she goes, Miss America!' And, wearing her crown as tenderly as it might be a brimful glass of beer, she floats with proper majesty along the runway and all the length of the looped silk curtain.

It is noticeable that there is not a flat chest, a bandy leg, a bird's-nest haircut, a craggy knee, a mini skirt, a mackerel foot in the lot. Is this bad? Well, fellow Americans, I dare to say it is. It reveals America back in the thirties, forties, and early fifties, resting on her laurels of long thighs, and unashamed bosoms; an America smugly disdainful of knobby knees and bloodless lips; an America content with clothes cut only for females, and with piles of glistening hair, superb figures, and the carriage of a Gibson Girl. Not only do they look in superlative health. They are—ugh!—physically clean! They restore us by a process of dangerous, perhaps subversive, nostalgia to an America where women had legs like pillars of gold, bellies like bushels of wheat, breasts like meringues.

If allowed to go on, this could undermine everything the 1960s have been working for: which is, I guess, the triumph of the neuter and the revival of tuberculosis.

8

Star Quality
[March 31, 1970]

The movie queen who decides, too soon, to take Broadway in her stride invites a cruel fate: simply, the inevitable contrast between her—possibly haunting—presence on the screen and her ineptitude at the different craft that is being expertly practised all around her. Connoisseurs of theatrical disaster still recall that evening, thirty-seven years ago, when Katharine Hepburn drifted airily on stage (in an appalling play called *The Lake*) in the fatal hope of mingling easily with such an old stage pro as Blanche Bates. Whenever Miss Bates came on, though, Miss Hepburn appeared to retreat upstage, downstage, as far away as possible. Could it be, mused Dorothy Parker, 'that Miss Hepburn was afraid of catching acting from Miss Bates?'

That mean line can now be recalled in all charity, for Miss Hepburn has burnished, down the decades, what was always an essentially theatrical talent as striking as her beauty. And in the current *Coco*, she has taken a resounding revenge on the Parker attack. Troops of worshippers nightly attest to the proclaimed consensus of the critics that Miss Hepburn now exhibits a theatrical presence that is unsurpassed.

Rather, she was unsurpassed until last night, when a second lady, assumed to be a fixed star hanging over Beverly Hills, hurtled into New York to be recognized as a comet: that is to say, according to the best technical definition, as 'a body with a star-like nucleus and a train or tail of light moving around the sun in an elliptical course or towards and from it in a parabola'. Nobody who has watched the stars in their courses needs to be reminded of the enchanting arrival on the screen of a flaxen-haired girl with a body as trig as a trout and a come-hither look unique among all previous come-hither looks, one that could invite its victim to bed or to butchery. Lauren Bacall, of course. After the early celebration, in the Bogart years, of her lynx-like glance, her mocking whistle and her youthful beauty, Miss Bacall suffered an embarrassing decade or so during which she was regularly required to be a romantic and fragile figure. But, temperamentally, as her last night's authors remarked, 'she is as fragile as a moose'.

For too many years, she withstood prodigies of miscasting. In the Hollywood casting directory, nubile girls with flaxen hair and yellow eyes must be either sirens or helpless fawns. Bacall was too young for a siren, unlikely to threaten Gale Sondergaard. So—how often did we see strong males—Kirk Douglas, Gary Cooper, John Wayne, Kenneth More—attempt to be tender with Miss Bacall, who is as susceptible of protection as a tornado? It took a close friend Nunnally Johnson, happily also a famous humorist and a director, to cast her as herself: a first-rate clown, and write lines for her that revealed her to be as malleable, as funny, as a monkey in a barrel. *How to Marry a Millionaire* was the day of epiphany, and some of us assumed that from then on she would fulfil her destiny as the obvious successor to Carole Lombard. It was not to be. She was soon back to the romantic grind and movies routinely described as 'pure Hollywood moonshine', 'overwrought melodrama', 'rudimentary heroics'. Maybe, it struck me at the time, since nobody—except Mr Johnson—would let her become a screen actress by simply 'behaving' as herself—perhaps what she needed for the full exercise of her elliptical and parabolic course was not a wider screen but a wider stage. Perhaps, after the sinking of a movie star in heaps of rubbish, she might prove she always had star quality by moving to the theatre, to Broadway.

She has, it is true, appeared on Broadway before. She was again miscast, as a hermaphrodite(!), in a woeful and short-lived play. Then, only three years ago, she became something more like herself in the Broadway version of *The Cactus Flower*. It was generally conceded to be a 'smash', if not a very good comedy. But it can now be seen to have been a rehearsal for the blinding triumph of *Applause*, which burst on Broadway last night and which may well outshine any other explosion in prospect until the crack of atomic doom.

Applause is neatly based, by the old team of Betty Comden and Adolph Green, on Joseph Mankiewicz's movie *All About Eve*, the story of an ageing actress adored by a stage-door slip of a girl who comes in like a waif and goes out like a werewolf. It is the old story, as durable as a Groucho–Chico vaudeville routine, of the old witch out-bitched by the new. It would be nice to say that the young girl puts up, as Anne Baxter did against Bette Davis, menacing competition. The truth is that Miss Bacall defuses and obliterates every other talent on stage. She tosses a line like a dagger and leaves it twanging there while the audience applauds over the victim's response. She sings, sort of, in a Bankhead growl but with a blissful *élan* which implies that Ella Fitzgerald is a pedant for singing on pitch. She dances (an astonishing talent, this) through an anthology of the popular dances of the past thirty years, with her train or tail of light moving in a parabola that leaves the audience with the breathless impression that Florence Mills and the Astaires have been resurrected in one flashing body.

It is academic to mention the modesty of the music, the inaudibility of the lyrics and the mere adequacy of the rest of the cast, gasping to stay above water. The theatre is Bacall's private heaven. And who asks that the Florida sky should be studded with other stars when *Apollo* is launched? It is enough that the surrounding script, actors and actresses should provide no clouds, no drizzle, no high wind or other intrusion on a clear view of the comet.

I'm not sure that all this triumph has much to do with acting.

[199]

We are talking about what makes a star. Peter Ustinov said it was useless for an actor to act his heart out in a close-up if Humphrey Bogart was smoking a cigarette in the background. Bogart never struck me as a remarkable actor, but he was mesmeric. The definition of a star comes down to this: someone you can't take your eyes off. Lauren Bacall, heretofore known as a movie sexpot with a slinky style, who was allowed to 'behave' as herself in just one rollocking movie, demonstrated in dazzling fashion last night that she is a theatrical star of the first magnitude. At the end, the lovely rascal threw her head up and her arms high, and the Palace Theatre resounded with a tumult unlike anything heard in this town since Laurence Olivier wiped the paint from his eyelids and bowed himself out as Oedipus. Quite simply, Lauren Bacall achieved a most surprising reincarnation: Groucho reborn as Dietrich, Judy Garland as Monroe. Better, Bacall as her true self.

9

The Duke
[May 31, 1974]

'**W**_hen_ it is finished,' says the guidebook, 'it may well be the largest cathedral in the world.' I am always leery of sentences that contain 'may well be'. But it is certainly a very large cathedral; namely, the Episcopal Cathedral Church of St John the Divine on the upper West Side in New York City. Its foundations were laid in 1892. They've been building it ever since, and the end is not yet.

On Monday, May 27, 1974, St John the Divine housed a ceremony that would have flabbergasted its architect and its early worshippers. Every pew was filled, and the aisles were choked, and there were several thousands listening to loudspeakers out on the street. And when the ten thousand people inside were asked to stand and pray, there was a vast rustling sound as awesome, it struck me, as that of the several million bats whooshing out of the Carlsbad Caverns in New Mexico at the first blush of twilight.

It is not the size of the crowd that would have shocked the cathedral's founders (they might have taken it jubilantly as a sign of a great religious revival). It was what the crowd was there for. A crowd that ranged through the whole human colour scale, from the most purple black to the most pallid white, come there to honour the life and mourn the death of a man who had become supreme in an art that began in the brothels of New Orleans. The art is that of jazz, and the practitioner of it they mourned was Edward Kennedy Ellington, identified around the world more immediately than any member of any royal family as—the Duke.

The Duke's career was so much his life that there's very little to

say about his private ups and downs, if any. He was born in Washington, DC, in 1899, the son of a White House butler, and perhaps
the knowledge that Father had a special, protected status inside
the white Establishment had much to do with the Duke's seeming
to be untouched, or untroubled, by the privations and public
humiliations we should expect of a black born in the nation's capital. Certainly he must have thought of himself as belonging to one
of the upper tiers of black society. But his upbringing could be
called normal for any of the black boys who were to turn into great
jazzmen. I'm thinking of men like Earl Hines and Fats Waller, the
sons of coloured parsons or church organists, who, almost automatically as little boys, were hoisted on to a piano stool. The Duke
took piano lessons but also took to sketching and thought of a
career as an artist. This dilemma was solved by his becoming a sign
painter by day and running small bands by night.

What got him going was the nightly grind and the daily practice. It is something that nightclub habitués seldom credit, it being
assumed that while classical pianists must follow a daily regimen,
people like Ellington, Hines, Waller, Tatum, simply have a 'natural
gift' and just rattle the stuff off on request. Nothing could be more
false. I remember ten or fifteen years ago running into an old and
engaging jazzman, a white who was employed in a poky little jazz
joint in San Francisco. Muggsy Spanier, a sweet and talented man
who had had a long experience of the roller-coaster fortunes of a
jazzman: one year you are playing before delirious crowds in a
movie theatre or grand hotel, three years later blowing your brains
out before a few nodding drunks in a crummy roadhouse off the
main highway in some place called Four Forks, Arkansas, or New
Iberia, Louisiana. Just then Muggsy was in a lean year playing in a
small band with Earl Hines, who was also at a low ebb (this was
before Hines, the father of jazz piano, had been discovered by the
State Department and the Soviet government, or been re-discovered
by a new generation). Well, Muggsy had left his trumpet in this

[202]

dreadful nightclub and found he needed it, on his night off, for some impromptu gig or other. So he had to go into the nightclub next morning, always a depressing experience, what with the reek of sour air and spilled alcohol and the lights turned down to a maintenance bulb or two. He told me that one of the unforgettable shocks of his stint in San Francisco was coming from the bone-white sunlight into the smelly cave and squinting through the dark and seeing Hines sitting there, as he did for two or three hours every morning, practising not the blues or 'Rosetta' or 'Honeysuckle Rose' but the piano concertos of Mozart and Beethoven. To the gaping Muggsy, Hines looked up and said, 'Just keeping the fingers loose.' To be the best, it's a sad truth most of us amateurs shrink from admitting, you have to run, fight, golf, write, play the piano every day. I think it was Paganini—it may have been Rubinstein—who said: 'If I go a week without practice, the audience notices it. If I go a day without practice, *I* notice it.'

This digression is very relevant to the character and the mastery of Duke Ellington. He was at a piano, but he was there as a composer, day in and night out. For a man of such early and sustained success, it is amazing that he not only tolerated the grind, after one-night stands, of the long bus rides through the day, and the pick-up meals, but actually cherished them as the opportunity to sit back and scribble and hum and compose. He did this to the end.

I knew all the records of his first period when I was in college, from 1927 through 1932. And when I first arrived in New York I wasted no time in beating it up to the Cotton Club to see the great man in the flesh. But, apart from a nodding acquaintance in nightclubs, and becoming known to him no doubt as one of those ever-present nuisances who request this number and that, I didn't meet Ellington alone, by appointment so to speak, until the end of the Second War. I went up to his apartment on the swagger side of Harlem. There is such a place, in fact there are as many fine shadings of Negro housing through the hierarchy of Negro social status as there are shadings of pigment from the high yaller to the coal black. Ellington was at the top of the scale, in a large Victorian building looking out on a patch of greenery.

The date had been for two in the afternoon. In my mind's eye I had the picture complete: the dapper figure of the Duke seated in a Noël Coward bathrobe deep in composition at a concert grand. In those days, bandleaders got themselves up in gold lamé and sequins. The Duke wore white tie and tails, and was as sleek as a seal.

Well, I was shown into a large and rambling apartment with a living room that had evidently seen a little strenuous drinking the night before. Off from the living room behind curtained French doors was a bedroom. The doors were open and there in full view was a large bed rumpled and unmade. Beyond that was a bathroom, and out of it emerged what I first took to be some swami in the wrong country. It was the Duke, naked except for a pair of underdrawers and a towel woven around his head. He came in groaning slightly and saying to himself, 'Man!' Then *his* man came in, a coloured butler, and they went into the knotty question of what sort of breakfast would be at once tasty and medicinal. It was agreed on, and the Duke turned and said, 'Now.' Meaning, what's your business at this unholy hour of two in the afternoon?

The breakfast arrived and he went at it like a marooned mountaineer. To my attempts to excite him with the proposal I had come to make, he grunted 'Uh-huh' and 'Un-un' between, or during, mouthfuls.

At last he pushed the plate away, picked up his coffee cup, and sat down and slurped it rapidly and nodded for me to begin again. I had come to suggest that he might like to record a long session with his band for the BBC. This was, remember, the peak period of his big band, and I suggested that we record him not, as we now say, 'in concert', but in rehearsal. He shot a suspicious glare at me, as if I'd suggested recording him doing five-finger exercises. But slowly and warily he began to see my problem, and to respect it. Simply, how to convey to a listener (this was before television) the peculiar genius of the Duke, since it was unique in the practice of jazz music. Which was somehow to be, and feel, present at the act of creation when it was happening to the Duke standing in front of the band in rehearsal. Everybody knows that the best jazz is impossible to write down to the usual musical notation. You can no more make a transcription of Hines playing 'I Can't Give You Anything But Love' or, worse, Art Tatum playing any of his cascading variations on 'Tea for Two', than you can write down three rules for the average swimmer to follow in doing the two hundred metres like Mark Spitz. Jazz is always improvisation done best by a group of players who know each other's whimsical ways with such mysteries as harmonics, counterpoint, scooped pitch, jamming in unison. Alone among jazz composers, the Duke's raw material was the tune, scribbled bridge passages, a sketch in his head of the progression of solos and ensembles he wanted to hear, and an instinctive knowledge of the rich and original talents, and strengths and perversities, of his players. They were not just trumpet, trombone, clarinet, E-flat alto sax, and so on. They were Cootie Williams, Lawrence Brown, Barney Bigard, Johnny Hodges, who had stayed with him for years, for decades. One of them, Harry Carney, played with the Duke on his first recording date in 1927, and he was with him on the last date, in Kalamazoo, Michigan, last March. In 1927 Ellington had created a weird, compact, entirely personal sound with his band. It was weirder still and richer, but it was just as personal at the end.

Eventually the Duke appreciated that what we wanted was not just another performance. He agreed, and we had a long and unforgettable session, in a hired studio on Fifth Avenue, where we recorded the whole process of the number dictated, the roughest run-through, with many pauses, trying this fusion of instruments and that, stopping and starting and transferring the obligato from one man to another, the Duke talking and shouting, 'Now, Tricky, four bars' and 'Barney, in there eight.' And in the last hour, what had been a taste in the Duke's head came out as a harmonious, rich meal.

The Duke was nicknamed as a boy by a friend who kidded him about his sharp dressing. He was an elegant and articulate man and, as I've hinted, strangely apart from the recent turmoil of his race. Not, I think, because he was ever indifferent or afraid. He was a supremely natural man, and in his later years devout, and he seemed to assume that men of all colours are brothers. And most of the immediate problems of prejudice and condescension and tension between black and white dissolved in the presence of a man whom even an incurable bigot must have recognized as a man of unassailable natural dignity. He had a childlike side, which—we ought to remember—is recommended in the New Testament for entry into the kingdom of Heaven. He was very sick indeed in the last few months. He knew, but kept it to himself, that he had cancer in both lungs. A week or two before the end, he sent out to hundreds of friends and acquaintances what looked at first like a Christmas card. It was a greeting. On a field of blue was a cross, made up of four vertical letters and three horizontal. They were joined by the letter O. The vertical word spelled 'Love' and the horizontal 'God'.

He has left us, in the blessed library of recorded sound, a huge anthology of his music from his twenty-eighth birthday to his seventy-fifth. He began as a minority cult, too rude or difficult for the collectors of dance music. For much, maybe most, of his time he was never a best seller. He never stuck in the current groove, or in his own groove. He moved with all the influences of the time, from blues to bebop and the moderns, and transmuted them into his own. And at the end his difficult antiphonies and plotted discords, the newer harmonic structures he was always reaching for, were no more saleable to the ordinary popular-music fan than they had ever been. Most people simply bowed to him as to an accepted institution.

In 1931 a college roommate of mine who was something of a pioneer as a jazz critic, on the university weekly, was graduating, and he wrote a farewell piece. He recorded the rise and fall—during his four-year stint—of the Red Hot Peppers and the Blue Four and McKinney's Cotton Pickers and Bix and Trumbauer. He ended with the phrase: 'Bands may come and bands may go, but the Duke goes on for ever.' Ah, how true! We thought it a marvel that the Duke had ridden out all fashions for four long years. In fact, his good and always developing music lasted for forty-seven years. And we have it all.

So I am inclined to paraphrase what John O'Hara said on the death of George Gershwin: 'Duke Ellington is dead. I don't have to believe it if I don't want to.'

1 0

Two for the Road
[December 23, 1977]

At the risk of seeming to take a short trot through a graveyard (something that only Dickens in one of his familiar morbid moods would do at Christmastime), I should like to say something about two tremendous figures who recently went off—along with Johnny Mercer—into immortality. Or upon what Mercer, the most poetic of jazz lyricists, called 'the long, long road'.

I hope there was no moaning at the bar over the death of Groucho Marx. He was very old, and for several years he had had only short lucid intervals in which he knew much about what was going on.

My first contact with him was about twenty-five years ago, when he wrote to me to say he would very much like to be on a television show that I was running. We were delighted to start negotiations, and at one point we thought everything was sewed up. Then, mysteriously, he backed out. In those days, television was done 'live' (no taping beforehand) and movie stars were petrified by it since they'd have to memorize a whole part instead of thirty-second bits. By the same token, stage actors were eager for exposure over a national network, and you could hire the best of them for a few hundred dollars. Groucho evidently didn't know this. And I soon heard from our business manager why Groucho wouldn't be with us: he had asked an enormous fee. We regretfully declined his services. There was an awkward interval of silence at both ends. Then he wrote to me: 'Like Sam Goldwyn, I believe in art. But my agent, a coarse type, believes in money. And who am I to argue with such a baboon?'

Shortly after that, I was in Hollywood. He invited me to lunch, and ever afterwards, whenever my wife and I were out on the Coast, we saw him and enjoyed him as the slap-happy anarchist he was in life just as much as he was in the movies. The great pleasure in him came from his finicky, and funny, respect for the English language. That, at first hearing, may sound incomprehensible. But, whatever his comic style was like when he started out in vaudeville, he had the luck in Hollywood to fall in with the supreme American humorist, S. J. Perelman, who wrote one or two of the early Marx Brothers movies. I dare say nobody alive has a quicker ear for the oddities and absurdities of the language that can spring from taking words—taking the tenses of English—literally. This gift passed over to Groucho and he made it his own. So much so that when I wrote a piece about Groucho's gift to the Library of Congress of his letters, I suggested in it that S. J. Perelman's scripts and letters should be sent along, too. Groucho, whose laughable view of human pomp did not extend to his own vanity, kicked up a great fuss and swore our friendship was an unpleasantness from the past. A vow he forgot the next time he embraced me.

The most memorable example of this language game I can think of happened when we were lunching with him at the most iuxurious of Jewish country clubs in Los Angeles. When the menu was passed around, I raised an eyebrow at what even then were outrageous prices. 'Fear not, my friend,' said Groucho, 'it's only money. The initiation fee at this club is ten thousand dollars, and for that you don't even get a dill pickle.' When the main course was over and the waiter came to take the dessert order, he stumbled several times over who was having what. Finally he said: 'Four éclairs and four—no, four éclairs and two coffees?' Groucho whipped in with: 'Four éclairs and two coffees ago, our forefathers brought forth on this continent a nation dedicated to the proposition—skip the dedication and bring the dessoit.'

On the way out, Groucho lined up, to pay his bill, behind a fat and fussy lady who was fiddling around in her bag for change. The young cashier gave a patient sigh, and Groucho—his cigar raking the air like an artillery barrage—said: 'Shoot her when you see the whites of her eyes!' The large lady turned around in a huff, which dissolved into a delighted goggle. 'Would you,' she gasped, 'be Groucho Marx?' In a flash, Groucho rasped out: 'Waddya mean, *would* I be Groucho Marx? I *am* Groucho Marx. Who would *you* be if you weren't yourself? Marilyn Monroe, no doubt. Well, pay your bill, lady, you'll never make it.'

The other great man was a world apart from Groucho—in geography, upbringing, temperament, and talent. I'm talking about Harry Lillis Crosby, who, for reasons as obscure and debatable as the origins of the word 'jazz', was known from boyhood on as Bing. Some years ago a friend of mine, a publisher, thought of persuading Bing to sit down in several sessions with a tape recorder and put out a book of reminiscences. My friend was very steamed up about this project and came to me one day and said he'd got the main thing, he'd got the title. He narrowed his eyes and said very slowly: 'My Friends Call Me Bing.' Four words too many, I said. And, truly, I don't suppose there are more than half a dozen people in the world who would be instantly recognizable by a single word.

It's been just over fifty years since we were first exposed to the Rhythm Boys and their lead tenor, who provided the first happy breakaway from the ladylike sopranos and resonant baritones of the London and New York stages, who were singing Youmans, Gershwin, and Rodgers as if they were still commuting between Heidelberg and Ruritania. Then the Rhythm Boys' tenor, never identified on the record label, broke loose on his own, and the word ran through the English underground that a genuine jazz singer—and a white man!—had appeared in the unlikeliest place: breezing along on the ocean of Paul Whiteman's lush 'symphonic' sound. For about six precious months, as I recall, from the fall of 1927 through the spring of 1928, Whiteman, of all people, permitted a small jazz group—Bix Beiderbecke, Frank Trumbauer, Eddie Lang, and Crosby—to be given its head. And on the long spring nights, the punts drifting along the Cambridge Backs gave out with the easy, vagabond phrases of Bing and the lovely codas of Bill Challis's orchestrations.

For several years after that, the underground went into mourning for the apostasy of Bing Crosby, who turned into a gargling crooner. We abandoned him as a traitor, until during the war years and afterwards he relaxed again into the unbuttoned troubadour, the mellower jazz singer known from El Paso to El Alamein as the Groaner, Der Bingle, and always Bing. For thirty years or so, there appeared a parade of male singers, from Russ Colombo through Como and Sinatra and beyond, who could never have found their own style if Crosby had never existed.

By then Bing had done everything he wanted to do in music and movies, and, having wisely appreciated the approach of the gentleman with a scythe, he countered him by developing other talents and went off to fire 3-irons in Scotland and repeating rifles in Africa. Never a man to push himself, at twilight or any other time, he crooned only to himself. Then, fifty years after his first record, he cut a final album. Well into his seventies, he was the same Bing, because he had the great good sense to know the right keys, the navigable modulations, where to go and where not to go, unlike some other star-studded egos who like to fancy that the rules of mortality have been suspended for them alone.

I first ran into him on the set of one of the Hope–Crosby *Road* movies, and I think I picked up a false impression of him right away. Because he was saucy, mischievous, almost gabby when he was working, especially with Hope. They ad-libbed so much and broke down in chuckles so often that at one point Bing turned to a writer who was sitting with the director and said: 'If you hear any of your own lines, shout Bingo!' Of course, Bing was witty, in a droll, tired way (nobody else would have described his face, with its flapping ears, as looking 'like a taxicab with both doors open'), but the movie image of Bing was a very high-pressure version of the man off the set. Once the lights dimmed and the director said, 'It's a take,' Bing visibly drooped into a character so shambling and low key that I got the impression he'd had a sleepless night and would soon be off for a nap. People used to ask me, 'What was Bing like playing golf, I'll bet he was uproarious, right?' In fact, he was relaxed to the point of boredom, good-natured boredom. It's true he always looked you in the eye, but he did it with the grey, tired eyes of a man who had seen everything—a lot of fun but also a lot of grief—and was never going to be surprised by anything said or done.

From his early success days with the Rhythm Boys and on into his movie career, there'd been all sorts of problems in and around his family: sickness, death, the bottle, truancy, spats and sulks with his sons. Until he came into port at last, after some stormy seas, with his second wife and his new family. It is possible that he talked about these things to very close friends, but even his butler couldn't recall any. To everyone except some missing confidant, he put up the quiet defence of offhand, easy-going small talk.

I can't think of another man of anything like his fame who was so unrattled by it and so genuinely modest. The accursed foible of show-business people is prima-donnaism: the massive ego, the implication that the whole world is revolving around them and their new picture, their new plans—which they pretend to find delightful but embarrassing. Not Bing. He was in this more mature than any actor or actress, author or musician, statesman or politician I have known in coming to sensible terms with great fame. His mail must have been staggering, with its appeals for favours and money from every charity and every crackpot in the world. He never mentioned it. He was polite to every nice fan,

[212]

and every child, and every moron who hailed him. All his later concerts and pro–amateur golf tournaments passed on the receipts to a raft of favourite charities.

When he died, there was a spate of film clips and replayed old interviews and the like. The most revealing of these was one done shortly before he died by the news interviewer Barbara Walters, who does have a knack for asking the childlike questions we'd all like to ask but don't dare. She asked him to sum himself up, and he allowed that he had an easy temperament, a way with a song, a fair vocabulary, on the whole a contented life. And she said, 'Are you telling us that's all there is—a nice, agreeable shell of a man?' Bing appeared not to be floored. After the slightest pause for deep reflection, he said: 'Sure, that's about it. I have no deep thoughts, no profound philosophy. That's right. I guess that's what I am.'

It was so startling, so honest, and probably so true, that it explained why he'd been able, through hard times, to stay on an even keel. Perhaps he was one of those people who, though not at all selfish, are deeply self-centred: what they call 'a very private person'. Because he couldn't identify deeply with other people's troubles, he was able to appear, and to be, everybody's easy-going buddy, and forget death and disaster in a recording date or a round of golf. He was the least exhibitionist celebrity I have ever known. And because death is so dramatic, so showy, some of us cannot believe he won't show up in the locker room tomorrow and say: 'Well, skipper, how's tricks?'

The Life, in the Music, of George Gershwin
[1987]

I remember it as one of those midsummer mornings in New York when the skies can take no more of the rising heat and dump on the city a cataclysm of warm rain. It was the fifteenth of July 1937, just four days after George Gershwin had succumbed to a brain tumour in Hollywood at the age of thirty-eight. Across the roadway from Fifth Avenue's Temple Emanu-El a thousand or more very drenched and very subdued New Yorkers were pressed against a police cordon. Wafting towards them came the chanting of psalms, the soaring voice of a cantor, and—at the dead man's request—some Bach, Beethoven, Handel and Schumann. Afterwards, the lofty doors parted and as the pall bearers, led by New York's stocky little mayor, Fiorello LaGuardia, pattered beside the casket, the organ sounded the long eerie glissando of the opening of the *Rhapsody In Blue*. More than all the splendid music that had gone before, it was a personal sound and seemed to let loose the spirit of the man into the roar of the city he had loved above all other places.

Since then, Gershwin has been written about, I suppose, as much as any other American composer—popular, classical or modern. And by now it is agreed on all sides that he is remarkable, if not an unquestioned genius. This is a very recent consensus. Throughout his short life, and for thirty years or more thereafter, Gershwin was, at best, patronized by the musical intelligentsia. It was the first performance of the *Rhapsody* that triggered this condescension. The leap from a Broadway theatre to Carnegie Hall was an audacity that was psychologically too much for the critics. Irving Berlin, Jerome Kern, Vincent Youmans, Richard Rodgers: all admirable in their popular way, but none of them had the gall to present himself in a concert hall as a 'serious' composer. The critics were not to be intimidated by the presence in the Carnegie Hall audience of Rachmaninov, Heifetz and Kreisler. While the *New York Times* alone hailed 'an extraordinary talent', the other papers echoed the most austere critic of the day in lamenting the 'lifelessness of the melody and harmony'. Barely two years later, while there was a general complaint that the *Concerto in F* was not in form a classical concerto at all, there was grudging praise for a work more 'serious' than the *Rhapsody*. Three years later, *An American in Paris* had the austere one repenting to the extent of calling it 'engaging, ardent, unpredictable', but the general view saw it as 'patchy . . . thin . . . vulgar'. When it was heard in London, there was no argument among the British critics. They were unanimous: it was 'innocent babble . . . tiresome . . . silly . . . pretty bad'.

It appears that Gershwin, a considerable ego, was strangely nonchalant about these strictures. So far as I can discover, he never joined in the squabble about the 'seriousness' of his 'serious' music. ('Serious', a word never defined, was the sign on the door that barred the entry of song writers into the company of real musicians.) He was always wryly tolerant and unresponsive to suggestions of how he might improve himself. So far as he was concerned, both the concert pieces and the musical comedy songs were facets of his talent. No contest.

He did, however, hope for great things from the reception of *Porgy and Bess*. It had been written after years of dither and forgetfulness, until the novelist DuBose Heyward put a fire under him with the word that the Theatre Guild was thinking of having the novel adapted by Jerome Kern for Al Jolson—in blackface! Gershwin sprang to attention, positively swore he was dying to write it and did so during the following two years. For once, there was not a dissenting voice among the critics: from—'sure-fire rubbish' to Virgil Thomson's 'a fake'.

The truth is that since his concert hall debut fourteen years earlier with the *Rhapsody*, the critics had a problem of their own making, which *Porgy* encapsulated. Serious operas and concertos were written by serious composers. Both the critics' judgement and their professional pride were threatened by the shocking novelty of a serious opera written by a popular song writer. Surely, it could not be done. It took about a dozen years for critics, musicians and opera company directors to agree that it had been done. It took another twenty years for *Porgy* to be admitted, without condescension, to the opera repertory of the Western world. And it took very much longer for the intelligentsia to join the naïve millions who had guessed from the beginning that Gershwin's songs were the thing, and that like the songs of Schubert, they were here to stay.

Today, as I say, he is everywhere accepted as a considerable, indeed a unique, talent. Which is not necessarily good news. The day a writer, a musician, artist, statesman, is installed on his pedestal, he is a target for brickbats. So, the fiftieth anniversary of his death seemed a felicitous time to look over his work and character before he is boxed and labelled and filed away for good.

For thirteen years, from the middle 1970s to the late '80s, Alan Owen, my BBC music producer, and I worked together on many series of radio programmes that charted, and enjoyed, the course of American popular music between the wars. Slowly—and surely, once the fiftieth anniversary loomed—the conviction grew on us both that of all the gifted men who made the 1920s and '30s a golden age of American song, Gershwin more and more looked like the truest original. For one thing, his life and character were a good deal more interesting than most. Son of a Russian immigrant who followed the familiar route of an escapee from military service. An East Side boy who, as a song plugger, played ragtime by day ('pounded on tin', as he put it) and pored over Dvořák and

[216]

Debussy by night. A Broadway idol who hankered after classical forms and the help—withheld—of such as Ravel. A famous lover of women who maintained touching friendships with all the old girls. An egocentric without a smidgen of malice. An immensely successful loner who ached, at the end, to be married but feared, like a priest, he would betray his mission: which was, at all times and by night and by day, his music. Much of this can be felt and sensed, without strained hindsight, in his music and gives it its special fascination.

Gershwin never had Richard Rodgers's talent for effortless, jetting melody. His songs are rarely as sheerly singable as Irving Berlin's. But his music—and I mean his popular music—seems to me to be the most memorable and recognizably individual, going beyond the surface expression of his pleasure in invention into the deeper layers of a wistful and lonely man. It is, I suppose, always pretentious to try and pin down in words the emotional quality of any composer. Let us pretend, with Gershwin.

It has something to do with an irresistible habit of putting a jaunty tune in a minor key, or intruding minor modulations into the sunniest melodies. This fascination was marvellously compounded by his brother Ira, a very different character, a droll, easy-tempered man who loved to write 'against' the mood of the music (as Gilbert liked to do with Sullivan) with cheeky or mocking rhymes to tunes that are infinitely sad. The result is to leave you halfway between a chuckle and a tear. Can sadness be delightful? Melancholy turn to roguishness? Can gaiety be poignant? The brothers showed it could be done. And in demonstrating it to an unseen, and unseeing, audience, we felt that this emotional counterpoint is subtle enough to be ruined by singers who trick up the melody, venture on their own variations, attempt cute cadenzas. The musical comedy stage today is howling with such performers, and we have nothing to fear quite so much as revivals of Gershwin's musicals, which are bound to come, in which these banshees

[217]

give their all.* In putting together our memorial series on the life and music of Gershwin, we junked limousine loads of celebrated vocalists and went—and stayed—with singers who appear to recognize a particular emotion and express it, and Gershwin's tunes, as simply as possible: Julie London, Rosemary Clooney, Fred Astaire, Dinah Shore, Tony Martin, Lee Wiley, Doris Day, Gene Kelly. Best of all, we raided the treasure house of *The Gershwin Songbook*, with Ella Fitzgerald in her prime (in the late 1950s) when she had the luck of the exquisite orchestrations of Nelson Riddle, a man who knew what Gershwin was all about and who, cruelly, came too late for Gershwin to salute and rejoice in.

At Gershwin's death, Arnold Schoenberg, bearing in mind the songs just as much as *Porgy and Bess* and the concert pieces, wrote a declaration of belief, which may be challenged but cannot be dismissed:

'It seems to me beyond doubt that Gershwin was an innovator . . . I am not forced to say whether history will consider him a kind of Johann Strauss or Debussy, Offenbach or Brahms or Lehár or Puccini. But I know he is an artist and a composer who expressed musical ideas—and they were new.'

They arrived, in 1993, with an enthusiastic travesty called Crazy for You.

[218]

1 2

Chaplin
[1989]

Sometime in the late winter (of 1988–9), I had a call from an overseas newspaper asking me to contribute to the Great Celebration, the centenary of the birth of 'you know who'. To this coy request, I put them off by saying—so you're going to do a big feature on Hitler. The man was baffled. Why Hitler? Because, I said, April 20, 1889 is a date that will live in infamy, the day of the arrival on the continent of Europe of the human who would do more than anybody in this century to shatter it.

They had no plans, but must have devised some pretty quickly. They were talking, of course, about the immortal Cockney who had been born four days before the Führer: Charles Spencer Chaplin. I turned them down on the ground that I had written, in a book, just about everything I should want to say about him. They were amazed to hear this. But then, I am getting healthily used to the discovery that my heroes, heroines, authors, jazzmen, movie stars are unknown to most people under sixty! In the past few years, when an anecdote occurs to me that might be received as riveting (bearable, anyway) I have learned to say: 'Does the name So-and-So mean anything to you?' 'Tell me,' I recently asked an enchanting woman in her mid-forties—educated, knowledgeable about theatre and movies, hip (or hep?) about many things—'does the name Ronald Colman mean anything to you?' Thoughtfully, after a pause, she said: 'He was a United States Senator, wasn't he?' All right, I admitted, no story. How about Charlie Chaplin? She snorted in a ladylike fashion: 'Of course!' Another winning pause.

'You know something? I've seen, I think, only two of his films—both at the Museum of Modern Art.' Which would *they* be? Never mind.

The overseas newspaper was not to be fobbed off. Another call: 'We understand from someone in this office that you once worked with Chaplin on a movie about Napoleon?' That's right, it's all in the book—goodbye.

So I write now in the full knowledge that the people who might like to hear a little more about Chaplin know a good deal about him already. And that to the rest, which is to say the great majority of the population anywhere, his name is one of those that come up in crosswords and television games, like William Pitt or Phineas T. Barnum. Consequently, none too soon, I seize the accident or incident of his centenary to have a last word about this extraordinary, irascible, generous, conscienceless, thoughtful, mischievous, overwhelmingly charming man. About whose work, I gather, the old and the not-so-old now agree to differ. At my end of the calendar, it is established as gospel that Chaplin was the first genius of film comedy (the *only* genius, Bernard Shaw declared, thrown up by the movies) and that nobody had touched him for weaving together slapstick and pathos in artful ways. I met only one member of my own generation who—as they say in the House of Commons— begged to differ. A university friend, a sly, unfooled Irishman, who enjoyed the Marx Brothers but found Chaplin from the beginning arch, self-conscious and nauseatingly sentimental. But old Heb Davidson, still—I hope and believe—of Donard Demesne, County Wicklow—was always an exception, a wicked dissenter from all conventional wisdom.

There are, I read, young critics (some of whom, I'm sure, took degrees in The Film—a woeful sign that the once scandalous pasttime of the movies, like jazz, has now gone beyond respectability into Graduate Studies!) who have used this centenary to resurrect Buster Keaton as the new god and to declare, in passing, that

Chaplin is, always was, sorry stuff. The young American critics are, I believe, behind the times in this apostasy, but it appears now to be the standard intelligentsia view in Britain. Sixty years ago, it was the intelligentsia who were the first people to rescue Chaplin from the masses who adored him and suggest that he was almost too good for them. The new view was put crisply by *The Economist*, which—remarking correctly that Chaplin's comedy was rooted in the Victorian music hall, both in its slapstick and its maudlin love songs—concluded 'this is why today his comedy is so unfunny and manipulative'. Manipulative! It is the new executioner's chop, as 'vulnerable' is the new laurel wreath.

Well, that's all that need or can be said about the comedian. For although people can be taught to enjoy a composer, a painter, a writer, there is absolutely no way that anyone can be instructed to find someone funny they find unfunny. (Years and years ago, I gave up—in the flesh or in print—ever trying to persuade anybody to enjoy my authors, my comedians, my jazzmen, or my favourite foods.)

But how about the man who one day in 1934 wrote to me? A miracle that. He rarely wrote to anyone. He asked me to go out to Hollywood that summer and help him with the script of a project-ed film on Napoleon. (I have written at length on how I, a very obscure journalist, came to know this dazzling figure; except to say that the previous year, as a graduate student at Yale, I had a com-mission from a London paper to interview him; that I met him one summer morning in his studio; that he took me afterwards up to his house in the hills; and that the rest of the summer I was up there many evenings. He was then forty-four: a tiny, dapper man, a graceful golliwog in an angora sweater, topped by a remarkably handsome face of almost sculptured bone structure. I was twenty-four, lean and gabby, hipped on the movies and certainly then bedazzled to be taken up by the most famous man in the world—an obvious title when you remember that since his pictures were silent, the natives of about a hundred and fifty countries had seen and laughed at him. The old cowboy philosopher, Will Rogers, put it in a nutshell: 'The Zulus knew Chaplin better than Arkansas knew Garbo.'

So, the second year, 1934, I drove off across the country, landed in Hollywood and next morning reported to his funny little rundown-bungalow studio. After that we went off each morning to a small workroom, something like a workingman's kitchen, rather shabby, peeling wallpaper, three straight-back chairs, a plain round table, an upright piano out of tune and with yellowing keys. The room was a shocker, an interesting reflection of something I'd noticed about one or two other rich men born into dire poverty. In Chaplin's case, it was not so much a reminder of where he'd come from as a visible reminder that—as he put it—'perhaps the new money is not there for keeps'. Although he had been very rich for at least twenty years, I'm told he preserved this anxiety all his days. It made him splurge with a flourish one minute and be extremely stingy the next. It explained, too, I think, his habit of never carrying money. In a restaurant, he either signed the bill or handed it over to an assistant director or other employee present.

Most afternoons I spent in the local library, boning up on the biographies and memoirs of Napoleon during his exile on St Helena. Some evenings I would mock up scenes and stretches of dialogue. Next morning, we would go over the stuff, and Chaplin would pad around the little room creating scenes in mime before he even looked at my dialogue. All that was necessary to set him off gesturing and murmuring (sometimes in gibberish or vaudeville double-talk) was the mention of an incident: a row with a British doctor, a complaint dictated back to Britain, mooning daydreams on the anniversary of a famous battle or a well-remembered assignation with Josephine or Waleska. An imperial attack of indigestion. (We did not know then that Napoleon had cancer of the stomach, but reports of gastric attacks occur constantly in some of the memoirs.)

[222]

The chronic stomach aches were something that Chaplin seized on, as comic punchlines to serious scenes and speeches. These mimicked attacks could have come straight out of *The Immigrant* or *The Gold Rush*, and I think I knew then that the grand project would never—as we were learning to say—work. He would be off on a bit of incomprehensible dialogue, slouching or strutting around the room looking morose or indignant or sombre—and he had an astonishing gift to look more like Napoleon than Napoleon (or, for that matter, more like any of the many real people he mimicked). But then he couldn't help making the point in dumb show that an emperor with a hiccup or a burp is as helpless as a baby. Several times, in the weeks we worked on this rough script, a serious scene—Napoleon re-writing his will, say—would gradually turn into a piece of pantomime that had us falling about. The third member, brought in as the public's stand-in for trying things out on, was an affable mountainous Swede, Henry Bergman, who had played in practically all of the early Chaplin comedies. At such times, we'd give up and go chuckling off to lunch.

One evening, after about a month of this, I went up to the house to dinner. At one point during drinks (of water: during the two summers I saw a lot of him, he never served alcohol. It was—I'm sorry to say—a sudden and, I believe, a temporary, crusade with him) he broke off for a telephone call and when he came back, I remember, he was twirling a toothpick. He sat back on a sofa and picked away. 'By the way,' he said, 'the Napoleon thing. It's a beautiful idea—for somebody else.' We didn't discuss it. Nobody discussed a personal decision once it was made by Charles Spencer Chaplin. When I was leaving to go back to my hotel, he said: 'Nobody wants to see Chaplin do an artistic experiment. They go to see the little man.' Nothing more was said, ever. A week or so later, I packed and took off East. I'm sure he was right, as some of his later, lamentable, impersonations proved.

This is not the place to go into his exile in Switzerland. It was generally reported as the price he had to pay for his offensive political ideas, at a time when the United States was ravaged by fear of the Soviet Union and of the contagious properties of communism. The truth is that Chaplin was never more than what in those days was called 'a parlour pink'. Throughout most of the Second World War, he shut himself up in the Hollywood hills and kept his political ideas, whatever they were, to himself. But in the last years, he appeared a time or two at wartime rallies at which he enjoyed carrying on, in the oratorical tradition of Victorian melodrama, about the courage of the Russian people and the glory of the Soviet 'democracy'. He was very soon accused of every radical crime in the book by malicious gossip columnists who resented, more than anything, his holding on to his British citizenship. His eventual banishment had, in fact, much to do with a paternity suit and with his cavalier attitude, in womanly matters, towards subpoenas and other court orders. The administration—a Democratic administration, by the way—hounded him but in the end found nothing indictable. However, it had its chance to be rid of this pestilent alien while he was off on the Atlantic on his way to a holiday in Europe. It quietly rescinded his re-entry permit. He was first shocked, then disgusted. He abruptly decided to stay in Switzerland for life. It was a sad end to his long American adventure. He loved this country, but he never forgave the Truman administration's final and shabby treatment of him.

Those paranoid years are long gone, and luckily the generations that don't know much about him will know even less of his old age. The homeless waif remains a universal type, and nobody did it better. Too often he crossed the fine line between what is touching and what is maudlin. But in impersonating this character he was, in all the middle and later films, as W. C. Fields described him (better than he meant), 'a ballet dancer'. As such, turning every ordinary social gesture into a tiny dance step, he was inventive—as Astaire on a larger scale was inventive—and to some of us uniquely funny.

This anniversary recalls also the special emotion everybody feels when a great comic dies. An emotion it would be difficult to put into words had it not been done finely for us more than a century and a half ago by Leigh Hunt on the death of the reigning comedian of the day, Elliston:

'The death of a comic artist is felt more than that of a tragedian. He has sympathized more with us in our everyday feelings, and has given us more amusement. Death with a tragedian seems all in the way of business. Tragedians have been dying all their lives. They are a "grave" people. But it seems a hard thing upon the comic actor to quench his airiness and vivacity—to stop him in his happy career—to make us think of him, on the sudden, with solemnity—and to miss him for ever. It is something like losing a merry child. We have not got used to the gravity.'

Jazz, San Francisco, and Jimmy Price
[1989]

This essay constituted the liner notes for a record I persuaded Jimmy Price and his men to make. It also happens to express, as well as I am able, my own attitude on jazz and its alleged progress.

Roving an American city these nights in search of jazz is a cheerless pursuit.

There are innumerable cocktail pianists tinkling away in hotel lounges and genteel bars. And in a few big cities the weekend 'Entertainment' listings bristle with groups offering bop, post bop, modern, post modern, and heinous exponents of Free Form ('You improvise in your key, I'll improvise in mine'). All of them advertised under the heading of available 'Jazz', which has come to be a blanket term embracing pretty much everything that bounces which is not Mozart or rock.

In New York City once, in a single city block on a single evening, you could drop in, as monotonously as a fire inspector, on half a dozen smoky clubs housing the separate talents of Art Tatum, Billie Holiday, John Kirby, Art Hodes, Joe Marsala, Lee Wiley and Jess Stacy. Today, if you are busy on Monday evenings and can't catch Woody Allen keeping the faith with his New Orleans Funeral and Ragtime Band, you have to scour the town for a fugitive jam session. There is nowhere to go for one solo (non-vocal) jazz pianist. The Carnegie Tavern, where Ellis Larkins stroked his plangent chords, turned into a Chinese tea shop! Hanratty's found few takers (old folks mainly who actually came to listen) for the marvellous stride piano of Dick Wellstood and closed up its back room as a music shop.

Of course, jazz was always a minority interest, a fact that astonishes the generation whose parents think back to their happy 'jazz' nights and are really thinking of the big hotel dance orchestras with their pumping brass and mechanical riffs. Bix and the early Louis, and the Blue Five, and Teagarden and Red Nichols, and Pee Wee Russell and Max Kaminsky never sold more than several thousand copies of anything, and they were gobbled up on both sides of the Atlantic by the aficionados, an order as small and fervent as that of Trappist monks. This is a truth about the quintessential American music that has been befuddled by associating the sacred word with the 'dance' orchestras of the twenties and thirties, and the big bands of the forties and fifties, which played—for a dancing public—'jazz' pasteurized for commercial consumption. (Through this happy confusion, though, there were Goodman's small groups and the towering figure who absorbed jazz triumphantly into the big band, digesting every new strain into his own sound, and never waned: Duke Ellington.)

So, we come to San Francisco. In the late fifties and on into the sixties, there was the haven of the Hangover on Bush Street, where Earl Hines and Muggsy Spanier and Jimmy Archey played their wonderful stuff—with the forgotten Joe Sullivan as fill-in pianist!—before an audience of gabby girls and slurping drunks. It should have been an omen. Even then, the population of listeners was sparse in numbers and thin on top. I had long ago given up thinking of San Francisco as a town in which you would automatically devote a late evening once a week listening to jazz until, two or three years ago, I dropped into the Fairmont on a Sunday or a Monday night. In the—shall we say?—Dorothy Draper Concourse, I was stopped short by the distant sound of the Right Stuff, apparently played by a spanking quintet. I hurried into the New Orleans Room. It was not a quintet but three men who enlarged the compass and sound of a trio by having a leader who alternated on trumpet, trombone and flugelhorn; a wizard of a pianist who straddled a baby grand *and* an electric keyboard; and a precise, restrained drummer with no prima donna ambitions. It was Jimmy Price and his men. Hallelujah!

Finally, after much urging, Jimmy has made a record of his splendid trio. And here it is. To define exactly what you are in for, let me say as plainly as possible—and at the risk of reciting an outworn mumbo-jumbo—that jazz arose in the early 1900s as black vocal music rooted in the twelve-bar blues; developed small combinations of brass, clarinet, saxophones; went on to records the day King Oliver took his men into the Gennett studios in Richmond, Indiana; hooked many gifted young whites; burst out all over Chicago in the twenties, then in New York in the thirties and forties; was lavishly recorded by the great originals and their protégés in the fifties; and then died, its mission accomplished.

It was not enough for a younger generation to recognize or admit that jazz was a form of music with a natural life span—like the sonnet, plainsong, Colonial architecture, the epic poem, like you and me. It had to be maintained as a twitching vegetable with life-saving injections of desperate harmonies and atonalities that can no more be fused into the honest original than John Cage's 'prepared piano' can be made to play Bach. Bebop was the death knell. After that, jazz had to be mystified and tortured to screech off into various expressions of violence, with Monk, Parker, Coltrane, Coleman and whatever came, or is coming, after. The critics, who had a living to make, padded along, puzzled at first like the rest of us, but then protected their tenure by telling us that all these tortuosities were a form of Progress which we must strenuously study and learn to like.

The musical history of Jimmy Price and his men might lead you, for one frightened moment, into thinking they too had made a career of incorporating all these discords and dissonances picked up at Juilliard. Jimmy Price has a BA degree from San Francisco State. Worse, Buzzy Daniels is a bachelor of musical education and survived the Philadelphia Conservatory of Music. Not to worry. Their saving grace, the guarantee that their talents for jazz are uncorrupted, is the reminder that Jimmy Price played with Red Nichols and Earl Hines; that Daniels cannot plant a chord or ripple through an arpeggio that does not proclaim the blues; that, simply, Dave Black worked—the only white man apart from Juan Tizol—with Ellington.

So far as this recording session was concerned, the trio might never have heard of 'Bird' or Coltrane. We are back with a group of undying classics, recalling Bix's 'San' and 'I Found a New Baby', Hines's 'Rosetta', Armstrong's 'Struttin' With Some Barbecue', King Oliver's forgotten 'Dr Jazz', Turner Layton's 'Way Down Yonder in New Orleans', and—best of all—a noble recollection of Mr T and Don Ewell, in Handy's tribute to a favourite town: 'Atlanta Blues', which, by the way, no other group I've ever run into has been able to play on request. In short, here is a spate of honest jazz, rude, poignant, undecorated by overlays from Scriabin or—why not?—Stockhausen: mostly from the twenties and thirties, the high noon of jazz performance.

It all comes down to Eddie Condon's test of what you prefer to think of as jazz: 'As it enters the ear, does it come in like broken glass or does it come in like honey?' If you prefer the sound of honey, Jimmy Price and his men are for you.

[229]

Screen Acting: 'Eyes Only'
[1991]

'Here is Universal, in Next Time We Love, *trying to turn James Stewart into a Fred MacMurray. They give him an old hat and a messy bedroom and they dress him like a lovable, uncouth tramp—but they don't get MacMurray. The way to get MacMurray is to get MacMurray.'*

Don Herold, 1936

No tributes are more predictable than the obituaries of famous men and women who were generally admitted to be supreme at a single trade: author, artist, musician. Actors and actresses get more attention than anybody because theirs is the most popular and envied of the arts. So, there were no surprises in the recessional columns devoted to Laurence Olivier and to Peggy Ashcroft. They were at the peak of their profession and, so far as I've read, nobody discovered in retrospect gifts and qualities that had not been justly celebrated during their prime.

But, from time to time, a lesser actor dies. And there will be no surprises in his obituaries either. Because he became identified in the beginning with one sort of comedy or drama or character, we soon took the measure of him. He is classified and filed away without a second thought. Sometimes, we were wrong. And when we are wrong, it is time to say so.

Fred MacMurray died last Monday (November 5, 1991) in Los Angeles, and next day we could read, in many parts of the country, ample tributes that struck a similar note. Thus the *New York Times*: 'the personable, unassuming actor who starred in some of the best film comedies of the 1930s and '40s and was later the protagonist in popular Walt Disney fantasies, and in a television situation comedy'. That's fairly unassuming itself. It is literally true, from the first fling with Carole Lombard in the 1935 *Hands Across the Table* throughout the next twenty-odd years, he was among the most engaging leading men. In life he was a casual character—not unlike Crosby—who never would or could have become a stage actor. But something in their make-up—a kind of vacancy, or inability to be put off by outside events (including the stare of a motion picture camera) destined them to be made for the movies, and turn into—not an actor acting to a camera but a human being happening to be photographed.

It is striking how often, by contrast, fine stage actors turned into mediocre or thoroughly bad movie actors: Cedric Hardwicke, Ralph Richardson, Walter Hampden. Barrymore was awful—a caricature of the stage actor at his archetypal worst: the large calculated gestures, the 'projected' voice, the sense that he knew he was being filmed and was determined to impress you. I suppose that Olivier was the most successful in both media, although in his youth, when he was the adored cavalier of the English stage, he derided Hollywood and film-making in general. But at some point he must have spotted, and acted on, an essential difference between the two arts that most stage actors never arrived at: he saw stage acting as a form of living sculpture, and film acting as a performance with the Face Only—the best film actors do best with the Eyes Only (*vide*—in no preferential order—George Macready, Jennifer Jones, Aline MacMahon, Edward G. Robinson, Conrad Veidt, Henry Fonda, Jeanne Moreau, Jean Gabin, Joan Plowright, Jessica Lange, above all Spencer Tracy). In, I believe, the last interview Olivier gave on American television, he was asked if there was any one actor or actress who stood out as the supreme film actor. He said quite quickly—'Oh, no competition—Gary Cooper.'

A similar unawareness, a gift to behave rather than act, belonged to Fred MacMurray too. But to say that is only to analyse what everybody noticed and praised in him in his usual role as a

[231]

light-hearted cut-up or a 'lovable, uncouth tramp'. My point in celebrating him here is to remark that, in four of his eighty-odd films,
he created one unforgettable male character that elevated him into
the top rank of quintessential movie actors. That we look back on
him now and forget or overlook this is probably nobody's fault but
his own, because it's true that throughout most of his career, over
seventy films were given over to light comedy, farce, playful fantasy, routine Westerns. And he was, in life, a very easygoing type:
'I take my movie parts as they come . . . I'm not dedicated . . . I'm
lazy in spurts. I am, I admit, no great screen lover. Sometimes,
scenes include people who just say "Hi" to indicate they're in love.
I play those scenes very well.'

Such a man is not likely to pressure agents and producers to
insist on finding variations on the role I think he played better
than anyone in the movies. What type? Well, to take the type I
have in mind to its extreme, am I saying that MacMurray could
have played Raskolnikov in Dostoevsky's *Crime and Punishment*? He
would have been very fine. The four matchless performances I
have mentioned are not so much of a recognizable American type
as a marvellously American representation of a fascinating, if
regrettable, male of the species: an agreeable, suspiciously affable,
offhand *fraud*. An on-the-ball insurance salesmen caught up with a
sleazy blonde and suddenly way out of his depth—in murder, no
less (*Double Indemnity*). A businessman philanderer available to be,
in a slightly shame-faced way, a pimp of sorts (*The Apartment*). A
nice cop turned shifty crook with the help of Kim Novak's razzle
dazzle (*Pushover*). And in *The Caine Mutiny*, the dreadful Keefer,
the Navy lieutenant who is the big rooter for his mutinous buddy
until—if you'll excuse me, I notice that my own career is at risk.
Interesting, I think, that of these four one should have been written by Dmytrik, the son of recent Ukrainian immigrants, and the
best two (*Double Indemnity* and *The Apartment*) were both written
and directed by Billy Wilder, a Viennese refugee from Hitler

[232]

whose mother and family died in concentration camps. Perhaps it takes a European early acquainted with grief to see the dark side of the country club wag.

The day after he died I brought up with one or two friends of my own, or the next, generation the MacMurray gift for playing affable heels. None of them knew what I was talking about. Not surprising, if you consider that they might well have seen everything he did except those four gems. But then I also remember that at the time MacMurray was performing those infrequent masterpieces, only two critics I was familiar with even hinted that here was a master. The day *Double Indemnity* was shown in London, the English critic, James Agate, wrote in his diary: 'This is a magnificent murder story, with the moral that a man and woman who put their heads together to murder her husband begin to loathe each other before the body is cold. MacMurray is, surprisingly, magical and touching. Barbara Stanwyck completely convincing as the common, bloody-minded hussy.' The other, unsurprised and more perceptive, note can be found in David Thomson's biographical dictionary: 'The ingredients of the MacMurray man . . . brittle cheerfulness; an anxious smile that subsides into slyness . . . a rare character who has let the tawdry con man grin through the all-American wholesomeness with a conjuror's swiftness.'

It is a pleasure to pay tribute to an artist who has had many tributes, mostly for the wrong things. In life, MacMurray was much like his comedy self without, I trust, the phoniness. More than acting, he liked to fish, paint, cook, play golf. For thirty-seven years, he was married to a former nun.

1 5

'Upstairs, Downstairs'
[1993]

Throughout the 1970s and '80s, I had the job, and often the pleasure, of introducing over American public television many series of British dramas, mostly—through the early years—adapted from English classics. It is a risky and generally, I think, a failed effort. Mainly, because the person who does the choosing (the producer, director, whoever) appears to make the automatic and fatal assumption that the author's great talent lies in plot and dialogue and not in the uniqueness of the running commentary on the characters. This was glaringly true of Dickens and Wodehouse; and in a recent adaptation of George Eliot's *Middlemarch*, done as a sumptuous costume drama and quite brilliantly acted, the pretence of 'adapting' George Eliot was in vain. There was one essential voice missing: it was the voice of George Eliot.

But there were some surprising successes. Of the classic novels, most notably Fay Weldon's script of *Pride and Prejudice*, in which the narrator is a double character: the heroine as participant, and the heroine as onlooker. Ms Weldon solved this challenge with felicitous ease by having Elizabeth seen as the central character and heard as the ironical (voice over) commentator. Almost as impressive were two adaptations of Henry James: *The Golden Bowl* and *The Spoils of Poynton*. James's own dramas were whimpering failures on the London stage, because—as Max Beerbohm regretfully noted—James's 'chamber music' was too finely spun for the theatre. But in Henry James's world, a polite refusal to take a walk can mark the shattering of a friendship, and a raised eyebrow be more ominous than an earthquake. The small box is an ideal medium for him.

Yet, after twenty years of these dramatic shifts and stratagems, there seems to me to emerge one true television masterpiece, a work made for television with no collateral debt to the theatre, the cinema or any published work of fiction. It was *Upstairs, Downstairs*. From the start it was an immense popular success, and superior people jumped to the condescending lifesaver that it was after all a 'soap opera'. Of course it was. Soap operas were the prevailing form. As well say that Dickens was a cliff-hanging serial hack because, like every other Victorian novelist great or small, he published his books in fortnightly parts, having the lure into the next part contrived accordingly.

Upstairs, Downstairs was the chronicle of a London household existing on one of those finely graded English social strata somewhere between the upper and the upper-middle class, between 1903 and 1930. Through fifty-two episodes we followed the fortunes of the Richard Bellamys of Eaton Place from the imperial days of Edward the Seventh's reign through the First World War and the wrenching social changes of the 1920s to the family's abandonment of its house and the scattering of its members and staff.

It came along in the backwash of applause for the BBC's dramatized *Forsyte Saga*, and there were fears that it might founder in the wake of Galsworthy's work which, after decades of ridicule, the intelligentsia now decided was formidable. The fears were groundless. And what can be seen now as the tantalizing element of its success, quite independent of its intrinsic merit, was the shrewdness of its appeal to the widest possible audience. The servants of the Galsworthy households carried trays, existed as lowly mechanics necessary to the maintenance of a prosperous upper-middle-class family. They were not developed as a parallel family of agonizing and rejoicing human beings. In *Upstairs, Downstairs*, both the Bellamy family and the staff were seen on their own planes in all their separate intimacy and complexity, and whenever the main story was being enacted upstairs, the downstairs team provided a counterpoint of commentary and concern. The television viewer was thus able, as he was not in the *Forsyte Saga*, to identify with the strong and whimsical humanity of the staff and, at the same time, enjoy the snobbish kick of living the upstairs life. It should have been seen as a foolproof formula for ensnaring a mass audience, and undoubtedly it would have attracted one if it had been done half as well. What gave it extraordinary distinction was the sure observation of character, the confidence and finesse with which social nuances and emotional upheavals between the two groups were explored, and the scrupulous accuracy of the period language, décor, mores, prejudices, and points of view.

It is only right, then, to say how this came about, what talents were so cunningly moulded into a writing and directing team. For it was a team job, a dramatic chronicle created by a dozen or so writers, five or six directors, and one producer: a rare example, like that of the translators of the King James Bible, of a committee producing a work of art.

The idea for the series came from Eileen Atkins and Jean Marsh (who played Rose), both of whom were born into families that had been in domestic service. They wanted to show the life of a country mansion seen through the double vision of a family and its staff. They took their idea to John Hawkesworth, who seized it, substituted a town house for a country house and who, through more than four years of the making, was the producer, often the writer, and always the paterfamilias of the whole production team and acting company. He had impressive credentials for such a challenging job of social exploration, though his dossier does not at first suggest it. Reading over its early entries without any prior knowledge of his later work, or meeting him today, you would assume he had wound up as a retired brigadier general: this genial hulk of a man, sixtyish, in rumply tweeds, with a hoarfrost sparkle

[236]

about him, dogs always at his heels, possibly a brisk and competent master of fox hounds (which, in fact, he is).

He comes of a military family and was routinely sent to Rugby and Oxford. But between school and university, he had atypical ambitions. He thought of a career in architecture, he had a yearning to paint, and his father indulged him to the extent of a year in Paris where he studied under Picasso, among others, and developed a considerable talent. After Oxford, and the coming of the Second World War, he reverted to the family role and served for five years as an officer with the crack regiment of the Grenadier Guards. He found himself in the peace with a wife, no job, and no prospects. He had, however, a backlog of paintings and tried a one-man exhibition, which had the luck to be seen and admired by the Korda brothers, the film producers, who promptly hired him as a draughtsman. From then on, his career was straightforward and unhalting. Very quickly promoted, he became art director (on, notably, *The Third Man*), then produced and wrote scripts for the Rank Film Company, and—when the British film industry unaccountably exhausted its postwar spurt of inventiveness—went on to television for two long writing stints, an award or two, and the decision to start his own television production company. Its first offering was *Upstairs, Downstairs*.

Every producer is duty-bound to a tedious stretch of preparation before anything can be filmed: the story line, the several drafts of the script, the reconnaissance of possible outdoor locations, the scrutiny of the art department's blueprints and much checking of proper period furniture, costumes, street lamps, automobiles, and the rest. (Hollywood has set the standard for pedantic accuracy about such things from cathedral exteriors to lamp shades, open-toed shoes, barroom accessories, and so forth, even when they provide the setting for improbable feelings and wildly anachronistic dialogue.) Much can be learned from Hawkesworth's research labours to explain the viewer's fascinated sense of being nowhere

[237]

but in the London of 1904 or 1924. He had been a history student at Oxford, and this training, allied to an acute perception of social differences, really turned him into a social historian who had gone into television.

He began by blocking out the story line and then abandoning the script until he had scoured the period artefacts, through the microfilm file of the London *Times*, through letters, memoirs, House of Commons debates, store and fashion catalogues, weather reports, songbooks, theatre programmes; noticing in passing details of contemporary slang, sporting events, deaths, reputations, best sellers, etc. He then assembled his team of writers, assigned each episode to one or two and allowed the team the interesting freedom to bring their separate views to bear on any or all of the characters. Thus, the character of Richard Bellamy or Lady Marjorie or Rose or Hudson was never a single conception; it reflected such unexpected facets of temperament, moments of growth, as one might learn from the pooled memories of a group of friends.

The value of this dual approach, strictly observing the social and historical facts of the time, yet giving free play to the delineation of character, can be gauged by two examples. One was the decision to construct in minute detail a blueprint of the five-storey house in which the drama was to be played. The other was the gradual emergence of a rather weak though amiable character—James Bellamy—as the moral barometer of the story and the period.

The Bellamy house, in Eaton Place, was not designed by Le Corbusier as a 'machine for living'. It was of the type designed by late-eighteenth-century men for the comfort and service of upper-class families. If it was a castle to such as the Bellamys, it was a gymnasium for the eighteen-hour acrobatics required of the staff. They slept in the attic rooms and worked out of the basement—covering many vertical miles a day fetching and carrying. It sounds like a dog's life, but it was better than the rat's life of the mines, the factories, and what Blake called 'the dark Satanic mills'. Domestic

[238]

service then, and for long after, provided poor people with a haven of good food, elegant surroundings, and a continuous feast of gossip. So the house was essentially a class structure, a microcosm of what its owners liked to think of as the social order, but was, in fact, a private fort protecting both Upstairs and Downstairs from the recognition of Disraeli's 'two nations', the blithe rich and the luckless poor. Hawkesworth and his writers were thoroughly at home with this ménage and its social and emotional pecking order. Unlike many professional television writers, they wrote about what they knew. And in their hands, the house and its rituals were enough to trace with absorbing and entertaining accuracy the life of one English family in one place through nearly thirty years.

Many of the rewards of the preliminary social and historical research were unlocked by the decision to give Richard Bellamy, the father of the household, political ambitions. What might otherwise have been seen as an over-protected household (living, like the hero and heroine of Hollywood comedies of the 1930s, an unemployed life of intermittent quarrelling and lovemaking in a vacuum of rich surroundings) was able to be subjected to a continuous wash and buffeting of events great and small, national crises, fads and festivals, the death of kings, stock market shenanigans, political scandals, the uproar of the suffragettes, the disruption of family life by the First World War, the General Strike, the coming to power of Labour governments, and eventually the Wall Street crash, the bell that tolled the end of the Bellamys' life. Out of all this, James Bellamy, the family's firstborn, emerged as the representative figure of the prime and decline of the Empire and its values, a symbol of the First World War generation at its most charming and unstable.

A few years ago, George Kennan, the American diplomat and historian, was talking about some work he was then deeply engaged in on the diplomatic history of Britain in the late nineteenth and early twentieth centuries. He mentioned some of the diplomatic material he had been ploughing through. 'But,' he said, 'I've come on one thing which shows, step by step, and more clearly and more ruthlessly than any diplomatic file, that it was the upper classes, not the lower, that cracked. And that is the television series *Upstairs, Downstairs*.' It is enough of a tribute to the firm grasp of events, to the seriousness, artfully hidden under a remarkable entertainment.

16

Genius as an Urchin
[1986]

Only three blocks east of Fifth Avenue's elegant museums, Ninety-Sixth Street takes a social dive and becomes a thoroughfare for the working class and its daily needs. There is on the south side a row of grimy, five-storey Victorian houses, shades permanently down, some of them perhaps permanently abandoned. On the north side, a corner lunch counter, basement locksmith, shoe repair shop, laundry, flower shop, hemmed in to the west by the slab of a high-rise apartment building. In the middle of the north block, planted deep and flat alongside the seedy or garish little stores is a church in sombre grey stone. It is the church of St Francis de Sales.

Here on a mild morning in April, the sidewalk opposite the church was lined with neighbours fenced in by a police cordon. They had come to see a rare event, the funeral of a film star. An old man, evidently not a local but a puzzled passer-by, wondered what it was all about. 'Which film star?' James Cagney. '*The* James Cagney?' The same. Humph! (St Francis de Sales became the Cagneys' church when, in the boy's teens, they had moved across town from his slummy birthplace to the still German-Hungarian section known as Yorkville.)

The old man mused for a moment. 'Was that his real name?' A nod was the polite response. The rude answer would have been: 'Of course it was his real name, he was an Irishman.'

When Cagney came along in Hollywood in the early thirties, the original film tycoons—the Mayers, Goldwyns, Zukors, the young Thalberg—were still very much in charge and had for long dictated the mores and folkways, among which was the custom of looking over a new name and if it was not an Anglo-Saxon name, making it one. They had flirted in the silent days with the notion of French and Spanish names as romantic magnets and, for native sexpots, anything wildly exotic (Theodosia Goodman, of Cincinnati, was set up in a house with snakes and incense and rechristened Theda Bara, an anagram for Arab Death!). But with the sound films and the requirement to speak literate or at least intelligible English, the old immigrants reverted to the Anglo-Saxon prejudice that the United States was an Anglo-Saxon culture, at least that the toniest stratum of its society had English names. Any arriving actor with a Russian, Polish, German or Lithuanian name had it promptly changed, by producers who themselves were Russian, Polish, German or Lithuanian. And because of the strong, if sometimes tacit, anti-Semitism (when I shopped around for a New York apartment in 1937, every building I looked at had a handsome sign posted outside the entrance with the warning word—'Restricted') all Jewish names were changed at once. Hence, Emmanuel Goldenberg became Edward G. Robinson, Marion Levy turned into Paulette Goddard, Issur Danielovitch Demsky into Kirk Douglas.

I can think of no Irishman, or woman, who was ever given a change of name. There was for the longest time almost as much social prejudice against the Irish ('No Irish Need Apply') as against the Jews. But the first producers were canny enough to know that in the cities where they picked up the most substantial revenue—in New York, Boston, Philadelphia, Chicago—the Irish might be the majority immigrant group and, in any case, were stalwart movie fans, particularly proud of their own. The day it got out that Paddy O'Neill had had his name changed to—say—Derek Wakefield, there would be a hot time in his old hometown that night. So no changes were anticipated or attempted when there appeared at the studios George Murphy, Maureen O'Sullivan, Ronald Reagan, and all the O'Briens from Edmond to Virginia. And James Cagney.

[242]

He was born and brought up on the Lower East Side, the son of a bartender who died, when Cagney was still in his teens, in the flu pandemic of 1918–19. It was a poor family of five children, and long before his father's death, Cagney was automatically expected, as soon as he could use his fists and jump to attention, to support his mother and the other children. The biography of his early manhood reads like a resumé of his early parts. He worked through several lowly occupations: waiter, office boy, poolroom racker. He made it through high school, but the Army Training Corps at Columbia paid no wages and he descended to a department-store basement as a daytime package wrapper. By night, he watched all the current vaudeville dancers and decided to be one himself. Which—if I had a thesis, it would be mine to maintain— he remained all his life, in all his movies. (This judgement contradicts my pet theory that the best film acting is done with the face only. There must be glaring exceptions: Chaplin, Astaire, Cagney require the whole screen—the full proscenium—to show how swiftly and subtly and fluidly emotion can be expressed with the whole body—whether or not there is any accompanying music.

He went into a Broadway chorus, he toured in vaudeville. Married at twenty-two, and just getting by, he grabbed a modest Hollywood offer and made seven inconsequential films in two years. But in one of them (*The Public Enemy*) he signalled his arrival as a tough guy, what was known at the time as a man's man (later, more pejoratively, a male chauvinist), by shoving a grapefruit into the face of his complaining girl friend, Mae Clarke. This outrage, *Variety* wrote, 'sent his stock soaring 100 percent as a heart palpitator among femme fans'. At any rate, that single scene, remembered by old folks who could recall nothing else of Cagney's career, guaranteed his continued stardom, and a life of wealth and fame, throughout thirty years and fifty films. (The scene did nothing for Mae Clarke, who rapidly declined into bit parts and what are fancifully known as cameos.)

[243]

In all the gangster and street-smart parts, while frighteningly true to type, he always had a documentary honesty about him, as if he had stalked into the picture by mistake to embarrass the fancy actors trying to impersonate people like him. This intrusion of actual street life into the filmed fantasies of it was often almost literally true, for Cagney was a born mimic and, from boyhood on, whether by intention or simple symbiosis, had observed and memorized in the flesh the physical gestures of the sailors, con men, bums, thieves and layabouts he had known. At one time, he went up to Sing Sing to entertain five of his old pals who were doing time, one of whom was subsequently executed.

It is a tribute to the verisimilitude of the low-life parts that so many movie-goers, otherwise intelligent and perceptive, disliked him for the oldest, as also the most flattering, reason—the first critical blunder: disliking the exponent of a milieu because you're uncomfortable with the milieu itself. (I once knew a man who couldn't abide the television series, *Upstairs, Downstairs*, because, it eventually came out, he didn't like rich people with servants!)

Everyone will have lasting memories of Cagney. Mine are not the more explicit gangster impersonations. They are what you might call the intervals of shameful self-knowledge in between the spasms of violence and meanness: his gratitude to the old saloon madam for taking him in when his self-respect was in shreds (*The Roaring Twenties*); his fusion of pride and embarrassment in seeing how right it is that his old girl friend, Priscilla Lane, should be married to the clean-cut DA; the hoodlum storming through *Love Me Or Leave Me*, as the husband of Doris Day, seething with jealousy he is trying and failing to contain. And there is, finally, the time he emerged from the chrysalis—or closet—where he had stealthily choreographed all the Hell's Kitchen gestures, of defiance, affection, belligerence, pathos, and was finally revealed (in *Yankee Doodle Dandy*) as the dazzling song-and-dance man he had been all along.

[244]

Nothing much can be done for those people, a considerable faction, who saw nothing more in Cagney than the vulgarity and general offensiveness of much of his material. But to anyone who saw the good man inside whatever he played, however malign, it was no surprise to discover from the obituaries that he was a man of principle (what we now call 'values'), a non-smoker, a rare, mild drinker, a lifelong Catholic living by fidelity (one wife for sixty-one years), thrift, his family and one or two close friends; and that he rarely if ever intruded into Beverly Hills, or any other chic, society, having a natural indifference or allergy to the whole *Vogue* view of life.

There are one or two surprises. He had seen, in his scraping urban youth, a big patch of Brooklyn where, indeed, grew many trees. He saw himself as a displaced countryman. He bought a farm, when he was in his thirties, in the beautiful Amenia Valley, at Millbrook up the Hudson, where he raised horses and—for the last twenty-odd years of his life—was a working farmer. Outside his family, he said in a rare interview, 'the prime concern of my life has been nature and order, and how we've been savagely altering that order'. He could be quite sententious about what he saw as the decline of American life. A former enthusiastic New Dealer, he admitted to turning more and more conservative in old age because he saw his country 'threatened by moral confusion'.

So it was entirely right and characteristic that he should come back to that frowzy stretch of Ninety-Sixth Street to be honoured in the church of St Frances de Sales. He knew where he came from and he went back to it at the end.

If there is a wishful strain in this catalogue of virtues, it may spring simply from a romantic desire to make the ideal, at the core of the Cagney character, realize itself in the flesh. At any rate, I am one who cannot lose the sharp image of that jaunty, bouncing, forever cocky little figure, successfully pretending through so many rowdy films to be a scamp but rarely managing to conceal the candid, decent Everyman underneath. A *brave homme*!

[245]

17

An Icon at Fifty
[1992]

While American commemorations come and go, and the Polish hero of the American Revolution gives way to the Puerto Rican, Bolivian and other South American heroes of *their* revolutions, Thanksgiving, the cardinal American festival, commemorating the first successful harvest of the original Massachusetts colony, retains all its pristine colour and its hold on the people. It is the great family reunion, more so for very many Americans than the Christians' Christmas. The original celebratory foods—the novelties the Indians introduced to their guests (or intruders)—are served from one end of Alaska to the Florida Keys: the turkey, the corn pudding, the cranberry sauce, the pumpkin pie.

But this year, Thanksgiving came and went in the shock of an anniversary so unexpected, so unproclaimed, that only now, a week or two later, can we see it as an American Event as bizarre as it was unique. The fiftieth anniversary of a motion picture. Something you might expect an expiring studio to organize and promote in the dim hope of reclaiming its former grandeur. If it was meant as a memorial to the men who made it, it came very late in the day, for the Warner Brothers, who produced it, the day-to-day producer, the director, and the stars are long gone. But showings of it exploded across the country on Thanksgiving night without prior warning and a baffling absence of advance studio hype.

It developed that for the past several years, film scholars busy about their separate specialties have reported bumping into a raft of memoirs and surveys about this film and have discovered an underground literature: massive, and massively silly, deposits of exegesis by Freudians, Jungians, sociologists, behaviourists, deconstructionists and paediatricians (the hero's rebelliousness is, it seems, a continuous protest against his lost boyhood!). Later still—and it might have been the cue for the sudden anniversary exploitation—one of those all-embracing statistical surveys that only *aficionados* bother to read revealed that more Americans picked this film over any other as their favourite film of the last fifty years. It was the best remembered.

What movie could this possibly be? In a private galloping poll, the votes poured in for *Gone With the Wind* and *The Sound of Music*. From loftier brows, who mistook the poll as an invitation to pronounce their own judgement on 'the art of the cinema', came *Citizen Kane*. One eccentric, plainly out of touch with the popular pulse, picked *Les Enfants du Paradis*.

The movie was *Casablanca*.

It was greatly liked around the country when it first appeared, but it did not break the box office, and a poll of 400 American critics voted it the *fifth* best film of the year. The upper-crust critics thought little of it. *The New Republic* found 'its kind of hokum lifted out of context', without saying what proper context that might be. The *New Yorker* thought it only 'pretty tolerable'. James Agee, the primate of American film criticism, admitted liking it but only on the odd ground of finding it 'obviously an improvement on one of the world's worst plays' (the play was never produced).

However, forty-six years later, in 1988, an act of Congress provided for its perpetual preservation as one of the twenty-five films of all time that are 'culturally, historically or aesthetically significant'. By the 1990s, the *New York Times*'s capsule review for every television revival of it was: 'the one and only'. Long before the 1990s, half a dozen of its lines had passed, as catch phrases, into the vernacular.

It was first shown on Thanksgiving night, 1942, in New York

City, and the timing of its release—as we shall see—gave the Warner Brothers ecstatic cause to bow down and thank the Lord.

It was filmed in just over two months through a hideous southern California heatwave in the summer of 1942, when air-conditioning was not yet an amenity of American life. Not for that reason alone, nobody connected with the picture was sorry when it was all over. It had been an orgy of disorder and improvisation for a cast never sure, from day to day, of the meaning or intended direction of any scene. Seven writers alternated in battling and tinkering with the script and, until the last days, were hurrying in with substitute speeches. 'Haphazard' was Ingrid Bergman's mildest word for the experience of working on her least favourite movie. The opening scene (a scramble of jostling refugees with a gaggle of accents) that looked so swift and disciplined on the screen was shot only a day or two before the end of everything. The last day of all was what they call a cleaning-up: odd close-ups of two of the film's three stars (Bergman and Paul Henreid) in a street scene that would be sliced into an earlier episode. Bogart was gone for good and off on his boat. He had struck no chord with Miss Bergman, nor she with him. But they were pros, they observed the courtesies, they played their parts. As for Paul Henreid, the noble Resistance leader, he had a nagging habit of bad-mouthing his co-stars. He thought Bogart 'a mediocre actor' and implied as much with generally haughty behaviour. Poor Ingrid Bergman, more than anyone the victim of a script that had eight different endings written for it, never knew until practically the last take which ending was for keeps and to which man she was meant to give her all. The director, the veteran Hungarian Mihaly Kertesz (a.k.a. Michael Curtiz), in America sixteen years yet never on easy speaking terms with English, howled impossible oaths at the bit players, and fawned indiscriminately over the stars, in four languages. He had his own set of troubles, being pelted throughout with hundreds of memoranda from producer Hal Wallis and watchful moral injunctions from the boss of the industry's Production Code. This downpour of criticisms, suggestions, reproofs, warnings obviously disoriented Curtiz's hold on things. At the end, there was no studio party. Some thought they had a good film, an indifferent one, a mess. But good or bad, special or routine, nobody had the glimmer of a conviction that they had produced an immortal.

The act of creation began the day after the Japanese bombed Pearl Harbor, a big point for the luck of this movie. If the script had appeared a year earlier, during America's anxious neutrality, the sting of the plot, the venom of the Nazis, would have had to be plucked. It might not have been made at all.

As it was, on Monday morning, December 8, 1941, there dropped on to the desk of a script reader at Warner Brothers the manuscript of an unperformed play, up for grabs by any studio that would buy it. It was the work of a 29-year-old schoolteacher who had spent the summer of 1940 in Austria. Two sharp memories stayed with him: the scary behaviour of the Nazis in occupied Vienna; and a smoky nightclub run by an American exile who had a black man for his piano player. The script was read by a studio hack who earned $1.12 an hour. He creditably reported it to have the makings of 'an excellent melodrama. Tense mood, timely background.' He explained to any studio mogul who might wonder where Casablanca was that it was 'in French Morocco, where European refugees fought and bargained and bribed for exit visas to Portugal and America'. Sophisticated hokum, he called it, 'a natural for Bogart or Cagney or Raft'. (Jack Warner chose Raft, Hal Wallis wouldn't hear of it.)

Well, it was bought outright (to the schoolteacher's subsequent pain) for $20,000 by Hal Wallis. After weeks of shooting, Wallis sent a memo instructing everybody that the original title of the play, and the movie, would be changed. From now on, it would be not *Everybody Comes to Rick's* but *Casablanca*. It was so re-named not

[249]

with any pre-vision of an American army invading Morocco but because one reader thought the script might aspire to the successful exoticism of a Charles Boyer-Hedy Lamarr movie called *Algiers*.

It is a very simple story, about an American expatriate with a dubious past running a nightclub under the tolerant eye of a corrupt French captain (Casablanca is an outpost of Vichy France). It is a hotbed of intrigue, blackmail and barely repressed panic among refugees of all sorts from Hitler's Europe who are desperate for exit visas to America. A famous Resistance hero appears and shortly thereafter an SS Major in the hunt for him. The American, if he cared, could help him. The Major is determined to trap him. The question, which strings the tension of the whole movie, is whether or not beneath the scar tissue of the American's cynicism there is a whole man and an honourable one. Like all first-rate movies—quite apart from aesthetic considerations—*Casablanca* is a spring of slowly coiling tension. It is about evil and the risks in a bad time of resisting it.

The film appeared when Hitler, throughout the decade of the thirties, had demonstrated something we had been loath to admit: the success of violence. What sort of hero could hope to triumph over a dictator acting out plots more monstrous than any the Warner brothers had contrived for their gangsters? No longer Leslie Howard, or Ronald Colman, not any of the suave white knights. Nor the simple giants of the prairie either: no Cooper or Wayne. What was needed, and what appeared perfect for the time (and the choice of actor), was a tough guy as subtle as Goebbels but on our side.

The movie was intended to be nationally released in the spring of 1943. But on November 8, 1942, we woke up to banner headlines: AMERICANS INVADE FRENCH NORTH AFRICA AT CASABLANCA. The Warner brothers, it was reported, were no sooner out of bed than they were down on their knees. The film was rushed into New York for a Thanksgiving opening. Coinciding with the first big military movement of the Americans in the European–African theatre, the film practically signified that America was now officially at war with Hitler on his home ground.

Somehow, against all the odds and Hollywood's long experience of a director's being paralysed by the encompassing bureaucracy, it all—as Leslie Halliwell put it—'fell together'. With respect to an old, and alas a late, friend, it did not fall together. It was pulled together, as all films are, by the one craftsman who never gets mentioned in the film cyclopaedias but who, more than any other person, can make or break a movie: the film editor. I can only gather from the considerable literature about the film who that might be. It would appear that Curtiz himself, badgered by Wallis, in the cutting room was more responsible than anybody. If so, the success may have, as Andrew Sarris wrote, killed off once and for all the *auteur* theory (that the director is the king, the supreme creator). His rôle as film cutter restores his laurel wreath.

There is a tremendous scene in which the denizens of Rick's bar join the band, in responding to a nod from Bogart, and drown out the German soldiers' singing of the *Watch on the Rhine* with the *Marseillaise*. During the final shooting of this scene, the cameraman noticed that half the cast were in tears. No wonder. There were seventy-five bit players in *Casablanca*, only a handful of them American born. Of the fictional refugees, temporary barflies, Nazi soldiers, stranded mistresses, old couples in Rick's bar, nearly thirty of them were recent Jewish refugees—from Germany, Austria and Hungary—being fed and sheltered by a fund set up by some of the lucky, prosperous old immigrants like Lubitsch, not forgetting generous help from the Warner brothers themselves. Most of these actors—some very famous at home, anonymous as exiles—had lost sisters, brothers, fathers, mothers, grandchildren to Dachau and other slaughter houses. Some of them found the scenes with the deadly believable Conrad Veidt hard-going.

At any rate, when Veidt, as Major Strasser, gave up conducting

[251]

the bawling chorus of his men, and the *Marseillaise* flooded the sound track, I shivered to find myself overcome by the most moving experience I have ever had in a theatre. Never before had I seen a whole audience of ordinary people rise and cheer, through a blur of tears.

Acknowledgements

Until I was seized, lamentably late in life, by the golfing virus, most of the sports pieces I wrote were overnight dispatches to the (then *Manchester*) *Guardian*, in the course of covering everything and anything in American life as the paper's chief American correspondent. Accordingly, the publishers are grateful to the present Editor for permission to reprint: all the boxing pieces, the two on cricket, Eric Tabarly's transatlantic race, the two golf pieces on Arnold Palmer and Gary Player, the piece on Pat Ward-Thomas, the three theatre reviews—of Lauren Bacall, *My Fair Lady* and 'Shakespeare in Loafers'—and the piece on 'The Coronation of Miss Oklahoma'. The first piece in the second section of the book ('Oasis in Baltimore') was submitted to the *New Yorker* but was rejected as too raunchy for the time. The pieces on Chaplin, Fred MacMurray, James Cagney, 'Screen Acting' and 'An Icon at Fifty' were broadcast talks, published here for the first time. The two after-dinner speeches, the one to the United States Golf Association, and the one to the All England Lawn Tennis and Croquet Club, were delivered *ad libitum*, but the recording of one, and the meticulous notes of the other, have produced faithful transcripts.

Thanks are also due, and are hereby tendered, to the following publishers for permission to reprint: 'Fun and Games at Blackpool' (from *Blackpool Football*, Robert Hale, London, 1972); 'Short History of Baseball' and 'Revised (Soviet) History of Baseball', 'The Road to Churchill Downs', 'Workers, Arise! Shout "Fore!"', 'The Money Game', 'The Legend of Gary Cooper', 'The Duke', and 'Two for the Road': all broadcast talks originally published either in *Talk About America* or *The Americans* (The Bodley Head, London, and Alfred A. Knopf, New York, 1969 and 1980); 'Breton Rules the Waves' (from *Single Handed*, Ebury Press, London, 1984); 'The Missing Aristotle Papers on Golf' (N.Y. *Herald Tribune*, Book Week, January 29, 1967); 'Pottermanship' (*Life* magazine, 1968); 'Walter Hagen': the US Golf Association; 'Make Way for the Senior Golfer' (*The Golfer's Bedside Book*, B.T. Batsford, London, 1971); 'Snow, Cholera, Lions and Other Distractions' (*Golf Magazine*, 1975); 'Movers and Shakers of the Earth' (from *The*

World Atlas of Golf, Mitchell Beazley, London, 1976); 'No One Like Henry' (from *The Best of Henry Longhurst*, Collins, London, 1979); 'The Written Record' (from *The Golf Book*, Arbor House, New York, 1980); 'The Making of the Masters' (from *Radio Times*, 1986); 'Nicklaus' (from the *New York Times*, July 9, 1972); 'History of the Scottish Torture' (from the *New York Times*, 1973); 'Golf: The American Conquest' (from the *New York Times*, March 31, 1985); 'Pudding Head' (from *The Hasty Pudding Theatre*, Anthony Calnek, New York, 1986); 'Garbo' (from *Garbo and the Night Watchmen*, Jonathan Cape, London, 1937); 'The Life, in the Music, of George Gershwin' (*Radio Times*, July 1987); 'Jazz, San Francisco, and Jimmy Price' (from album sleeve, the Jimmy Price Recording Co.); 'Upstairs, Downstairs' (from *Masterpieces*, The Bodley Head, London, and Alfred A. Knopf, New York, 1981).

A.C.

A note on the typeface

This book is set in Linotron Baskerville, 10/15 point.

John Baskerville (1706–75) lived in Birmingham and spent seven years designing his typeface and finally completing his first book. He once wrote, 'Having been an early admirer of the beauty of Letters, I became insensibly desirous of contributing to the perfection of them.'